AF528101

Child Labour: Different Dimensions

Child Labour
Different Dimensions

M.S. Gupta

Madhav Books
GURGAON (HARYANA)

© M.S. Gupta

First Published – 2011

ISBN: 978-93-80615-04-2

All rights reserved with the Publisher, including the right to translate or reproduce this book or parts thereof except for brief quotations in critical articles or reviews.

Published by

MADHAV BOOKS
F-2562, Palam Vihar
Gurgaon-122 017 (Haryana)
Phone : 0124-2365193, 9810373248

Contents

SECTION - II

Child Labour–Problems and Strategies

SECTION - III

Child Developmental : Some Issues

SECTION - IV

Child Labour and Human Rights

Preface

Child labour is a curse upon society, a malady wrecking the economic backbone of a country. Above all, it is a disgrace for the development of entire human civilization. It is a matter a fact that children are the future of the nation and thus they should be given adequate opportunity and facility for developing themselves into good citizens. Children in India and elsewhere in the world have not been given proper attention and are being exploited by the people for the accomplishment of their selfish ends. They have been exploited more or less in all periods, though varied in nature and dimension depending on the existing socio-economic structure of the society. Poverty, caste, tradition, size of the family, labour scarcity, wage rate, ignorance, schooling facilities, etc. are the major factors of occurrence of child labour. As the problem of child labour is a global phenomenon, it exists in almost all the countries of the world, the difference if any, is only of degree and form. But it is very saddening to note that India is one of the nations of the world which has the unique distinction of being a large employer of child labour. A plenty of legislations have been made to prohibit the employment of children but it is still rampant in India. Various organizations have also joined the campaign to stop the exploitation of child labour and protect their rights. Attempts to eradicate child labour at various levels have also been made. The sincere, massive and joint efforts by all concerning organizations and international agencies like ILO, UNICEF, UNESCO, WHO, NGOs and world communities are trying to eliminate this menace from the world.

Hence, the burgeoning problem of child labour requires appropriate solution as early as possible. There is an urgent need to evolve the most suitable development schemes for the economic development of the parents of children involved in various occupations. Greater amount of public awareness is to be created and effective machinery must be implemented to protect the rights of children and further destruction of this valuable resource. It is the high time for all to be very serious towards it to ensure better social and economic lives to all, at least in the interest of human dignity.

The book "Child Labour–Different Dimensions" is an attempt to deal with such debatable and burning topic not only of India but the entire world. It is divided into four sections. Section I deals with case studies of child labour while Section II analyses problems and strategies. Section III focuses on some vital issues of child development while Section IV discusses the human rights of child labour. About thirty eminent economists/researchers from different backgrounds and different countries have contributed their research papers. The coverage of this book is quite comprehensive, the papers do not only study the results of ongoing problem of child labour but attempt has also been made to provide futuristic insights too. The scholars have tried to highlight the various issues related to child labour. The book will certainly provide sufficient matters to the readers for understanding child labour.

In this endeavour, I have received help from numerous eminent research scholars across the countries who have ably undertaken the tedious task of preparing research papers despite of their heavy engagements well within prescribed time. I would like to place them on record my deep appreciation and gratitude to all contributors.

I feel highly privileged to express my profound regard to Dr. Alakh N. Sharma, Institute for Human Development, New Delhi; Dr. N.K. Choudhary, Professor and Ex-HOD, Department of Economics, Patna University, Patna; Dr. S.S. Gupta, Professor and Head, Post-Graduate Department of Commerce, Magadh University, Bodh-Gaya, Bihar; Dr. Asha Singh, Professor and

Head, Department of Economics, Magadh Mahila College, Patna University, Patna; Dr. S.D. Sharma, Retired Professor and Head, Department of Economics, R.D. & D.J. College, Munger for their help and encouragement in my academic pursuits. I am also thankful to Dr. Meera Verma, Professor, Department of Economics, Magadh Mahila College, Patna; Dr. T.K. Shandilya, Pro Vice-Chancellor, V.K.S. University, Ara, Bhojpur; Dr. M.C. Prasad, Reader in Commerce, Department of Applied Economics and Commerce, Patna University, Patna; Dr. Bipin Kumar, HOD, Department of Economics, R.R.S. College, Mokama, Patna and Shri Raj Rajesh, In-charge, Department of Economic Analysis and Policy, Reserve Bank of India, Patna for their help in the form of good discussion over the present issue.

I am thankful to all my colleagues, friends and relatives who have helped me directly or indirectly in completing and finalizing the manuscript. I also appreciate efforts and support of my wife, Manju Sahu and children, Mallika Aishwarya and Kumar Manorath in completing this manuscript and achieve this target.

Lastly, I am grateful to Shri S.K. Jha of M/s Madhav Books, Gurgaon, Haryana for publishing the book in present form within minimum possible time with such a professional approach and zeal.

M.S. Gupta
Patna, Bihar (India)

List of Contributors

M. Kasiram, School of Social Work and Community Development, Durban.

R. Sathiparsad, School of Social Work and Community Development, Durban.

D. Holscher, School of Social Work and Community Development, Durban.

Asha Singh, Professor and Head, Department of Economics, Magadh Mahila College (Patna University), Patna, Bihar.

Aparajita Chowdhury, Department of Home Science, Berhampur University, Orissa.

Mohammad Reza Iravani, Islamic Azad University of Khomeinishahr, Iran.

M.S. Gupta, Department of Commerce, R.K.D. College (Magadh University), Patna.

Sajitha O.G., Gujarat Institute of Development Research, Ahmedabad.

R. Parthasarathy, Gujarat Institute of Development Research, Ahmedabad.

Md. Mosiur Rahman, Department of Population Science and Human Resource Development, University of Rajshahi, Rajshahi-6205, Bangladesh.

Mahesh Chandra Prasad, Department of Applied Economics and Commerce, Patna University, Patna, Bihar.

Mithilesh Kumar Sinha, Head, Department of Economics, Nagaland University, Mokokchung, Nagaland.

Md. Reyazuddin, Reader in Commerce, Vanijaya Mahavidyalaya, Patna University, Patna.

Shahnaz Mirza, Lecturer, L.N. Mishra Institute of Economic Development and Social Change, Patna, Bihar.

Nanjunda D.C., Project Director, Center for Advanced Development Research and Policy Management, Kushal Nager, Kodagu Dist., Karnataka.

Md. Mahfuzar Rahman, Research Fellow, Department of Population Science & Human Resource Development, University of Rajshahi-6205, Bangladesh.

Tapan Kumar Shandilya, Pro Vice-Chancellor, V.K.S. University, Ara, Bhojpur.

Md. Rafiqul Islam, Associate Professor and Chairman, Department of Population Science & Human Resource Development, University of Rajshahi-6205, Bangladesh.

Anjali Prasad, Department of Economics, T.P.S. College, Patna.

Syed Eqbal Afzal, Department of Commerce, Oriental College, Patna City, Patna.

Pushpa Sinha, Department of Economics, Patna Women's College, Patna University, Patna.

Bipin Kumar, Head, Department of Economics, R.R.S. College, Mokama (Patna).

Savita Bajaj, Member, National Commission for Protection of Child Labour, 36 Janpath, New Delhi.

S.K. Khandelia, Research Scholar, Department of Applied Economics and Commerce, Patna University, Patna.

Nibha Kumari, Department of Economics, Magadh Mahila College, Patna.

Kumkum Jha, Lecturer, Department of Economics, B.S. College, Danapur.

Meera Verma, Professor, Department of Economics and Co-ordinator, BBA Programme, Magadh Mahila College, Patna, Bihar.

Vineeta Mishra, Faculty, Usha Martin Academy, Patna.

Ravikanth B. Lamani, Research Scholar, Department of Anthropology, Karnatak University, Dharwad-580 003.

SECTION – I

CHILD LABOUR – CASE STUDIES

1

Level of Living of Child Labour— A Case Study

M.S. Gupta

Introduction

The problem of child labour does not exist with the third world countries only. It has been more or less a global problem. The difference, if any, is only of degree. It is directly linked with socio-economic and cultural factors. Karl Marx proclaimed that the result of purchasing children at an immature age by the capitalist is not only a physical deterioration but a social degeneration as well. It is a matter of satisfaction that worldwide awareness regarding upliftment of child labour is increasing now. In this regard, the UNO and its agencies especially ILO have gone through many resolutions, programmes and regulations. Being enlightened by the activities of the world organigations and government of different nations all over the world irrespective of their political ideologies adopted so many measures protected its constitution and laws either to eliminate child labour or at least to regulate their wages and working conditions. No doubt, much has been done and a lot has to be done. India has also taken so many legislative measures for welfare of the children but slur of child labour still remains on its head. The problem of child labour is very intense in India though there is difference in estimates of magnitude of child labour.

Concept of Child Labour

The term 'child labour' is generally used to refer "any work by children that interferes with them in their full physical development, the opportunities for a desirable minimum of education and of their needed recreation". Children aged between 4 to 14 years doing work on family farms or in occupations without wage or in factories, farms outside home for wages constitute child labour. Now-a-days child labour is a widespread phenomenon. It is not only confined to work on family farms or in traditional family jobs and occupations, but it has also extended to other fields. They work in agriculture and allied activities, unorganised small scale sector and even in organised industries.

The phenomenon of child labour, which is a consequence of the exploitative system operating at the national and international levels, not only closes the future of millions of children in the third world countries, but it also restricts the development prospects of these countries drastically. The existence of child labour is a threat to overall world development, to the solidarity and peace in the world.

The problem of child labour is symptom of the disease, which is widespread due to exploitative structure, lopsided development, iniquitous resource ownership with its correlates of large-scale unemployment and abject poverty among the countries. The existing international economic order perpetuates this harsh reality because powerful multi-national corporations operate and use child labour directly or indirectly, to maximise profits and minimise costs. The poor third world countries faced with acute foreign exchange crisis, permit and encourage export of goods using cheap and vulnerable child labour in the hope of improving their foreign exchange reserves and balance of payments crisis. Indian carpet industry, lock industry, gem and precious metals, etc. are examples. It is true that extreme poverty and unemployment force the poor to send their children to work as a part of their survival strategy; greed for profit and desperate competition for markets in the developed world encourage employers to use child labour for economic advantage. Lack of firm commitment to the goal of eradication of child labour results in a haphazard and ineffective intervention from the government, which is quite conducive to the interest of M.N.G. and other vested interest.

Causes of Child Labour

Although there is no single factor responsible for the participation of the children below 15 years of age in the highly competitive job market, poverty seems to be one of the most dominant reasons. In spite of high claims by the government, the study by Institution of Public Opinion reveals that 41.2 percent of the population is still below the poverty line. Therefore, child labour is no longer a medium of exploitation but it is necessitated by the economic necessities of the parents and in many cases that of the child himself. Inadequate income of the parents does not fulfill the minimum requirements of the children, which in most of the cases inspires the children to inter into the job market.

Poverty is most often supplemented by other socio-economic factors to expose the child to manual jobs. Due to high degree of illiteracy and ignorance of the parents, the children are deprived of getting proper counseling for building up their future career and at the time of economic necessity, the children move into the job market to take out their subsistence. Most of the times, a bigger family size adds to the misery of the parents to maintain the children properly, which motivates some of them to search or a job even in their teens to supplement the family income. Since education has become expensive these days, those who cannot afford to educate their children, indirectly encourage them to go for a job instead of sitting idle. As unemployment creates havoc in our country and there is no adequate provision for maintenance allowance to the unemployed, the children of unemployed parents immediately jump to the job market. Besides these handicaps of the children, the employer finds child labour as the cheapest labour, malleable and can be easily controlled. Hence, the encouragement also comes from the profit-seeking employers to engage a child to get a good return out of his investment.

Absence of provision for compulsory education is another cause of child labour. Non-availability of school going facilities tends children to do some job as an alternative. National Commission on Labour (1969) states the main obstacle in the way of making education compulsory to all children upto a prescribed age in the following words: "An artisan cannot afford to educate his wards though education is free. For him, an uneducated child is an asset, desire to be educated becomes a double liability because of (a) loss of earnings if the child does not work and (b) expenditure on education howsoever small".

Migration is another cause of child labour. When family head moves from one area to another due to agricultural cycle, his wife and young children either move with him or stay back to look after the family plot in his absence. In both cases, they seem to have bad experiences. In the urban areas, when the whole family moves from their village to the cities, they face problem of lack of shelter, hunger, joblessness, etc. and it forces the children to join the labour force.

It has also been reported in some cases that in areas where green revolution is becoming a stabilised reality and wages of agricultural labourers has substantially gone up, labour families have pressed into service their child population tempted by relatively good earnings.

Further, a large percentage of children start working because of being orphaned, dejected by parents or because of broken families and other domestic problems. Here, it is also important to note that the children are not voters and hence, they do not constitute a political pressure group; this eventually makes no politician interested to think about and solve the problems relating to child labour. Further, the children are mostly silent listeners or non-listeners of the policies/programmes meant for them and hence, their problems are not properly realized.

Profile of Patna Town

Patna, the headquarters of the district as well as the capital of the state, is the largest city in Bihar, having a population of million plus (more than ten lakhs) as per the provisional population figures of 2001 Census. The position of Patna among the cities of India, so far as population is concerned, is quite low. The city has a glorious past and can boast of a very rich cultural heritage. During the decade i.e. 1991–2001, the city of Patna has shown comparatively higher decadal growth rate (50.12 percent). In 1911, the geographical area of Patna was mentioned as only 23.04 square kilometers while it has increased to 99.45 square kilometers in 2001 Census.

Objectives

The major objectives of the study are mentioned below:

- To know the ratio of the child labour in comparison to the total strength of the employees in the 55 establishments.
- To throw light on mode of employment, wage, working hours, educational background, reasons for dropping school and joining the establishments at such an early stage and leave facilities available to the child workers, etc.
- To analyse as to how far the child workers enjoy the statutory benefits provided to them in the various child labour welfare legislations.

Hypothesis

Child labour is basically a socio-economic problem and these problems are increasing day by day despite of adequate safeguards and numerous legislations. The working conditions of child labour in various organizations are far from satisfaction and against the spirit of child welfare legislations.

Methodology

The present study is based on primary data made available through a questionnaire of envisaging different aspects as well as to test the impact of socio-economic conditions of child labour. As the study has been applied to examine the different variables of the problems of child labour and correlation among them, sampling is based on random samples. It has been collected from the area concerned on interview basis. Utmost care has been taken and respondents from all castes, categories and religions have been included in our sample. Hence, the source of information is based on primary data.

Sample Size

The present study is confined to the tea-stalls, sweet-shops and dhabas located at Musallahpur area in Patna, Bihar. We have selected a few pockets of these establishments to analyse the working conditions of the child workers. The reason for making selection of 55 establishments is that it is not possible to conduct a comprehensive survey of the entire tea-stalls, sweet-shops and dhabas located in Patna. Thus, 55 samples establishments have been chosen for the study. Among them; there are 12 tea-stalls, 16 sweet-shops and 27 dhabas. These are mainly located at Musallahpur area in Patna.

Obstacles during Fieldwork of Research Study

During the fieldwork of research study, we have faced a variety of obstacles from child labour and their employers, which has taken additional time in completing the fieldwork. The major obstacle we faced was that majority of the respondents were either illiterate or less educated and incapable to understand the questions asked by the investigator while few of them were not giving much importance because there was no any advantage from such surveys. We also found lack of awareness among child labours and this was mainly due to poor economic condition, illiteracy also threat from employers. Some respondents also tried to furnish wrong information, which was detected through supplementary and counter questions during filling up of questionnaire.

Finding of the Study

Child labour, which constitutes a large section of the workforce in India, is probably the most deprived and disadvantaged group in the country. The Government has initiated several measures since independence to ameliorate their conditions. Although their levels of living have somewhat improved particularly during the previous decade, the child labourers have been largely bypassed by the general socio-economic development witnessed after independence. Various public works programmes and social security measures sponsored by the state have played an important role in India towards mitigating the plight of child labour.

Workers Allocation

The study of 55 establishments revealed that 212 workers were working in these establishments, carrying out all sorts of jobs which include cooking, cleaning, sweeping, serving, preparation of the tea and sweets, etc. It is revealed from the study that 80 child workers were engaged in various services by their owners of the tea-stalls, sweet-shops and dhabas. It is evident from the Table 1.

Table 1
Workers Allocation

Nature of Establishments	*Number of Establishments*	*Total Employees*	*Adults*	*Children*	*Percentage*
Tea-stalls	12	34	19	15	44.11
Sweet-shops	16	67	44	23	34.32
Dhabas	27	111	69	42	37.87
Total	55	212	132	80	

Source: Personal Investigation

Table 1 shows that out of 212 total workers, the number of children were 80. It constitutes 37.74 percent of the total employment given to the workers in the 55 establishments. The number of adults was 132, which comes to 62.26 percent when compared with the child workers in the establishments surveyed.

Mode of Employment

Further Table 2 reveals that the mode of employment followed by the owners of the establishments are of three kinds viz., employment through self, employment through relationship and other sources. Out of 80 child workers; 20 have got employment through self-persuasion, 36 through their relationship and remaining 24 have been introduced to the owners through other sources.

Table 2
Mode of Employment

Mode of Employment	*Number of Children*	*Percentage*
Self	20	25
Through Relations	36	45
Other Sources	24	30
Total	80	100

Source: Personal Investigation

Age Composition of Child Workers

Table 3 reflects light on the age composition of the child workers in the 55 establishments surveyed by the researcher. During the survey, it was found that 14 children were less than 9 years of age, which constitute 17.5 percent of the total child workers interviewed. There were 38 children between the age group of 9-12 years and 28 children between the age group of 12-14 years, which constitute 47.5 percent and 35 percent respectively of the total child workers.

Table 3
Age Composition of Child Workers

Age-Range in Years	*Number of Child Workers*	*Percentage*
Less than 9	14	17.5
9-12	38	47.5
12-14	28	35.0
Total	80	100.0

Source: Personal Investigation

Wages Earned by Child Workers

Similarly, the study of Table 4 discloses that the wage-range of child workers varies from Rs.0 – 350 and above. Out of 80 child workers; 15 get their wages below Rs.150, 44 child workers are given wages between Rs.150 – 250 and 19 get their wages between Rs.250 – 350. There are only 2 child workers who have stated their wages above Rs.350. Thus, it is quite evident that only 2.5 percent working children get their salary above Rs.350 and remaining 97.5 percent child workers draw their wages below Rs.350. There are 23.75 percent child workers who have their wage between Rs.250 – 350 and 18.75 percent get a poor wage of Rs.0 – 150 from their employers.

Table 4
Wages Earned by Child Workers

Wage-Range in Rs.	*Number of Child Workers*	*Percentage*
Below 150	15	18.75
150—250	44	55.00
250—350	19	23.75
350 and Above	2	2.50
Total	80	100.0

Source: Personal Investigation

Working Hours of Child Workers

It is also evident from the statements of the child workers that they have to work without rest pauses from morning till late night. It is revealed from the study of Table 5 that all the child workers are to work from 8 – 15 hours without any rest. 15 percent of the total child workers have stated that they work for 8 – 12 hours a day, 72.5 percent child workers have stated that their working hours vary between 12 – 15 hours and 12.5 percent have mentioned that they have to work tirelessly for 15 hours or above every day. It is generally found from the statement made by child workers that their employers do not follow any child labour welfare legislation. As the child workers are whole-time servants and live in the premises provided by their employers, they usually work from early hours of the morning to late hours in the night without taking any rest.

Table 5
Working Hours of Child Workers

Working Hours	*Number of Child Workers*	*Percentage*
0—8	0	0.0
8—12	12	15.0
12—15	58	72.5
Above 15	10	12.5
Total	80	100.0

Source: Personal Investigation

Leave Availed by Child Workers

Table 6 deals with the nature of leave allowed by owners of these establishments to the child workers. The study reveals that 70 percent of child workers have been allowed no leave in any shape. However, 1.25 percent of them have mentioned that their employers have allowed them 10 days as the leave with full pay, 13.75 percent have reported that they have been given 12 days as a leave period with full benefits annually, 5 percent have stated that they avail annually 15 days as a leave period with full wages while 2 workers (2.5 percent) out of 80 child workers have committed in their response that they avail 24 days as leave period and their owners make full payment for the above said days and 3 child workers (3.75 percent) of the sample units have mentioned 36 days as the leave period with full wages as agreed to by their owners. It is also clear from the Table 6 that 3 child workers (3.75 percent) get 52 days leave annually.

Table 6
Leave Availed by Child Workers

Leave Availed (Annually)	*Number of Child Workers*	*Percentage*
No Leave	56	70.0
10 Days	01	1.25
12 Days	11	13.75
15 Days	04	5.0
24 Days	02	2.5
36 Days	03	3.75
52 Days	03	3.75
Total	80	100.0

Source: Personal Investigation

Entertainment Facilities for Child Workers

Similarly, the data collected and tabulated under Table 7 represents the mode of entertainment provided to the child workers in these establishments. According to the study, 58.75 percent of the child workers have mentioned that there is no entertainment facility provided to them. However, 25 percent of child workers have stated that they entertain themselves through radio and tape recorders and 15 percent have mentioned that their employers have given them television. The child workers have made it clear in their statements that they can avail the entertainment facilities only in the late hours in the evening and night when there is no rush of work for want of customers.

So far as nature of their duties is concerned, they are engaged in washing utensils, cleaning of tables and chairs, sweeping of rooms, preparation of tea and sweets, etc. Despite of large number of such establishments, they are not covered by any law or regulation and are supposed to carry out jobs of mixed nature.

Table 7
Entertainment Facilities for Child Workers

Mode of Entertainment	*Number of Child Workers*	*Percentage*
No Provision	47	58.75
Radio	11	13.75
Tape Recorder	10	12.50
Television	12	15.00
Total	80	100.00

Source: Personal Investigation

Educational Profile of Child Workers

Table 8 shows the educational profile of child workers in these establishments. It reveals that 36 child workers (45 percent) of the total child workers are illiterate, 35 child workers (43.75 percent) are those who had joined the study but could not complete even fifth standard. The study further reveals that 9 child workers are those who have passed primary education but could not go beyond the middle standard. The percentage of these child workers is recorded as 11.25 percent when compared with the total strength of the child workers of 55 establishments. It is also important to note that none of the 80 child workers was matriculate or above as evidenced from the educational profile of child workers given in Table 8.

Table 8
Educational Profile of Child Workers

Education Level	*Number of Child Workers*	*Percentage*
Not Educated	36	45.00
0—5th	35	43.75
5th—8th	9	11.25
Above 8th	0	0.00
Total	80	100.00

Source: Personal Investigation

Conclusion of the Study

The data collected in the present survey depicts a clear picture of the working conditions of the child workers in tea-stalls, sweet-shops and dhabas located at Musallahpur area in Patna Town.

The child workers have stated that they have got the occupation through three different modes viz., self, through relationship and other sources. It is clear from the survey that 25 percent child workers got their occupations by their individual initiative, 454 percent through media of their relationship and 30 percent could get their employment through other sources. The main reason of joining the occupation by these child workers is stated as "poverty". It is the poverty, which seems to have been responsible to generate the evils of child labour in each and every establishment of our society.

The survey also reveals that the working conditions of the child workers are far from satisfaction. The owners of these establishments do not adhere to laws made to regulate the hours of work as prescribed under the Child Labour (Prohibition and Regulation) Act, 1986. It has been observed that the daily working hours of child workers vary between 8 to 15 hours as against 6 hours prescribed under Section 7, Clause (3) of the Child Labour (Prohibition & Regulation) Act, 1986. To the surprise of the investigator, 10 child workers have stated that they are forced to work even for more than 15 hours a day without any rest. The data collected reveals that the child workers are not allowed for any rest during the entire course of their work in a day. Almost all the child workers interviewed have mentioned that there is no specific period given to them for the purpose of rest. This practice is highly in contravention to Section 7(3) of the Child Labour (P & R) Act, 1986 wherein every employer is under statutory obligation to arrange the period of work on each day in such a manner that no period should exceed three hours and no child should work for more than three hours before he had an interval of rest for at least one hour. It is also observed during the interview of child workers that they have to work even in the late hours of the evening and there is no bar on the employers to restrain them as the employment of the children between 7.00 P.M. and 8.00 P.M. is totally prohibited under Clause 4 of Section 7 of the Act.

It is also quite evident that the child workers do not get any weekly holiday. 70 percent of the child workers interviewed have stated that they are not entitled to any kind of leave. Only 30 percent of the respondents have mentioned that they get annual leave ranging between 10 to 52 days. The survey results, therefore, show that the mandate of Section 8 of the Child Labour (P & R) Act, 1986 is not at all obeyed by the owners of tea-stalls, sweet-shops and dhabas.

So far as the wage is concerned, it has been generally observed from the study that they are poorly paid and even get their wages between a poor range of Rs.0–350 which claims 97.5 percent of the total child workers. There are only two children who have mentioned their wages above Rs.350 per month. The survey, therefore, discloses that the poor child workers are not paid even the minimum wages by their employers which is sheer in contravention to the decision of the Supreme Court given in M.C. Mehta Vs State of Tamil Nadu

(AIR) 1991 (SC 417). The Hon'ble Court in this case has held that the child workers must get at least minimum wages which comes to 60 percent of prescribed minimum wage for adult employees doing same job to be given to child in view of special adaptability of child's tender age to such work.

It is also observed from the survey that the educational profile of the child workers is very poor. None has stated his education above 8th standard. 45 percent of the child workers have been found totally illiterate and only 55 percent of the child workers upto 8th standard. It is observed that the majority of child workers have joined these occupations because they were basically poor and need wages as a source of their livelihood. There is hardly any night school for those who want to continue their studies. It is also revealed from the study that there is lack of appreciation on the part of their employers to give them education while serving in their establishments. The findings of the study, therefore go against the spirit of the decision of the Supreme Court in M.C. Mehta Vs State of Tamil Nadu.

Suggestions of the Study

On the basis of previous discussion, the following points may be considered useful for reappraising the strategy for preventing child labour as well as ameliorating their conditions:

- A constitutional obligation of providing free and compulsory education to all children upto the age of fourteen years of age must be fulfilled without any further delay. Education should be made compulsory.
- There is a need to bring consciousness among the children so that they may be aware of their constitutional rights and get relief accordingly. This is again possible with the help of radio, television, spread of education and literacy campaign.
- The problem of child labour is directly connected with the poverty and illiteracy of Indian people. There should be every possible effort on the part of Government and NGO's.

- Further, supportive measures for child labour such as removal of poverty and unemployment ensuring minimum wages, meaningful education policy, medical and health support, proper nutrition, recreation and cultural activities, family planning, apprenticeship and vocational training facilities etc. must be given much importance besides legislative measures.
- The raising of public awareness and supporting community action should be given top priority in any scheme concerning child labour.
- Government should implement such action plans in the areas where child labour concentration is much higher. These areas should get priority.
- Unemployment allowance, old-age pension and red-card schemes for supplying the grains at half price among the poor all should be properly and fairly implemented. Benefits should reach genuine and needy people.
- Poverty alleviation programmes should be formulated and implemented in a decentralized manner with the participation of people at the grass-root level through village panchayats, panchayat samitis, zila parishads, etc.
- In urban areas; slum dwellers, casual workers, small artisans, vendors, minority community people, SC/ST and Backward Classes of the population should be the main beneficiaries of anti-poverty programmes.
- Productivity may be augmented through land-based activities like minor-irrigation, dry farming, horticulture and even farm forest tree.
- Land reform programmes should be strictly implemented. Land to the landless must be provided as most of the families of child labour and landless.
- Since more than 80 percent people of the state still depend on agriculture, this sector should be developed

in a proper way. It provides employment to a sizeable population.

- Child labour should not be under the jurisdiction of the Ministry of Labour. The rehabilitation programmes come under Education Department, Health Department, Rural Development Department, etc. Co-ordination with these departments is often a major hurdle. Therefore, child labour should be under the Ministry of Welfare because it would be better suited to deal with the problem in its various dimensions.
- Minimum Wages Act should be strictly followed and the act concerning it must be amended and reformulated to avoid loopholes in them.
- Apart from general education, vocational training should be imparted to the children to make them economically independent in their adulthood.

To sum up, a strong political will power and dedicated welfare activities are necessary to check this evil practice. There is the need for change in social attitude and in this context; mass media should be assigned a constructive role. This will certainly help in reducing child labour and eliminate it through improving enforcing legislations, promoting school enrolment, raising public awareness, supporting community action and targeting hazardous environment. Last but not the least, the prevailing corruptions in the government machinery must be checked very effectively and properly otherwise our all efforts in elimination of child labour will be like filling a vessel which has a whole in it.

References

Hirway, Indira, Cottyn J. et.al. (1991) (Eds.), Towards Eradication of Child Labour, Oxford and IBH Publishing Company, New Delhi.

Marx, Carl, Capital, Translated from German Edition by S. Moore and E. Aveling and Edited by F. Engels, George Allen & Unwin, London.

Rodgers, G. and Standing, G. (1981), "The Economic Roles of Children: Issues for Analysis" in Child Work, Poverty and Unemployment (Eds.), ILO, Geneva.

Stein, E. and Davis, J., 1940 (Eds.), Labour Problems in America, F. Farraer and Richer, New York.

Singh, B.P.and Mahanty, Shukla (1993), Children at Work, Problems and Policy Options (Eds.), B.R. Publishing Corporation, Delhi.

Shandilya, T.K. and Khan, S.A. (2003), Child Labour-A Global Challenge, Deep & Deep Publications (P) Ltd, New Delhi.

Sharma, Alakh N. (1979), Child Labour in Patna, A.N. Sinha Institute of Social Studies, Patna.

Government of Bihar (2001), Census of India, Provisional Population Totals, Director of Census Operations, Bihar.

Government of India, Economic Survey, 2002-03.

2

Socio-Economic and Demographic Determinants of Child Workers Out of School: A Study of Gujarat

Sajitha O.G. and R. Parthasarathy

Rationale

The problem of child labour in India tends to associate with various reasons like traditional attitude, urbanization, industrialization, migration, capital market imperfections, poor quality, accessibility and reluctance towards education and extreme poverty (Gangrade 1980, Hirway 1991, Kanhere 1993, UNICEF 1997, Leclercq 2002). Empirical attempts to precise the quantitative magnitude and the strength of the relationship between the level of poverty and the incidence of child labour started recently rather than assuming the causes of child labour. However attempts done were mostly with GNP per capita, national averages of population below poverty line, share of agriculture in GDP, adult literacy etc. (Ahmed, 1999), which were having the limitation as crude rates in explaining the sophisticated process of household decision making to send the child to do work than to study or enjoy childhood. Axioms and theories regarding household income, role of parental decisions, exploitative work at hazardous situations are of very recent origin (Basu and Van 1998, Dessy and Pallage 2001).

The researchers argued that child labour arises due to variety of factors but whatever be the factors the situation where a parent compromises to exploit their lovely kids is to be reduced to the extent possible.

Child labour would bring physical, mental, social and labour repercussion in the later life of the child (Mendelievich, 1980); but work, which does not detract from other essential activities of children namely leisure, play and education, can be considered as less harmful. In general the works of children under hazardous situations were considered as exploitative child labour. The work without considering the time duration involved, payment received, hazardous working environment etc. can be termed as exploitative in nature if it hinders the child from enjoying his rights as a child particularly education if viewing through a right perspective. Even though child labour is not a unique mechanism, which keeps the children out of school (Lieten 2000) the other view of it, children never went or enrolled or not going to school (drop outs) to earn for the family or to do household work or looking after siblings and family members is exploitative. This 'exploitative child work' would be more dependent on the socio-economic and demographic household characteristics. Hence the household characteristics of the children away form school (both drop outs and never enrolled) to do work was done under the assumption that exploitative child work is a function of household characteristics.

Data and Methodology

Data from National Family Health Survey II, 1998-99 (NFHS II) for Gujarat, one of the industrialized states in India was analyzed. In NFHS the required sampling rates for rural (village as primary sampling unit) and urban (census enumeration block as primary sampling unit) were determined by allocating the sample proportionally to population of the two areas. That is at the first stage it was probability proportional to the population size and then in the second stage every household in the domain is given the same chance of being included in the survey (IIPS and ORC Macro, 2000)

The National Family Health Survey II, 1998-99 did not have a direct question on child labour. The criteria applied to select those who come under the definition of 'exploitative child work' is as follows. NFHS II collects data on 'main reason for never went to school' to those who never enrolled and if enrolled and currently not going 'main reason for not going to school' to all the household members. The data is given up to the maximum number of members enumerated in the household. The reasons coded were:

- School too far away
- Transport not available
- Education not considered necessary
- Required for household work
- Required for work on farm/family business
- Required for outside work for payment in cash or kind
- Cost too much
- No proper school facilities for girls
- Required for care of siblings
- Not interested in studies

From the reasons coded, each child in the age group 10-14 were treated as doing 'exploitative child work' if they never went to school (never enrolled) or not going to school (drop outs) due to the reasons 'required for household work', required for work on farm/family, 'required for outside work for payment', and 'required for care of siblings' and a new variable is created as "household having exploitative child work (HECW)" and used as dependent variable.

The main source of the data on child labour were labour force sample survey and national census and such traditional enquiries systematically undercover the economically active children primarily because of the existing national laws and regulations on minimum age for entering into labour market and secondly due to the non-coverage of unpaid child workers (Visaria, et.al 1995). Hence this methodology used to identify the 'exploitative child workers' in the present analysis would cover a good sample than from other studies to study the child workers outside the school. It would also help to identify the household characteristics of those child workers who never enrolled or dropped out studies to do work either in house or outside.

Analysis

The underestimation of child labours in India is attributed due to the inadequacy of the concepts and methods used in Census and NSSO surveys and lack information on pertinent factors like children's use of time (Hirway, 2002), the household characteristics or the extend of exploitation. These limitations of data in actual fact restricted researchers from studying the exact causes of child work than finding the causatives of variations in child labour at cross country levels. Most usually the studies included the case studies or data from family having child labour only. Here the relationship between household characteristics and 'exploitative child work' is drawn from household data having households having 'exploitative child work' and those with out.

Levels and Reasons for Not Enrolling/Droping-out

Figure 1 shows the rate of children not attending schools among school age population 6-17 by age and sex in the state. The school non-attendance rate harshly increased among both sexes in 11-14 and 15-17. However, the high rates of non-attendance among females in all the age groups points to the gender inequalities in the society preventing female children to access education.

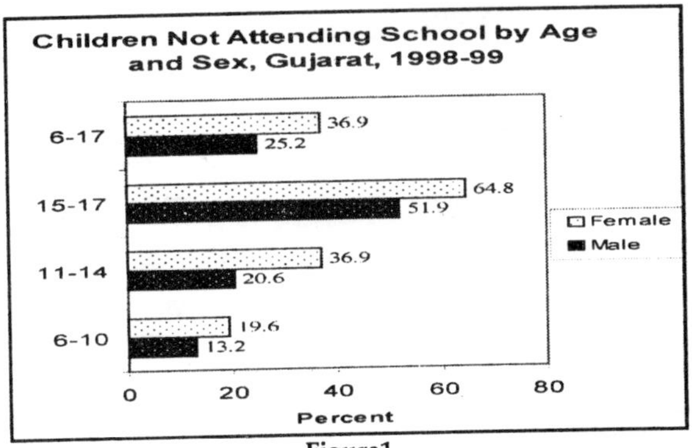

Figure1

Table 1 shows the main reason for the non–enrollment and drop out among school going children in the state. The three direct reasons that can trim down the school enrollment namely 'School far way', 'Transport not available' and 'No proper school facilities for girls' under the category of physical facility structure is found low for both male and female children in Gujarat. Yet the reason 'Education not considered necessary' seemed as one of the major reasons for female non-enrollment (18 %) compared to male non-enrollment (7.2 %) in the state. From Figure 2 it is clear that non-enrollment and dropping school studies to do work is high compared to other reasons listed in Table 1 among both sexes with significant gender preference in nature of work. If the sum of the percentages of the four reasons ('required for household work', required for work on farm/family, 'required for outside work for payment in cash or kind', and 'required for care of siblings) is considering, 31.8 per cent of male non-enrollment and 42.8 per cent of female non-enrollment in the state were due to the demand of child in the family to do work than any other reason. The picture becomes more sober as 39.3 per cent of male children and 34.6 percent of female children of the total drop outs compromised for their right to have education and stopped school going due to demand as a worker.

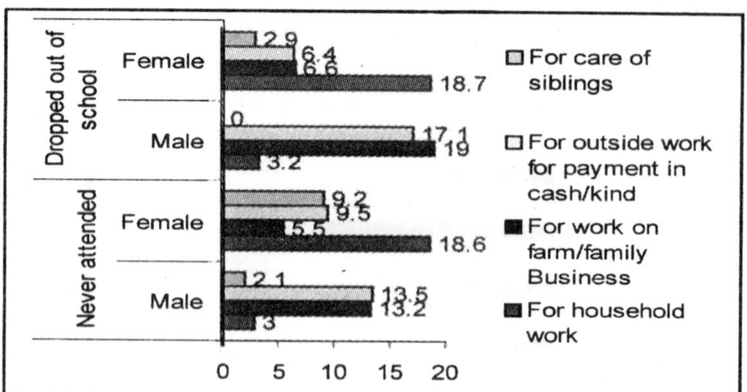

Figure 2: Children-Out of School to Do Work for Those Who Never Attended and for Those Who are Dropped-Out of School by Sex, Gujarat, 1998-99

Table 1

Main Reasons for Never Went and Not Currently Going to School by Sex, Gujarat, 1998-99

Main Reason	*Never Attended School*		*Who have Dropped Out*	
	Male	*Female*	*Male*	*Female*
School too far away	5.6	4.3	0.5	3.9
Transport not available	0	0.2	0.0	0.8
Education not considered necessary	7.2	18.0	1.6	3.7
Required for household work	3.0	18.6	3.2	18.7
Required for work on farm/family Business	13.2	5.5	19.0	6.6
Required for outside work for payment in cash or kind	13.5	9.5	17.1	6.4
Cost too much	5.1	7.1	1.8	1.6
No proper school facilities for girls	0.0	0.5	0.0	2.3
Required for care of siblings	2.1	9.2	0.0	2.9
Not interested in Studies	26.8	13.5	31.6	29.9
Others	23.5	13.6	25.2	23.2
Total Number	235 (100%)	424 (100%)	437 (100%)	514 (100%)

Source: Computed from NFHS II, 1998-99

Characteristics of Households with Exploitative Child Work

Among the school age population 6-17, the middle age 10- 14 is selected for in-depth analysis to study the characteristics of households having children not enrolled or stopped school going to do work (any one of the four reasons - 'required for household work', 'required for work on farm/family', 'required for outside work for payment in cash or kind', and 'required for care of siblings) and compared with the percentages at national level. The results were presented in Table 2.

Table 2
Percentage of Households with Children in Age Group 10-14 having 'Exploitative Child Work by Household Characteristics in Gujarat and All India, 1998-99

Household Characteristics	*Gujarat*		*All India*	
	Percentage	*Total No*	*Percentage*	*Total No*
Type of Place of Residence				
Urban	4.9	611	3.5	11955
Rural	19.5	893	9.2	28023
Household Standard of Living Index				
Low	28.5	372	13.2	11883
Medium	12.5	736	6.4	19327
High	1.5	394	1.9	8232
Ethnicity				
Scheduled Caste	14.8	237	8.9	7028
Scheduled Tribe	23.8	332	12.5	5443
OBC	13.8	363	8.1	11187
Others	6.6	516	4.3	14294
Agricultural Land				
Yes	16.1	659	8.4	21035
No	11.6	845	6.5	18939
Sex of the Household Head				
Female	18.8	112	7.8	3512
Male	13.1	1392	7.4	36466
No of Family Members				
7+	17.6	510	8.9	17452
Upto 6	11.5	994	6.4	22526
Exposure to Mass Media				
No TV	20.4	864	10.4	24906
Own TV	4.4	640	2.7	39978
Total	13.6	1504	7.5	39978

Source: Computed from NFHS II, 1998-99

Table 2 suggests that the percentage of rural households having children in age group 10-14, never went to or not going to school to do work either in house or outside is very high in Gujarat (19.5 per cent) compared to the national average (9.2). However, the difference between national average and for the Gujarat is observed low for the urban population. The cross tabulation with household standard of living index shows that 28.5 per cent of households in low standards of living have 'exploitative child work' in Gujarat, where as the percentage is only 1.5 per cent for those who are in high standards and 12.5 per cent among those who are in medium level.

It is noted that the households with 'exploitative child work' is almost double among scheduled tribes in Gujarat (23.8 per cent) compared to the scheduled tribes at all India level (12.5 per cent). It is interesting to note that there exists only modest variation between the households having agricultural land and not having the land both in Gujarat and All India compared to other household characteristics studied.

To study the influence of mass media in reducing child labour at household level instead of having their basic human right of having education the effect of presence of television in the household is studied. It is found that the difference is very high as the percentage of households with television is 20.4 per cent in Gujarat where as it is only 4.4 per cent among those having television. Even though the difference is high the percentages were observed low at the national level.

Results of Logistic Regression Predicting Household Characteristics

To identify the effects of variation of socio-economic and demographic household characteristics on the decision to send/opt the child to work instead of going to the school, logistic regression was done with presence of 'exploitative child work' (Yes = 1 and No = 0) as dependent variable. The predicated variables included were type of place of residence, standard of living index, ownership of agricultural land, sex of the household head, exposure to mass media and ethnicity.

However the suggested variables explained only 21.37 percent of total variation in the presence of 'exploitative child work' in the household. This may be due to the exclusion of factors like the highest educational level of household members, poverty level other than household standards of living, attitude towards female education and female literacy.

Table 3
Results of Multivariate Logistic Regression (Binary) Predicting the Variation in 'Household having Exploitative Child Labour (HECL)', Gujarat, 1998-99

Household Characteristics	*B*	*Wald* X^2	*p*	*Exp(B)*
Type of Place of Residence				
Urban	-0.90	12.69	.000	0.41
Rural (R)				
Household Standard of Living Index				
Low	2.35	23.74	.000	10.51
Medium	1.56	11.99	.001	4.77
High (R)				1.00
Ethnicity				
Scheduled Caste	0.25	0.85	.356	1.29
Scheduled Tribe	0.53	4.73	.030	1.69
OBC	0.23	0.84	.360	1.26
Others (R)				1.00
Agricultural Land				
Yes	0.06	0.10	0.75	1.06
No (R)				1.00
Sex of the Household Head				
Female	0.50	3.03	0.082	1.64
Male (R)				1.00
No of Family Members				
Greater than 6	0.59	11.56	.001	1.80
Up to 6 (R)				1.00
Exposure to Mass Media				
No TV	0.51	3.66	.056	1.66
Own TV (R)				1.00
Constant	-4.02		.000	

Source: Computed from NFHS II, 1998-99
Total sample: 1504- Households having at least one child in age group 10-14 enumerated in NFHS II, 1998-99 Gujarat state

The results of the logistic regression (Binary) results were shown in Table 3. It is found that the odds ratio is 0.41 for urban area compared to rural area and is highly significant.

Being other factors kept constant, the standard of living index also found highly significant in predicting the 'exploitative child work'. The probability of presence of 'exploitative child work' is found 10.5 times higher among those who are in low standards and 4.77 times higher among those who are in medium level compared to those who are in high standard of living. The ethnicity factor found that presence of 'exploitative child work' is higher among Scheduled Castes, Scheduled Tribes and Other Backward Communities compared to others in Gujarat. However the variation in prevalence among scheduled tribes (69 per cent high compared to others) is significant compared to other ethnic groups.

It is very much argued that the share of agriculture in Gross Domestic Product is a determinant factor of variation in child labour at cross country levels, even pertinent than poverty indicator (Ahmed,1999). In Indian situation also, it is argued with less empirical testing that possessing agricultural land would hinter parents from sending children to schools rather than to farms (Lieten 2000). In the present analysis, it is found that there is no such significant difference between the households having land and not having land in the presence of 'exploitative child work' at household level.

The presence of 'exploitative child work' is found 1.64 times higher among those households headed by females compared to males, even though the relationship is significant only at a low level ($p = 0.08$). It is also found that the probability of presence of 'exploitative child work' is 80 per cent higher among family with higher numbers (more than 6 in present study) compared to small families and is highly significant. Household exposure to mass media (measured in terms whether they are having television or not) is found that compared to those who are having television the chances of presence of 'exploitative child work' is 1.66 times higher among those who are not having.

Conclusion and Suggestions

The present analysis found that 'exploitative child work' as defined as the work preventing child from having education is a function of household characteristic and high among those who are in low standards of living, in lower ladder of ethnic groups, in female headed households, in large size families and among those with limited exposure to mass media. Hence the analysis suggests that banning of the child labour would work scarcely if the household characteristics of the poor and underprivileged like tribes are not improved. If the fruits of fastly growing science and technology are incorporating to improve the income level of poor, required means can be achieved even in the absence of maximized employment at the family level which can reduce the child labour in families which are trying to maximize output by maximizing employment in the family.

References

Ahmed, Iftikhar (1999), "Getting Rid of Child Labour", *Economic and Political Weekly*, July 3-9.

Basu, Kaushik and Pham Hoang Van (1998), "The Economics of Child Labour", American Economic Review, 88(3), June, pp. 412-427.

Dessy, Sylvain E. and Stephane Pallage (2001), "Child Labor and Co-ordination Failures,"*Journal of Development Economics*, 65, pp. 465-476.

Gangrade, K. D. (1980), "India-Socio cultural Background", in *Children at Work* (ed.) Elias Mendelievich, International Labour Organization, Geneva, pp. 81-85.

Hirway, Indira (1991), "Child Labour in the Developing Economies Today", in Indira Hirway *Towards Eradication of Child Labour*.

__________ (2002), "Understanding Children's Work in India: An Analysis Based on Time Use Data", in Nira Ramachandran and Lionel Massun (eds.), *Coming to Grips with Rural Child Work*, Institute for Human Development and United Nations World Food Programmes, New Delhi.

IIPS and ORC Macro (2000), International Institute for Population Sciences and ORC Macro, *National Family Health Survey II (NFHS II), India, 1998-99*, Mumabi.

Kanhere, Usha (1993) "Child Labour in India–Nature, Causes and Eradication" in Kamala Srinivasan and Veena Gandotra (eds.), *Child Labour Multi Dimensional Problem*, Ajanta Publications, Delhi.

Lecelercq, Fracois (2002), "Child Work, Schooling and Household Resources in Rural North India", in Nira Ramachandran and Lionel Massun (eds.).

Lieten, G.K. (2000), "Children, Work and Education II Field Work in Two UP Villages", *Economic and Political Weekly*, June, pp. 2171-78.

Mendelievich, Elias (1980), "Children at Work" International Labour Organization, Geneva.

UNICEF (1997), "The State of the World's Children", Oxford University Press, New York

Visaria, Praveen, Kebebew Ashagrie and Paul Jacob (1995), "Surveys of Child Labour and Activites of Children: Concepts, Methods and Procedures", International Labour Office, Geneva and Gujarat Institute of Development Research, Ahmedabad.

3

Factors Affecting on Child Survival in Bangladesh: Cox Regression Analysis

Md. Mosiur Rahman

Introduction

Infant and child mortality is the mortality during the first year of life and during 1-4 years of life respectively has traditionally been considered an important indicator for describing mortality conditions, health progress and indeed the overall social and economic well-being of a country (Anne T and Elizabeth R ,2002). The rate of loss in the first year and in the 1-4 years of life has attracted particular attention because: i) mortality if relatively high in these periods, the contribution of the probability of dying in the 0-4 years of human life is substantial, ii) it has a considerable impact on the average expectation of life and the arte of population growth, iii) it is sensitive to environmental and sanitary conditions and iv) the level of infant and child mortality is a useful indicator of the state of health and standard of a society or a country. Child mortality is therefore needed to be investigated in addition to infant mortality.

Infant and child mortality in Bangladesh has long been a topic of interest to population and health researchers because of its apparent relationship with fertility and indirectly with acceptance of modern contraception (Black, Morris and Bryce, 2003). The children of Bangladesh are particularly more victimized than those in other parts of the world. Because of poverty, neither mothers have access to medical facilities available in the country nor do their children. Moreover, the nutritional status of mother and children are very poor, about a quarter of infants in Bangladesh had low birth weights (NIPORT, 2003). According to BDHS Report 2004, the infant mortality rate is about 65 deaths per 1000 live births and a child mortality rate is 24 per 1000. Though the infant and child mortality rate has decreased but it is still a burning problem in Bangladesh. Despite or recent decline in infant and child mortality the level is one of the highest in the world. Again the situation of mother is aggregated than the health condition of the total population. It is also noted that maternal mortality and morbidity is also highest in Bangladesh (NIPORT, 2002).

The children who constitute a large proportion of the total population of Bangladesh are a vulnerable or special risk group, deserving special health care as the child mortality and morbidity risks are much higher than at older ages. Child mortality is determined by enormous number of complex and interrelated factors (YU VY, 2003). This paper focuses mainly on the impact of utilization of heath care services on child mortality. Availability and utilization of health personnel and facilities directly affect the mortality and morbidity of the children through standard biological treatment of diseases and injury and making available the most important immunizations as well as other ante-natal and intra-natal care to both pregnant mothers and their children.

Data Sources and Methodology

Data Sources

This paper utilizes the data extracted from 2004 Bangladesh Demographic and Health Survey (BDHS), which were conducted under the authority of the National Institute of Population Research and Training (NIPORT) of the Ministry of Health and Family Welfare. The BDHS 2004 is a nationally representative survey from 11,440 ever married women of age 10-49 and 4297 men age 15-54 from 10,500 households covering 361 sample points (clusters) throughout Bangladesh, 122 urban areas and 239 in the rural areas. The data has collected from six administrative divisions of the country- Barisal, Chittagong, Dhaka, Khulna, Rajshahi and Sylhet. Data collection took place over a five-month period from 1 January to 25 May 2004. Out of 11,440 ever-married sample, 8860 women has taken who have at least one child (live or dead) under consideration the time interval 1990-2004 and considers the sample according to the time span 2000-2004 in order to achieve our objectives. In the time span 2000-2004, 4873 sample has identified.

Methodology

The analysis of survival data requires special techniques, because the data are almost always incomplete, and familiar parametric assumptions may be unjustifiable. Three are many types of models that have been used for survival data. Among these, one popular and most extensively used model is Cox proportional hazards model (Cox 1972). The proportional hazards model is non-parametric in the sense that it involves an unspecified function in the form of an arbitrary baseline hazard function. In consequence, this model is more flexible. The Cox model is based on a modeling approach to the analysis of survival data. The purpose of the model is to simultaneously explore the effects of several variables of survival. In this model, the survival time of each member of a population is assumed to follow its own hazard function h(t). Let T is the associated failure time, than the proportional hazards model is specified by the hazards relationship;

$$h(t) = h(t;X) = h_0(t)\exp(X\beta) \qquad \text{..........(1)}$$

Where $h_0(t)$ is an arbitrary and unspecified baseline hazard function, X is the vector of measured explanatory variables for k individuals and β is the vector of k unknown regression parameters associated with the explanatory variables. The vector b is assumed to be the same for all individuals.

The survivor function can be expresses as,

$$S(t;X) = [S_0(t)]^{\exp(X\beta)} \qquad \text{..........(2)}$$

Where $S_0(t) = \exp(-\int_0^t h_0(u)du)$, is the baseline survivor function.

The population under study may consist of a number of sub-populations, each of which has its own baseline hazards function. Under the stratified model, the hazard function for the i-th stratum is expressed as,

$$h_j(t) = h_{jo}(t)\exp(X_j\beta) \qquad \text{..........(3)}$$

Where $h_{jo}(t)$ is the baseline hazards function for the jth stratum, and Xj is the vector of explanatory variables.

To estimate, Cox (1972, 1975) introduced the partial likelihood function. Let the set R (t_1) of indivusals at risk at t1-0. The conditional probability that ith item fails at t1 given that the items R (t_1) are at risk and that exactly one failure occurs at t_1 is;

$$\frac{h(t_i;X_i)}{\sum_{l\in R(t_i)} h(t_i;X_i)} = \frac{\exp(X_i\beta)}{\sum_{l\in R(t_1)} \exp(X_i\beta)}; \text{ for i= 1,2,...K} \qquad \text{..........(4)}$$

Since $h_0(t)$ is completely unspecified, no additional information about β is obtained from the observation that no failure occurs in (t_{i-1}, t_1) (i = 1, 2,........k). This is intuitively the case since we can account for this observation merely by taking $h_0(t)$ to be very close to zero over this interval. The partial likelihood for β is now formed by taking the product over all failure points $t_1$of (4) to give

$$L(\beta) = \prod_{i=1}^{k} \frac{\exp(X_i\beta)}{\sum_{l\in R(t_1)} \exp(X_i\beta)} \qquad \text{..........(5)}$$

Equation (5) is identical to the marginal likelihood. Now solving the equation (5), the estimate of *b* can easily be obtained. Partial likelihood function eliminates the unknown baseline hazards $h_0(t)$ and accounts for censored survival times. The partial likelihood of Cox also allows time dependent explanatory variables.

Results and Discussions

Trends in Childhood Mortality in Bangladesh

Mortality rates for children under five years of age are presented in Table 1 for the five-year period preceding the four BDHS surveys. The under-five mortality rate for the most recent five-year period (which roughly corresponds to the period 1999-2003) is 88 deaths per 1,000 live births, and infant mortality is 65 deaths per 1,000 life births. This means that 1 in 11 children born in Bangladesh dies before reaching the fifth birthday, while 1 in 15 children dies before reaching the first birthday. A child's risk of dying is highest during the first month of life. Almost half of all under-five deaths occur during the neonatal period about a quarter occurs during the post neonatal period, and another quarter occurs between ages 1 and 4 years.

Table 1
Trend in Early Childhood Mortality Rates

Data Source	*Approximate Reference Period*	*Neonatal Mortality (NN)*	*Post Neonatal Mortality (PNN)*	*Infant Mortality (1q0)*	*Child Mortality (4q1)*	*Under-five Mortality (5q0)*
BDHS 2004	1999-2003	41	24	65	24	88
BDHS 1999-2000	1995-1999	42	24	66	30	94
BDHS 1996-1997	1992-1996	48	34	82	37	116
BDHS 1993-1994	1989-1993	52	35	87	50	133

Comparisons of mortality estimates over time show continued declines in child (age 1-4 years) and under-five mortality (Table 1). Between the two most recent five-year periods, there was a 20 percent decline in child mortality and a 6 percent decline in under-five mortality. Infant mortality seems to have leveled off during recent years. For infant mortality to decline significantly, the Bangladesh program may need to focus on reducing neonatal deaths since most infant deaths occur during the first month of life

Effects of Maternity Care on Child Survival

Proportion hazard model indicates that the covariates such as mothers education, sources of antenatal care, assistance during delivery, place of delivery, duration of breastfeeding, father's education, sources of drinking water, electricity in the household and household assets index have potential significant effect on the child survival of mothers. Child mortality is 2.15 times and 3.09 times higher among the mothers with receiving insufficient antenatal care and avoids any care as compared to the mothers who were taking sufficient antenatal care from doctors, nurses or other government medically trained persons.

Table 2
Relative Hazards of Mortality between Ages 2000-2004 Years Associated with Explanatory Variables

Characteristics	*Coefficient β*	*Odds Ratio*
Antenatal Care Received		
Sufficient ®	——	1.000
Insufficient	0.61	2.158*
No care	0.98	2.79***
Assistance During Delivery		
Medically trained person ®	——	1.000
TBA	0.815	1.492**
Other's	1.069	2.937**
Place of Delivery		
Respondent's/others home ®	——	1.000
Govt,/Private hospital	-0.399	0.861***
others	0.586	1.172*
Mother's Education		
No education ®	——	1.000
Primary	0.108	1.251
Secondary	-0.115	0.448***
higher	-0.450	0.185**

Contd.

Characteristics	*Coefficient β*	*Odds Ratio*
Father's Education		
No education ®	——	1.000
Primary	-0.259	0.664
Secondary	-0.513	0.603*
Higher	-0.461	0.213***
Duration of Breast feeding		
Never breastfeed	——	1.000
< 11 months	-0.785	0.733*
11-23 months	-0.506	0.451***
23+ months	-0.279	0.390**
Sources of Drinking Water		
Piped water ®	——	1.000
Well water	0.387	1.462*
Others sources	0.519	1.738**
Household has Electricity		
Yes ®	——	1.000
No	1.041	1.328***
Household AssetsIndex		
Lower ®	——	1.000
Middle	-0.493	0.726**
Upper	-0.506	0.538*

Note: ® represents reference category.
Significance level: * = < 0.05; ** = p < 0.01; *** = p < 0.001.

Delivery assistance has positive significant effect on child mortality. Mothers who received assistance during delivery from TBA and other persons, child death rate is 1.4 times and 2.93 times higher than mothers taking assistance from medically trained personnel. Mother's place of delivery has also strong positive effects on their child mortality. Child death rate is 0.8 times lower among mothers whose place of delivery was government or private hospitals than respondent's or others home. On the other hand, this rate is higher among mothers whose place of delivery was in others sides such as public place than mother's delivery place in their homes or other relative or friends home.

It is observed from the analysis that even after controlling demographic factors, the utilization of antenatal care (ANC), and assistance during delivery provides moderate significance upon child mortality. Mothers' higher education has strong positive effects on child mortality. Women's with primary education are reported 1.25 times more child death rate compared to those who have no formal schooling. But mothers who are secondary and higher educated are 0.44 times and 0.185 times respectively less reported child death rate compared than mothers with no education. Fathers' with higher education, secondary education and primary education are 0.66 times, 0.60 times and 0.213 times respectively less reported their children deaths compared who has no formal schooling. The results suggest that certain socioeconomic factors like mothers' and father' education related to child mortality risks

An increase of one month in the duration of breast feeding by mothers decreases the hazards risk of child mortality. Mothers who breast fed their child in 11 to 23 months and more than 23 months are reported less child mortality in 0.45 times and 0.39 times than mothers whose children were never breastfed. Safe drinking water is one of the most important factors for leading a safe life. Child who was using well water for drinking purposes among mothers are reported 1.46 times more mortality rate than the mothers whose children were using piped water. This rate is also increasing for others sources of drinking water.

The household infrastructure variables like, electricity and household assets index seems to have little insight relationship with child mortality. The mortality hazard is 1.32 times higher if there is no provision of electricity in the household. Child mortality was reported 0.72 times and 0.53 times less in whose households' assets position is medium and higher than lower index.

Conclusions and Implications

From the trend analysis, we observed that 1 in 11 children born in Bangladesh dies before reaching the fifth birthday, while 1 in 15 children dies before reaching the first birthday. A child's risk of dying is highest during the first month of life. Almost half of all under-five deaths occur during the neonatal period about a quarter occurs during the post neonatal period, and another quarter occurs between ages 1 and 4 years. From relative hazards we found that child mortality is higher among mothers who do not take sufficient ANC and also not receive assistance from medically trained personnel. Mothers whose place of delivery is any hospital were reported less child mortality as against their opposite counterparts. Mother's higher education has strong positive effects on child mortality. Women with primary education are reported 1.25 times more child death rate compared with women who have no formal schooling. But mothers who are secondary and higher educated are 0.44 and 0.185 times less reported child death rate compared than mothers with no education. Fathers' with higher education, secondary and primary education are 0.66, 0.60 and 0.213 times less reported their children deaths compared who have no formal schooling. The result suggests that certain socio-economic factors like mothers and father's education are related to reduce the child mortality risks.

An increase of one moth in the duration of breast feeding by mothers decreases the hazard risks of child mortality. Mothers who breast feed their child in 11 to 23 months and more than 23 months are reported 0.45 and 0.39 times less child mortality than mothers whose children were never breastfed. Safe drinking water is one of the most important factors leading to a safe life. Mothers whose child using well water for drinking purposes is reported 1.46 times more mortality rate than the mothers whose children were using piped water. This rate is also increasing for other sources of drinking water. The household infrastructure variables like household electricity and household assets index seems to have little insight relationship with child mortality. The mortality hazard is 1.32 times higher if there is no provision of electricity in the household. Child mortality was reported 0.72 and 0.53 times less among mothers whose household's assets position is medium and higher than lower index.

Based on the discussion of this study, some policy implications, comment and recommendations have been suggested that would help the government to take initiative to promote child health care and child survival.

- Improving the household sanitation, provision of pure water i.e., clean water can help to prevent diarrhoea. Water supply and health programme should give emphasis on hygiene education to encourage the use of safe water for hygiene. Hygiene sanitation facility can reduce morbidity to a great extent. So, initial steps should be taken with this regard for survival of the children.
- Toilet facility should be developed and encourage people to build hygiene toilet at their home.
- Female education should be encouraged particularly in the rural areas and working facility should make available to them. Education gives mothers more decision making power and increase the knowledge about the health facility for better survival of their child.
- Mass media promotion programme should be taken to understand morbidity and encourage taking treatment.

References

Anne, T. and Elizabeth, R. (2002), Health Mothers and Health Newborns: the Vital Link, Population Reference Bureau (PRB), Connecticut Avenue, Washington.

Black RE, Morris S.S. and Bryce J. (2003), Where and Why are 10 Million Children Dying Every Year? Lancet 2003; 361: 226-34.

Cox DR (1970), The Analysis of Binary Data, London, Chapman and Hall.

NIPORT (2003), Bangladesh Health Services and Mortality Survey 2001, Dhaka and Claverton: National Institute of Population Research and Training (NIPORT), ORC Macro, John Hopkins University and ICDDRB.

NIPORT (2002), An Ethnographic Research on Newborn Care Practices in Rural Bangladesh. National Institute of Population Research and Training, Azimpur, Dhaka.

YU VY (2003), Global, Regional and National Perinatal and Neonatal Mortality, Journal of Perinatal Medicine; 31: 376-379.

4

Adolescent's Exposure to Family Violence: Effect on Psycho-Social Health

Aparajita Chowdhury

"Adolescence"–as a distinct stage of preparation for adulthood–is emerging or expanding in length in virtually all parts of the world, as a product of earlier puberty, later age of marriage, longer schooling and more engagement in peer worlds" (Larsen *et al.*, 2002). The future of world societies rests, in part, on how well they succeed in preparing adolescents to be productive adults who contribute to their communities. As we are in early years of 21st century, there are new reasons to worry that this vital life stage may be at peril. New demands of adulthood, frenetic lifestyles, entrenched poverty, adolescent alienation and a geopolitical climate marked by conflict within and outside the four walls of the family, jeopardise the transition to successful adulthood for many young people of our society.

Adolescence is often thought of as the healthiest time of life, embracing a definition of health that goes beyond a narrow focus on disease to incorporate emotional and social health. According to World Health Organisation (1999), the broad view of adolescent includes physical, social and psychological well-being as well as their collective contribution to the well-being of others. Eccles *et al.* (1997) advocates a developmental perspective of health and well-being that views adolescent's interactions with the context of daily family life as the primary determinants of their preparation for healthy adulthood. "Adolescents' lives are mostly directly shaped by their interactions with more proximal institutions and settings, including families, schools, occupational worlds and community organisations" (Larson, 2002). There are many more individuals involved such as: parents, teachers, relatives, peers and siblings, whose actions and behaviour affect adolescents' experience and preparation for adulthood.

However, today's adolescents are living in an exciting time of unprecedented changes, especially within family, that is posing threat to their healthy development and wellbeing. Most of the threats to adolescents are products of their immediate environmental interactions with parents and other family members. Families are without doubt the most important institution in adolescents' interpersonal lives, yet they have been changing dramatically in ways that affect both adolescents' interpersonal experiences and what will be required of them as adults. Many of the threats to adolescents are as much to their emotional well-being and mental health, as to their physical health and well-being. Close examination of evidence suggests multiple trends such as family size and composition; connections to other social institutions; parent-adolescent relationships and exchange have both positive and negative implications. Good parenting skills, shared family activities and positive potential role modelling have all documented positive effects on adolescents' healthy development (Hair *et al.*, 2005; Parker and Beson, 2004 and Resnick *et al.*, 2004).

Thus, adolescents' experiences and exposures to positive and negative family environment and interactions have tremendous impact on their future well-being. Factors that promote adolescents' healthy development are found in the families that nurture and encourage them to make good choices in their everyday life situations and act in ways that enhance their healthy development. However; Larson, Wilson and Mortimer (2002) were of view that "violence is a frequent experience for adolescents in many parts of the world". We are in the 21st century high-tech world and it is important to examine whether, the primary social institution, that is, the "family" and its mechanisms that have been relied on in the past, to foster adolescent health and wellbeing can be relied on in the future or not?

Today's Indian families are encountering complex and disturbing problems of various nature and magnitudes. The majority (roughly 75 per cent) of Indians, who live in villages and rural areas, are still poor, lacking in social resources and supports and generally isolated from the mainstream. Urban dwellers are also experiencing a multitude of difficulties which are challenging for traditional family structures and relationships and putting marriage and families at risk. More recent crises in Indian families encompass many of the same kinds of problems that have plagued countries in the West at least since 1960s. These include, for example – marital strain and dissolution, parent-child and parent-adolescent conflicts, various forms of family violence, substance abuse, juvenile delinquency, school dropout or low school attainment among the lower class; and excessive pressures in many middle and upper middle class families for adolescents and young adults to achieve academically. Given these conditions and difficulties, the future and well-being of the Indian family is uncertain (Chowdhury, Carson and Carson, 2006). Perhaps most notable in educated families are the extreme pressures on children and adolescents to achieve and excel academically, so that they can gain entrance into the prestigious colleges and universities. This pressure tends to increase the vulnerability of older children and adolescents to various personal and relational difficulties.

Adolescents in Contemporary Indian Family

Family shape the lives of their children from birth through adulthood. In case of adolescents, the influence of peers and friends take on greater importance. However, researches clearly demonstrate the continued significance of family environment on adolescents' overall health, shaping their behaviours and choices, as they face the challenges of growing up as adults (Bharat, 1997). Growing as a female adolescent in India carries with it the connotation of inferior status and less privileges, as compared to a male adolescent. It cut across all social classes of the society and through entire life-span. For a girl, the onset of puberty implies more restrictions on her movement, fewer interactions with boys and men and more active participation in household chores. Boys begin to exercise greater freedom to move about, expected to seek educational and vocational pursuits as a priority and to take adult roles. On the surface, there does not appear to be any gender discrimination in the families of these adolescents but covertly they do exist.

Despite unparalleled modernisation and mobilisation in recent decades, millions of Indian families, both rural and urban, have remained undeniably close and resilient. Family has always been at the foundation of Indian society and contemporary people of India continue to take pride in the centrality of marriage and family life. Children and adolescents are given a special place in the family. Interdependency, support, and nurturing across the generations are uniquely valued in the Indian family system (Chowdhury, Carson and Carson, 2006).

Contemporary Indian family is in "transition", affecting the general health and well-being of its members and specially having direct bearing on adolescent's development. Sinha (1988) maintains that socio-economic changes in Indian society have induced certain changes in family experiences that serve as antecedents to various behavioural and psychological consequences. He further stated that changes in contemporary Indian family are not entirely accompanied by psychological changes. Thus, according to Sinha, it has resulted in ambiguity in setting roles and expectancies for the growing child. With the help of several studies Sinha points out that in the changing family pattern there are unstable and contradictory patterns of rearing the children and adolescents, which generate anxiety and conflict among them. Moreover, due to lack of proper role model within family, adolescents are growing up aimlessly and becoming easy victims of negative peer pressures. Exposure to Western thinking has brought about changes in the attitudes towards traditional methods of disciplining the young adolescents but because of traditional attitude and mindset on the part of the parents (which have not been given over completely), a spurious sense of permissiveness alternates with strictness thereby creating anxiety and confusion with far reaching implications for children and adolescents (Bharat, 1997).

Further, nucleation has also depleted the emotional surround of adolescents and made them more vulnerable. The growing feelings of competitiveness, consumerism and materialism are replacing the traditional Indian family values of sharing, accommodativeness, mutual dependence and conformity with greater feelings of individualism, personal freedom, autonomy and self-determination. Accordingly, adolescents in the Indian families are being socialised to adapt and adjust to the changing value system and ethos. Mishra (1995) summarises the transitional state of Indian family and its influence on family members as follows:

"Family members are questioning the roles, obligations and relationship which have been nourishing the inherently social texture of Indian family. The tension experienced in the course of pursuing personal goals and familial goals are becoming an important source of stress................"

Thus, adolescents within families are facing host of problems and difficulties of various natures, due to this transitional nature, function and structure of Indian families. However in India, adolescents are not properly understood and perceived as individuals with potentials to grow naturally. Parental confusion, anxiety, stress and strain, along with varied types of family problems, are creating barriers for normal adolescent growth and development. Excessive pressure for academic excellence, lack of proper parental care and support, parental violence, lack of role model to follow are few reasons for making the adolescents aimless and engaging in warranted behaviour and activities (Baral & Chowdhury, 1999). These pressures tend to increase vulnerability of adolescents to various personal and relational difficulties (Nanda & Dash, 1996). Serious marital maladjustment in families is more likely to result in adolescent abuse, juvenile delinquency and mental health problems (Baral, Das and Dash, 1999). Study conducted by Carson *et al.* (1999) in Orissa State of India suggest that certain family processes (e.g., enmeshment, low or inadequate emotional expressiveness) were found to create a greater risk for adolescent behavioural difficulties.

Violence in Indian Families

Globally, violence within family is universal across culture, religion, clan and ethnicity. Despite their widespread prevalence, however, family violence in India is not customarily acknowledged and has remained invisible. It is such problem thought unworthy for any immediate attention, especially in the context of legal or political attention (Vindhya, 2003). The social construction of the divide between public and private underlines the hidden nature of family violence against adolescents and children in India. Rather, it is considered as disciplining and essential for maintaining the rule of authority within the family, especially for children and adolescents.

Family violence is an everyday occurrence in Indian family life irrespective of class, community, status, society and religious affiliation. It is a private affair with a few or no bystanders and no real time or opportunity to help the victim (may be women or children or adolescent or aged). The accused is often times the only witness to the violence. The family in India, once considered a fortress of safety and security for women, children, adolescents and aged; and a place of peace and solace has turned out to be breeding ground of violence (Ahmed-Ghosh, 2004). It is an irony, as Martin (1978) observes, "... family, the most intimate association to which the majority of people belong, is an unrivalled source of strength and comfort. But its very closeness can also intensify the worst of human relations. Love may be corrupted to envious possession and discipline to cruelty. And above all the private focus of hopes and fears may foster dual standards of private and public behaviour".

The pervasiveness of family violence problems in India has not been fully documented. It is one of the least reported of all crimes relative to actual frequency of occurrence (Chawla, 2004). Except for police records that are loosely maintained and a few privately conducted investigations, no nationally represented study provides data concerning the incidence of family violence in India (Ahmed-Ghosh, 2004; Chawla, 2004). Despite the absence of any uniform national investigation into the problem, there is enough evidence to show that family violence does occur in India, and that marital violence in particular is widespread though largely hidden (Chawla, 2004; Fernandez, 1997).

However, due to the private, personal and sensitive nature of the problem in India, scholars have not yet been able to overcome the theoretical and methodological issues involving family violence (Vindhya, 2003). Increased privacy, inequality between the sexes and legitimisation of violence through cultural and social norms, are some of the factors responsible for family violence (Williams, 1992). Since, the family is a source of comfort and nurture of its members are regarded as sacred, family members who are victims of violent behaviour rarely seek outside help, when it occurs. Outside intervention and assistance for personal or family problems is generally looked down upon in India (with few exceptions). Thus, violence within the family tends to be trivialized or ignored. Yet, the collection of empirical data on family violence in India began in the 1980s and ever since the rate of violence has increased. One such study conducted by International Centre for Research on Women (ICRW, 1999) indicates that, 40 per cent of the women under study reported experiencing at least one form of physical violence within family. Fifty per cent of the women experiencing severe physical abuse reported being beaten three or more times in their life time and at least once during pregnancy (INCLEN, 2000, Vasaria, 1999).

Why Violence against Adolescents?

Families today face innumerable stresses as they attempt to raise adolescents into healthy and productive adults. Undoubtedly, families with adolescents have long faced severe challenges but new elements have entered the old mixture of problems that make success or even more tenuous outcome. Adolescents' abuse within family is due to very many reasons but the most important among all are:

- *Adults' Perception Regarding Adolescents:* Adults often perceive that adolescents are less likely to be innocent victims of abuse, because they are not small, powerless, and helpless and with large size, physical ability with more developed cognitive ability and are expected to be able to protect themselves. In reality, adolescents are not that strong enough to protect themselves from any type of abuse. Further, parents often report confusion, anger and fear of being unable to control their adolescents' behaviour. This confusion and frustration lead to violence against adolescents on the part of the parents. Parents fail to understand that adolescents have a need for greater independence and need to explore for themselves. This need for exploration and independence often stresses family relationships that lead to frequent disagreements between parents and adolescents. In many cases, adolescents may be more likely to respond to parental abuse with mutual assault. Hence, parents may then feel that the adolescent is more deserving of physical abuse.
- *Parental History of Abuse:* Parents who were abused during their childhood and adolescent years, tries to transmit the violence to their own children. This intergenerational transmission of violence seems to create a cycle of family violence, which is hard to go away.
- *Family Poverty:* Family living with poverty tend to develop few typical characteristics of resource crunch,

lack of services and day-to-day provisions, which further leads to lack of education, unemployment and then to poverty again. Adolescents growing up in poverty tend to develop and experience violent behaviour often, which in turn have long lasting impact. Families growing up in poverty experience and exposed to different forms of violence and violent behaviour among its family members.

- *Presence of Step-parent:* Families with step-parent have been observed to be at risk for both physical and psychological abuse of adolescents. Presence of step mother in the families are seen to have increased risk of psychological and sexual abuse in Indian families, especially adolescent girls are the victims.
- *Family Functioning:* Families at high risk for adolescent abuse and violence have shown poor adaptability, low cohesion, low levels of support; inconsistent use of parental discipline; inadequate family problem solving and coping skills; and high levels of inter-parental conflict. Families may be more chaotic (lack of structure and organisation) or enmeshed (excessive dependence on each other) showing more violent atmosphere towards adolescents. Further, parenting styles such as, authoritarian and over indulgent parenting usually associated with abusive families.
- *Being Adolescent Girls:* Adolescent girls in India are most vulnerable and susceptible to violence within and outside family. It is mainly because of their upbringing and as there is an absence of legitimate, indigenous adolescent culture enabling their harmonious development. Further, the system of inequalities within Indian households makes the adolescent girls more discriminated, suffers abused by different forms within the family. Thus, familial views on what should be an adolescent girl's expectations take precedence over the right to a greater individual entitlement and on the whole, reinforce her

growing sense of marginalisation, powerlessness as well as vulnerability. According to UNICEF (1990), the young adolescent girls are considered as the "perils of neglect, exploitation, physical stress and depletion, mainly because of early assumption of domestic responsibilities and sibling care, discontinuation of education, engagement in hazardous work and high rates of morbidity and malnutrition due to early marriage and pregnancy".

A recent Government of India Survey states, one in every four Indians under the age of 16 is sexually abused, 50 per cent of these children are victimised by those in positions of their trust (mostly family members). Moreover, every second child is a victim of some kind of abuse – physical or emotional. This clearly indicates towards family dysfunctionality, hyper-sexuality and criminalisation, which further cascades into the next generation.

Association between Family Violence and Adolescent's Psycho-social Health

It is increasingly being recognised that family violence has adverse effects on the physical and mental health of adolescents. In addition, exposure to violence also can have implications for their subsequent behaviour (Jejeebhoy, 1998; CORT, 2000). Family violence was conceptualised as both family violence and adolescents' abuse. The construct of family violence emerged from a family events affecting the adolescents in recent past. The construct of adolescent family violence include: (a) exposure to parental fights; (b) witnessing paternal violence towards the mother; and (c) witnessing or experiencing abuse and/or violence on the part of the adolescents. According to a study conducted by Kliewer and colleagues (2001), violence against a family member was positively correlated with depressive symptoms and anxiety in adolescents. Exposure to violence in the family has become a major public health problem in Western world, particularly in children and adolescents who live in environments characterised by extreme danger. These toxic environments also are associated with maladaptive behaviour responses such as substance use and abuse in youths (Klevens, Bayon and Sierra, 2000; Maya *et al.* 2000).

Family violence and adolescent maltreatment are stressors that put adolescents at heightened risk for adjustment problems, including depressive and anxious symptoms, aggressive behaviour and the lower social competence (Doumas, Margolin and John, 1994; Jouriles *et al.* 2001; and Lynch and Cicchetti, 1998). Considerable developmental work has been documented pathways from family violence experiences to serious delinquent behaviours (Mejia, Kliewer and Williams, 2006).

Recent literature has focussed on pathway from family violence to adjustment in adolescents. Becker and McCloskey (2002), for example, examined the impact of family violence in the development of attention and conduct problems in 287 adolescents, who were 6 to 12 years old at the start of six years prospective study. Family violence was defined in this study as marital violence, including physical and escalated violence, and the frequency of father's abuse toward children. Results showed associations of family violence and attention and conduct problems in girls as well as the development of delinquent behaviour. Boys who developed attention-deficit hyperactivity disorder (ADHD) were more likely to show conduct problems that lead to adolescent delinquency.

The child and adolescent abuse literature in India indicates that their maltreatment has its own set of negative consequences or harmful developmental outcomes for children and adolescents (Chowdhury *et al.* 1994, and Chawla, 2004). For instance, abuse tends to lead to more abuse, contributes to delinquency and aggressive behaviour in children, and increases the likelihood of adult criminality. Hence, violence tends to beget violence (Patnaik, 2007). The children inherit a legacy of violence, a gift of tyranny, which they in turn will pass into their children – one generation of violence begetting another and so on. There is considerable evidence for the inter-generational transmission of family violence. The continuance of this syndrome erodes the basic structure of the family and society.

Maltreated children also express more anger toward and have more conflict with their family members than non-maltreated children. They exhibit more internalizing disorders (e.g., depression and various anxiety disorders) than non-abused children and are less pro-social. In addition, abused children and adolescents tend to manifest a variety of other cognitive, emotional and social difficulties including troubled relationships with peers, impaired social cognition, lack of empathy, and poor performance. Sexually abused children and adolescents often suffer from a variety of behavioural and emotional problems. These include depression, guilt and shame, learning difficulties and higher rates of school dropout, sexual promiscuity, runaway behaviour, somatic complaints and sudden changes in mood to name a few (Gelles and Coute, 1990).

Experience and Exposure of Adolescents to Family Violence

Witnessing and experiencing family violence is equally hazardous for the development and well-being for the adolescents. According to Chawla and Kang (2007), "Children in homes where domestic violence occurs are physically abused or seriously neglected at a rate 1500 times greater than the national average in the general population". Further, hearing or visualising the abuse and/or violence against one parent by other take a huge toll on children and adolescents. It leads to following conditions, such as:

- Adolescents develop physical and/or mental problems that can last for lifetime;
- Adolescents grow up, believing violence is a normal part of family life;
- They become more likely to be abusive as adult leading to cycle of violence;
- Live in daily fear, filled with confusion, chaos, anger, and tension, leading to lifelong inability to trust others;
- Adolescents get caught in the middle of a domestic violence, as they feel responsible for the abuse and powerless to stop it.

Parent-adolescent violence and inter-parental violence witnessed were significant predictors of both externalising and internalising behaviour problems. Further, study conducted in western world stresses on the consequences of witnessing family violence on children and adolescents in terms of physical and biological functioning, behaviour, emotions, cognitive development and social adjustment. According to Osofsky (1995), "For adolescents, particularly those who have experienced violence exposure throughout their lives, high levels of aggression and acting out are common, accompanied by anxiety, behaviour problems, school problems, truancy and revenge seeking."

Various researches conducted in India have proved that witnessing family violence can cause long term effects on children. Nair (1997) and Sunny (2003) reported that children who witness family violence have more physical and mental health problems and more likely to be abusive as adults. Findings of Jaya and Narasimhan's (2003) study showed that from children exposed to family violence, 7% wanted to get rid of their parents and 4% wanted to run away from the family because they were frightened to the inconsistent characteristics of the parents, felt low and rejected due to their parents violence.

Consequences of family violence vary with the sex of the child and adolescent. Boys were more prone to exhibit behavioural problems than girls, especially externalising behaviour, such as hostility and aggression (Chowdhury and Patnaik, 2007), while girls exposed to family violence demonstrate more internalising problems such as depression and somatic complaints. Further, the duration and intensity of the family violence has impact on child and adolescent's developmental outcomes. Adolescents witnessing traumatic events like family violence may feel helpless and see the world as unpredictable, hostile and threatening. Researches indicate that children who live in households affected by family violence may suffer extensively and are vulnerable to developing a host of short and long term physical and mental health problems.

Adolescents are at less risk for immediate and direct exposure to family violence. However, long term effect exists, leading to future well-being and adjustments. Specially, sexually abused adolescents are at greater risk for unintended pregnancy, depression, suicide, anxiety, feeling of vulnerability, powerlessness, sexual identity confusion, substance use and abuse. In case of physically abused, adolescents are at greater risk for anxiety, depression, extreme adjustment and acting out problems, academic problems, sleeping problems, drug use, self-destructive or reckless behaviour, suicidal ideation, suicidal actions, violence against siblings and even parents. Family violence exposure is a potentiating factor within the environment of adolescents. Thus, on the basis of these fundamental issues, this paper tries to understand the issue of family violence in the context of adolescents' psycho-social health and well-being.

Key Findings of the Sample Study

Family violence against adolescents is an area that has not been adequately addressed in the existing literature, policies and programmes. To address this gap in knowledge, a small sample study was undertaken that aim to understand forms of violence as perceived by adolescents, the actual reported experiences of violence against adolescents and their mothers. These data were collected as part of a Master's Studies project work carried out in Berhampur town of Orissa State in India. Investigator interviewed one hundred adolescents (Boys = 50; Girls = 50) aged 10 to 13 from middle and lower middle class families using semi-structured questionnaire. During these interviews, the adolescents were asked about quarrels and fights among their parents and about violence within family that they may have experienced directly.

Forms of Family Violence against Adolescents- During the free-listing exercise, researcher asked adolescents to list different forms of violence they experience within families, presented in Table -1. On average 37.4 % boys and 49.6 % girls mentioned experiencing violence within family (Table 1). Both adolescent boys and girls indicated that verbal abuse is more (84%)

followed by psychological abuse (60.5%). Among the verbal abuse, scolding for every act and behaviour, arguments, asking for explanations and using bad language is very common, as stated by the adolescents. Psychologically, they were abused through constant criticism, demeaning in front of others, neglecting, comparing with other siblings or peers too often. Boys reported more physical abuse than the girls, being slapped or beaten, having objects thrown at them, tying hands and legs for longer hours to restrict movements, locking inside a room without food and water, etc. Adolescents did mentioned sexual harassment during the individual in-depth interview.

Table 1
Forms of Family Violence Experienced by Adolescents

(in per cent)

Forms of Family Violence	*Boys*	*Girls*	*Total*
Physical	29	20	24
Psychological	46	75	60.5
Verbal	83	85	84
Financial	12	21	16.5
Sexual	04	18	11

Source: Personal Investigation

Patterns of Violence against Adolescents- About 20.5 % of adolescents reported violence (including physical and verbal abuse) by their fathers against their mothers. A greater proportion of girls (27%) than boys (14%) reported having witnessed their fathers beating their mothers. Though it is not clear what accounts for the difference, one possibility is that girls were more expressive and boys were more introverts to express their family internal matters (against their fathers)openly (Table–2). In case of experiencing violence by fathers, about 27% adolescents were of the view that their father beat them (Boys – 33% and Girls – 21%) at home for slightest mistake and even some time without any reasons. It is interesting to note that about 15.5 % adolescents (Boys – 18% and Girls – 13%) were of the view that their mothers and they were beaten by their fathers at several occasions.

Table 2
Adolescent's Experience of Family Violence by Fathers Against Mother or Self

(in per cent)

Patterns of Violence	*Boys*	*Girls*	*Total*
Beats mother alone	14	27	20.5
Beats adolescents alone	33	21	27
Beats both mother and adolescents	18	13	15.5

Source: Personal Investigation

Frequency of Violence- When asked about the frequency of verbal abuse and physical violence against their mothers, around 10% boys and 19% girls reported that such abuse occurred *"always"*, 75% boys and 70% girls said *"sometimes"* and 15% boys and 11% girls said *"rarely"* (Table–3). About 13% boys and 26% girls reported experiencing violence against them directly by their fathers "always", 27% boys and 54% girls "sometimes" and 60% boys and 30% girls experienced "rarely". The adolescents and their mothers were also experiencing violence against them together. Around 14% boys and 17% girls reported it to occur always, 63% boys and 65% girls reported it to occur sometimes and around 23% boys and 18% girls reported it to occur rarely (Table–3).

Table 3
Frequency of Family Violence Experienced by Adolescents

(in per cent)

	Boys			*Girls*		
Patterns of Violence	*Always*	*Sometimes*	*Rarely*	*Always*	*Sometimes*	*Rarely*
To mothers	10	75	15	19	70	11
To self	13	27	60	26	54	30
To both	14	63	23	17	65	18

Source: Personal Investigation

Reasons Leading to Violence- While investigating the reasons of situation leading to violence against adolescents, it was found out that, there were few typical reasons associated with boys and girls separately. Boys mentioned poor academic performance, not attending school regularly and not doing homework timely, not obeying their parents, conflicts about being forced to go to work and earn money, quarrels with friends and neighbours, smoking, getting involved in parent's fights, gossiping were few major reasons leading to violence against them. Whereas, girls reported not complying with their gender roles, not attending to household chores, talking to boys, coming late from school or work and going out without informing parents as the main reasons for violence against them.

Coping with the Violent Situation- In spite of facing abuse against them, some (36%) adolescents freely expressed that it is a part and parcel of their family life and nothing unusual about it. Both boys and girls mentioned that they usually stopped talking or eating, spending more time with friend or relatives, when faced with such situation. Some reported feeling like crying; being alone, even feel like running out of the house. As Parson (1994) mentioned that adolescents witnessing or experiencing violence within family attach themselves to peer groups and gangs as substitute family and incorporate violence as method of dealing with disputes or frustration. Still few mentioned that they used to get angry with their fathers and would like to hit back and take revenge. For example, one 13 year old girl mentioned her anger saying, "my father beats me, my sister and my mother regularly after consuming alcohol for no reason. I feel like killing him so that we can have some peace in our lives".

This study provides a glimpse into the violence witnessed and experienced by adolescents in middle and lower-middle class families of Berhampur town. There is a need for a deeper understanding of the dynamics and consequences of violence including sexual violence, which may have both short-term and long-term implications for both victims and perpetrators. In addition, an in-depth understanding of the factors that lead to violent behaviour could help point to strategies to curb such family violence and provide healthy and enriching environment for our adolescents. To achieve this, more in-depth and systematic research is needed in various settings.

Strengthening Families and Parents for Adolescent's Well-being

Despite greater pressures due to globalisation, most adolescents are rising to the challenges and developing higher levels of skill and maturity than were common in the prior generations. There is a need for today's adolescents for a *"safe haven"* in the family to develop their potentials, capabilities and competencies to face the challenges of future. Close parent-adolescent relationships, good parenting skills, shared family activities and positive parent role modelling all have well-documented effects on adolescent health and development (Hair et al. 2005; Parker & Benson, 2004; and Resnick et al. 2004).

Families are found worldwide and are considered most significant social context for youth development, despite its variability and vulnerability. They not only foster development in children and adolescents, but also shape the quality of their lives by serving as a source of nurturance, emotional bonding, and socialisation. The family has the potential to provide stability, support and act as a safety net in the face of crises in the environment (Choudhury & Chowdhury, 2007). Therefore, families need to be strengthened to provide scope and opportunities for its younger members to enhance their potentials and develop resilience against any forms of challenges. Thus, strengthening families and parents are of prime importance for healthy psycho-social development among adolescents within family, which may include:

- Parent-adolescent closeness and communication;
- Parental monitoring;
- Eating meals together;
- Parental health behaviour;
- Family resourcing

Conclusion

Family violence against children is a social problem with which India as a developing nation has yet come to understand or be able to provide concrete futuristic solutions. The most significant cost to society due to family violence is the direct and indirect impact on children and adolescents in the form of physical and psychological trauma. Family violence continues to be an epidemic that kills and tortures its members within family in different forms including adolescents. It damages the quality of family life, not only of the victim but also of the entire family. Children and adolescents become the silent sufferers of this violence having long lasting impact on them. Even though most societies denounce violence, the reality is that violence is often sanctioned under the cover of cultural practices and norms of misinterpretation of religious tenets. In case of adolescent boys and girls who are also the victim of this epidemic in different forms need to be specially protected. Violence against adolescents is not at all acceptable. Like adult men, adolescent boys need access to services to help them deal with any violent behaviour they may have experienced or exposed to. Support services need to address associated behaviour patterns such as drug and alcohol problems or the risky sexual behaviour in which adolescent girls and boys may indulge as a result of being victimised themselves.

In sum, adolescent exposure and experience of family violence is influenced, not only by the strength and vulnerability of individual adolescents but also by the character of the family setting in which they live and the ways in which they connect to their outside family and social world. To reach these hidden victims, however, all agencies, institutions and service providers for children and adolescents must increase efforts to identify adolescents who are exposed to family violence and provide assistance to counsel them accordingly. Thus, changes in social policy, effective law enforcement, evaluation of rehabilitation programmes, family life education and training can help combat the problem to some extent. A multilevel effort to improve the capacity of families in building safety nets, social controls coupled with positive and enriching school experience and reduced opportunities for engaging in crime and other risk behaviours can prove beneficial in the long run.

References

Ahemed-Ghosh, H. (2004), Chattels of Society: Domestic Violence in India. *Violence Against Women*, 10 (1), 94-118.

Baral, J.K. and Chowdhury, A. (1999), *Family in Transition: Power and Democracy*, New Delhi, Northern Book Centre.

Baral, J.K., Das U. and Dash, S. (1999), Power Equations in Family. In J.K. Baral and A. Chowdhury (Eds.), *Family in Transition: Power and Development*, New Delhi: Northern Book Centre, pp. 57-82.

Becker, K.B. and McCloskey, L.A. (2002), Attention and Conduct Problems in Children Exposed to Family Violence, *American Journal of Orthopsychiatry*, 72: 83-91.

Bharat, S. (1997), Family Socialisation of the Indian Child. In: *Trends in Social Science Research*, Vol. 4, No. 1, pp. 201-216.

Carson, D.K. and Chowdhury, A. (2000), Family Therapy in India: A New Profession in an Ancient Land? In: *Contemporary Family Therapy*, 22 (4), 387-406.

Carson, D.K., Carson, C.K. and Chowdhury, A. (2007), *Indian Families at the Crossroads: Preparing Families for the New Millennium*, New Delhi: Gyan Publishing House.

Carson, D.K., Chowdhury, A., Perry, C.K. and Pati, C. (1999), Family Characteristics and Adolescents' Competence in India: Investigation of Youth in Southern Orissa. In *Journal of Youth and Adolescence*, Vol. 28, No. 2: 211-233.

Centre for Operations Research and Training (CORT) (2000), Baseline Survey for Action for Slum Dwellers Reproductive Health Project (Monograph), Baroda.

Chawla, A. and Kang, T. (2007), Domestic Violence: Impact on Children. *Social Welfare*, December, 30-33.

Chawla, S. (2004), International Perspectives on Family Violence and Abuse: A Cognitive Ecological Approach. In K. Malley-Morrison (Ed.), Mahwah, NJ: Lawrence Erlbaum.

Choudhury, R. and Chowdhury, A. (2007), Nurturing Youth Potentials within Indian Families. In David K. Carson, Cecyle, K. Carson and Aparajita Chowdhury (Eds.), *Indian Families at the Crossroads*, New Delhi: Gyan Publishing House, pp. 281-298.

Chowdhury, A. (2007), Domestic Violence Against Elderly Women in South Orissa: A Study of Incidence, Patterns and Perspectives.

Project Report Prepared for National Commission for Women, New Delhi.

Chowdhury, A. and Patnaik, I. (2007), Effects of Family Life on Child Mental Health. In David K. Carson, Cecyle, K. Carson and Aparajita Chowdhury (Eds.), *Indian Families at the Crossroads*, New Delhi: Gyan Publishing House, pp. 123-145.

Chowdhury, A., Carson, D.K. and Carson, C.K. (2006), *Family Life Education in India: Perspectives, Challenges and Applications*, New Delhi: Rawat Publications.

Chowdhury, A., Pattnaik, S. and Patro, A. (1994), Psycho-social Profile of Abused Children in India. *Early Child Development and Care*, 104: 85-93.

Doumas, D., Margolin, G. and John, R. (1994), The Intergenerational Transmission of Aggression Across Three Generations, *Journal of Family Violence*, 9: 157-175.

Eccles, J.S., Lord, S.E., Roser, R.W., Barber, B.L., and Jozefowicz, D.M.H. (1997), The Association of School Transitions in Early Adolescence with Developmental Trajectories Through High School. In: J. Schulenberg, J.M. Maggs, and K. Hurrelmann (Eds.), *Health Risk and Developmental Transition during Adolescence*, Cambridge: Cambridge University Press, 283-320.

Fernandez, M. (1997), Domestic Violence by Extended Family Members in India: Interplay of Gender and Generation, *Journal of Interpersonal Violence*, 12(3): 433-455.

Gelles, R.J. and Coute, J.R. (1990), Domestic Violence and Sexual Abuse of Children: A Review of Research in the Eighties. *Journal of Marriage and the Family*, 52: 1045-1058.

Guilamo-Ramos, V., Jaccard, J., Turrisi, R., & Johansson, M. (2005), Parental and School Correlates of Binge Drinking among Middle-School Students. American Journal of Public Health, 95(5): 894-899.

Hair, E., Moore, K., Garrett, S., Kinukawa, A., Lippman, L. & Michelson, E. (2005), The Parent Adolescent Relationship Scale. In: K. Moore & L. Lippman (Eds.) *What Do Children Need to Flourish*, New York: Springer Science, 183-202.

International Center for Research on Women (ICRW) (1999), Domestic Violence in India: A Summary Report of Three Studies, Washington DC.

International Clinical Epidemiologists Network (INCLEN) 2000. In Domestic Violence in India 3: A Summary Report of a Multi-site Household Survey, Washington D.C.: International Center for Research on Women and the Centre for Development and Population Activities.

Jaya, N. and Narasimhan, S. (2003), Violence on Children between 10-18 Years in Varied Family Contexts. *Indian Psychological Review,* 60: 2-9.

Jejeebhoy, S.J. (1998), Wife Beating in Rural India: A Husband's Right? *Economic and Political Weekly* (India) 23: 558-562.

Jouriles, E.N., Norwood, W.D., McDonald, R. and Petas, B. (2001), Domestic Violence and Child Adjustment. In J.H. Grych & F.D. Fincham (Eds.), *Inter-parental Conflicts and Child Development: Theory, Research and Applications,* New York: Cambridge University Press, 315-336.

Klevens, J., Bayon, M. and Sierra, M. (2000), Risk Factors and Context of Men Who Physically Abuse in Bogota, Colombia. *Child Abuse and Neglect,* 24: 323-332.

Kliewer, W., Murrelle, L., Mejia, R., Torres, D., Galvis, Y., and Angold, A. (2001), Exposure to Violence against a Family Member and Internalising Symptoms in Colombian Adolescents: The Protective Effects of Family Support, *Journal of Consulting Clinical Psychology,* 69: 971-982.

Larsen, R. (2002), Globalisation, Societal Change and New Technologies: What They Mean for the Future of Adolescence, *Journal of Research on Adolescence,* 12: 1-30.

Larson, R.W., Wilson, S., and Mortimer, J. T. (2002), Conclusion: Adolescent's Preparation for the Future. In Larson, R. W., Brown, B.B., & Mortimer, J.T. (2002) edited book on: *Adolescents' Preparation for the Future: Perils and Promise.* A Report of the Study Group on Adolescence in the 21st Century. Miami: The Society for Research on Adolescence. pp.159-166.

Larson, R. W., Brown, B.B., & Mortimer, J.T. (2002), Edited Book on: *Adolescents' Preparation for the Future: Perils and Promise.* A Report of the Study Group on Adolescence in the 21st Century. Miami: The Society for Research on Adolescence.

Lynch, M. and Cicchetti, D. (1998), An Ecological Transactional Analysis of Children and Contexts: The Longitudinal Interplay Among Children Maltreatment, Community Violence and

Children's Symptomatology, Development and Psychopathology, 10: 235-257.

Martin, J.P. (1978), *Violence and the Family*, England: John Wiley & Sons.

Maya, J.M., Torres de Galvis, Y., Murrelle, L., Rodriguez, M.A., Mejia, R., Gavaria, D. (2000), Use and Abuse of Psychoactive Substances and Associated Factors in Juvenile Delinquency, Medellin, Colombia: Institute of Health Sciences-Colciencias and Inter-American Development Bank.

Mejia, R., Kliewer, W., and Williams, L. (2006), Domestic Violence Exposure in Colombian Adolescents: Pathways to Violent and Pro-social Behaviour, *Journal of Traumatic Stress*, 19 (2) April: 257-267.

Mishra, G. (1995), Reflection on Continuity and Change in the Indian Family System. *Trends in Social Science Research*, 2 (1): 27-30.

Nair, G.R. (1997), An Anatomy of Child Abuse. *Social Welfare*, 44: 76-78.

Nanda, G.K. and Dash, A.S. (1996), *Disadvantaged School, Competence and Invulnerability*. Panchajanya, Bhubaneswar.

Osofsky, J.D. (1995), Children Who Witness Domestic Violence: The Invisible Victims, Social Policy Report of Society for Research in Child Development. Chicago.

Parker, J. and Beson, M. (2004), Parent Adolescent Relations and Adolescent Functioning: Self-esteem, Substance Abuse, and Delinquency, *Adolescence*, 39 (155): 519-530.

Patnaik, M.M. (2007), Family Violence: Impact of Family Life: In Carson and Chowdhury (Eds.), *Indian Families at the Crossroads: Preparing Families for the New Millennium*. New Delhi: Gyan Publishing House. pp. 35-50.

Resnick, M., Ireland, M. and Borowsky, I. (2004), Youth Violence Perpetration: What Protects? What Predicts? Findings from the National Longitudinal Study of Adolescent Health, *Journal of Adolescent Health*, 35(5): 424e1-424e10.

Saraswathi, T.S. and Pai, S. (1997), Socialization in the Indian Context. In H. Rao and D. Sinha (Eds.), *Asian Perspectives in Psychology* (New Delhi: Sage Methodology Series), 74-92.

Sinha, D. (1988), The Family Scenario of a Developing Country and its Implications for Mental Health: The Case of India". In P.R.

Dasen, J.W. Berry and N. Sartorius (Eds.), *Health and Cross-cultural Psychology: Towards Applications.*, California: Sage.

Sunny, C. (2003), Domestic Violence Against Women– Rεport on a Situational Analysis in Ernakulam District, Kerala, *Social Change,* 33: 26-54.

UNICEF (1990), The Girl Child in India – SAARC Year of the Girl Child, New Delhi.

Vindhya, U. (2003), Private Crimes and Public Sanction: Violence against Women in the Family. In Margrit Pernau, Imtiaz Ahmad, and Hrelmut Reifeld edited book on: Family and Gender: Changing Values in Germany and India. New Delhi: Sage Publication, pp. 322–348.

Visaria, L. (1999), Violence Against Women in India: Evidence from Rural Gujarat, In: *Domestic Violence in India: A Summary Report (Ibid.).*

Williams, K.R. (1992), Social Source of Marital Violence and Deterrence: Testing and Integrated Theory of Assaults between Partners, *Journal of Marriage and Family,* 54 (3): 62-629.

World Health Organisation (1999), *Programming for Adolescent Health and Development: Report of a WHO/UNFPA/UNICEF Study Group,* Geneva, Switzerland.

5

Determinants of Children Ever Born (CEB) Among Slum Mothers: A Multiple Classification Analysis

Md. Mahfuzar Rahman and Md. Rafiqul Islam

Introduction

Bangladesh, situated in South Asia, is one of the developing countries in the world and emerged as a unitary and independent country on December 16, 1971 through a bloody-shed war. The population of Bangladesh is increased from about 42 millions in 1941 (BBS, 1998) to 129.25 millions in 2001 (Census, 2001). It is now 149 millions with growth rate 1.47 and total fertility rate (TFR) 3.0 (World Population Data Sheet, 2007).

The number of CEB to a particular woman is an aggregate measure of her lifetime fertility experience up to the moment at which the data are collected. Fertility is the reproductive performance of woman. It is the variable, which may have to be manipulated by policy interventions in order to reduce population growth (Nas, 1971; UN, 1973). Thus "the problematical factors in determining the course of population have been levels and conditions of fertility and the prospects for their change" (UN, 1979). Fertility behavior is an important indicator for understanding the trend of population dynamics of any country. Over the past four decades the developed and developing worlds have been witness to important changes in reproductive behavior among their adult and adolescent population.

In Bangladesh, fertility is high even by the standards of developing nations. Although teenage fertility rates were declining throughout the late 1960s and early 1970s, their reproductive behavior emerged as a major concern in many developing countries. The people of Bangladesh are often criticized for having many children when they are too poor to provide for them. Recent evidence suggests that fertility has started to decline in Bangladesh (Amin et al., 1993). There have been considerable social and economic changes in the country and contend that these have changed couples attitudes about family size in such a way as to lead to decline fertility (Caldwell et al., 1999). The medium variant scenario of the United Nations Projection indicates that Bangladesh will achieve replacement level fertility (2.1 children per women) around 2025 (United Nations, 1991).

Modernization has been claimed to be an instigator of fertility decline in many societies (Caldwell, 1976; Coale, 1973). Innovations in health care, increased education and improved communication are thought to bring about forces dissolving traditional tendencies toward large families and to reduction in the need to have many pregnancies to achieve the desired number of surviving children. Similarly, lower child mortality might also reduce the pressure for women to start childbearing at younger ages in order to meet their family goals.

In Asian countries, rates of childbearing vary widely where fewer than 10.0 % of the women had childbirth before age 20 (UN, 1989). When family planning programs both private and public were initiated in the 1960's in Bangladesh, older women became the principal beneficiaries, finding modern contraceptive methods more acceptable than the traditional methods. Thus, fertility among older women has fallen more acceptable than fertility among younger women.

To reduce the civic problem already exists in slum areas, it is necessary to identify the demographic, socio-economic, cultural and programmatic factors associated with these. Then, strategic and programmatic measures should be undertaken to get maximum benefits from available facilities. In the background of this situation, it seemed vital importance to undertake an exploratory study concerning mean number of CEB of slum mothers. This exploratory endeavour is further expected to contribute to the development and proper implementation of existing health and fertility control programs through necessary changes in customs and laws that will address the indispensable wants of the slum population in Bangladesh.

Therefore, the main aim and objective of this study is to investigate the contribution of some selected variables on CEB among slum mothers by MCA.

Data and Methods

The data of this study were collected from 8 different slums of 3 wards of RCC, Bangladesh. These data were collected purposive sampling technique through personal interview method from 700 married women in their reproductive ages who had at least one child under five years of age at the time of interview and it had been taken into consideration that the selection should be consistent with our objectives.

In 1934, Yates developed the multiple classification analysis (MCA) and, it was later expanded and detailed by Anderson and Bancraft in 1952. In 1963, the computerized MCA program was prepared by a group of researcher at the Survey Research Center of the University of Michigan. Since then, the MCA program has been widely used in social science research. MCA requires one dependent variable and two or more independent variables. The dependent variable can be either a continuous or a categorical variable, but all the independent variables must be categorical variables. MCA can equally handle the nominal and ordinal variables and can also deal with linear and non-linear relationships of predictor variables with dependent variables. Mathematically, the model can be expressed by the following equation:

$$Y_{ijk} = \overline{Y} + a_i + b_i + c_k + ... + e_{ijk}$$

where,

Y_{ijk} = The value or score of an individual who falls in the ith category of the factor A, jth category of the factor B and kth category of the factor C.

$\overline{Y}$ = Grand mean of Y

a_i = The effect due to the ith category of the factor A, which is equal to the difference between $\overline{Y}$ and the mean of its category of factor A.

b_j = The effect due to the jth category of the factor B, which is equal to the difference between $\overline{Y}$ and the mean of its category of factor B.

c_k = The effect due to the kth category of the factor C, which is equal to the difference between $\overline{Y}$ and the mean of its category of factor C.

e_{ijk} = The error term related with score of the individuals.

There are two effects in MCA- gross/unadjusted effect and net/adjusted effect. These effects measure those of the predictor alone after taking into account the effects of all other predictors. The unadjusted, eta-square (h^2) coefficients are correlation ratio, which explain how well the predictor variable explains the variation in the dependent variables. Similarly, the beta-square (b^2) coefficient indicates the proportion of variation explained the dependent nariable by the other predictor variables.

The mean number of CEB is used as dependent variable and some selected variables such as age at marriage, family planning, family's income, household asset index, birth place of respondent, respondent's education, religion, husband's occupation and current age of respondent are used as independent variables in this model.

Results and Discussion

Mean Number of CEB

The number of children of a woman has ever born is a cohort measure of fertility. Because, it provides a somewhat different picture of fertility levels, trends and differentials than do period measures of fertility such as crude birth rate (CBR) and TFR. It is obvious that fertility is directly proportional to current age. That is, for women of higher age, number of CEB and number of living children will be high as compared to women of younger ages. The following table is shown the percentage distribution of mothers by the number of CEB.

Table 1
Percentage Distribution of Mothers by CEB

	Current Age of Respondent			
Children Ever Born	*<20*	*20-29*	*30-49*	*All*
1	83.4	32.9	4.3	39.9
2	13.2	41.7	19.4	30.1
3+	3.4	25.4	76.3	30.0
Total	100	100	100	100
N	175	386	139	700
Mean	1.21	2.01	3.53	2.11

From the Table 1, it is seen that for the age group <20, 83.4% of women have one children. The proportion of mothers decreases as the number of CEB increases. For age group 20-29 and 30-49, 32.9% and 4.3% have one child, 41.7% and 19.4% have two child and 25.4% and 76.3% have 3 and above children respectively. The mean number of CEB for <20 years age mothers are 1.21 which is high enough and indicates that in the slum areas of RCC, women marry at early age e.g. below the legal age at marriage (18 years) and start child bearing just after marriage and before reaching age 20 they have on average more than one children.

Mean Number of CEB by MCA

The mean number of CEB by some selected socio-economic and demographic characteristics are demonstrated in Table 2.

The result is indicated that the proportion of variance explained by MCA is multiple R^2=0.486 and multiple R=0.697. Of all the variables, respondent's education and current age of respondents appear as the important determinants of CEB and other variables play relatively less important role on CEB.

It is observed that current age of mothers is closely related to the CEB. The current age of respondents among the selected factors is the most effective one and showing the 1st strongest association (η^2= 0.631) with CEB even if, the effect of respondent's current age remains high after adjusting the effects of all other predictors employed in the model (β^2=0.589). The respondents whose ages are 30-49 (3.53) and 20-29 categories (2.01) tend to have higher fertility than the average, but for the age <20 are lower (1.21). The result is indicated that the CEB are higher in accordance with higher ages. This may due to the lack of respondent's proper awareness living in slum areas about the complications of health, which may occur with childbirth in higher ages. Even the life may be lost if mothers give child due to higher ages, which is not clear to them. Among the respondents, while higher levels of education are associated with lower probability of giving births, the direction of causality is less clear. Findings are also indicated that educational attainment is the 2nd strongest association (η^2 = 0.412) with mean number of CEB. The effect of educational levels remains high after adjusting the effect of all other predictors in the model (β^2 = 0.269). It is important to note that secondary+ level educated women have been found to have lower fertility than the illiterates. The mean number of CEB is 2.48 for women who are illiterate and 2.03 and 1.68 for women who have primary and secondary+ level education. So, it may be concluded that the respondents with more education in the slum areas have lower fertility.

Respondent's age at marriage seems to be less effective factor than respondent's current age in explaining the variation in mean number of CEB (η^2 = 0.007 and β^2 = 0.084). The women whose age at marriage below 20 years has the mean number of CEB of 2.12, while it is 1.28 for women whose age at marriage 20years. It indicates that the mean number of CEB is higher for those women who marry at below 20 years than the women who marry at 20 years. This means that the women of the study area whose age at marriage is below 20 is not so conscious about their family size than the women whose age at marriage is 20. Family planning is another factor that shows weak strength in explaining variation in mean number of CEB (η^2 = 0.013) and its effects are also low after adjusting for the model (β^2 = 0.001). The mean number of CEB for women of practicing family planning is (2.10) which is less than the women who not practicing family planning (2.12). Thus, it could be said that the practices of family planning by the women of the slums have very little effect on lower fertility.

Family's monthly income also shows relatively very low strength in explaining variation in mean number of CEB (η^2 = 0.071, β^2 = 0.037). The women whose family's monthly income are TK. 4000> have lower childbearing (2.04) than the women whose family's monthly income are TK. <3000 (2.10), though the childbearing is (2.16) for women whose family's monthly income are TK. 3000-4000. So, it may conclude that the family's monthly income effectively change the childbearing pattern in the slum areas with higher monthly income. Household asset index appears to be a weak predictor of CEB (η^2 = 0.039) but the effect of household asset index increases after adjusting for the effect of all other predictor in the model (β^2 = 0.055). The mean number of CEB for the lower class women is 2.07, which is much higher than the women of upper class (1.96). But at the same time, the mean number of CEB for the middle class women (2.19).

The effect of birthplace of respondents remains low on mean number of CEB (η^2 = 0.030, β^2 = 0.011). The women, whose birthplace is in rural, have mean number of CEB (2.07), which is less than the women whose birthplace is in urban (2.11). That is, the women living in slums whose birthplace are urban contributes higher in CEB than the women who are from rural areas although both of them reside in the same location. Although Muslim women have higher (2.11) fertility than their non-Muslim counterparts (1.92), religion becomes less important factor in explaining vitiations in mean number of CEB ($\eta^2 = 0.001$, $\beta^2 = 0.016$) when other socio-economic factors are controlled. This may happen because of less exposures of Muslim to contraception practicing behavior than the non-Muslim who are always more exposure.

Table 2
Mean Number of CEB by Some Selected Variables Applying MCA

Explanatory Variables	*Unadjusted Mean*	*Adjusted Mean*	*Correlation Ratio*	
			η^2	β^2
Age at Marriage			0.007	0.084
<20	2.11	2.12		
20	2.18	1.28		
Family Planning			0.013	0.001
No	2.00	2.12		
Yes	2.11	2.10		
Family's Income			0.071	0.037
<3000	2.02	2.10		
3000-4000	2.21	2.16		
4000>	2.14	2.04		
Household Asset Index			0.039	0.055
Lower	2.08	2.07		
Middle	2.17	2.19		
Upper	2.03	1.96		
Birth Place of Respondent			0.030	0.011
Rural	2.22	2.07		
Urban	2.10	2.11		
Respondent's Education			0.412	0.269
Illiterate	2.70	2.48		
Primary	1.89	2.03		
Secondary+	1.51	1.68		
Religion			0.001	0.016
Muslim	2.11	2.11		
Non-Muslim	2.13	1.92		
Husband's Occupation			0.041	0.037
Service	1.97	1.98		
Business	2.16	2.14		
Labor	2.11	2.12		
Current Age of respondent			0.631	0.589
<20	1.21	1.25		
20-29	2.01	2.03		
30-49	3.53	3.43		
Grand Mean		2.11		
Multiple R		0.697		
Multiple R^2		0.486		

Table 3 produces the results of zero order correlation coefficients of CEB with various demographic and socio-economic variables. Here an attempt is made to look at the extent of influences of the variables on CEB on the basis of the results produced by MCA. Using the value of b^2 from Table 2 with the values of Table 3, the indirect effect of the variables can be estimated. The salient features of the in Table 3 are as follows.

Table 3
Zero-order Correlation Co-efficient of Mean Number of CEB by Some Selected Variables

	Y	X_1	X_2	X_3	X_4	X_5	X_6	X_7	X_8	X_9
Y	1.000	.007	.013	.052	.020	-.030	-.404**	.001	.021	.616**
X_1		1.000	.018	.098**	.051	.009	.018	-.014	-.190**	.163**
X_2			1.000	.040	.014	.046	-.020	.015	-.017	.020
X_3				1.000	.467**	.034	.092*	.007	-.406**	.132**
X_4					1.000	.080*	.145**	-.020	-.468**	.083*
X_5						1.000	.076*	-.089*	-.129*	-.025
X_6							1.000	.015	-.200**	-.214
X_7								1.000	.010	.028
X_8									1.00	-.108**
X_9										1.000

* indicates at 5% level of significant
** indicates at 1% level of significant

Y = Children ever born
X_1 = Age at marriage
X_2 = Family planning
X_3 = Family's income
X_4 = Household asset index
X_5 = Birth place of respondent
X_6 = Respondent's education
X_7 = Religion
X_8 = Husband's occupation
X_9 = Current age of respondent

Respondent's education has a significant contribution on CEB, producing a negative association with CEB. The correlation coefficient is found to be r = -0.404. Among the included variables, respondent's education has the 2nd strongest influence on CRB. Respondent's education has the direct effect on CEB and also has the indirect effect through age at marriage, birthplace of respondents and family planning. The indirect effect of education on CEB through age at marriage, birthplace of respondents and family planning is 0.0015, 0.00084 and 0.00002 respectively.

The correlation coefficient between age at marriage and respondent's education is r =0.018 which implies that the respondent's education increases their age at marriage. So, age at marriage affects CEB through respondent's education. The indirect effect of age at marriage on CEB through respondent's education is 0.005

The correlation coefficient between family's income and household asset index show a significant association (r =0.145). The indirect effect of family's income on CEB through household asset index is 0.008.

It has been observed that husband's occupation has a significant association with household asset index (r = -0.468). So, the indirect effect of husband's occupation on CEB through household asset index is 0.026.

Conclusion and Policy Recommendations

This study is indicated that the mean number of CEB (2.11) for all mothers is very high in the slum areas of RCC. From the study, it is also showed that the current age of mothers is closely related to the CEB and the most effective one among the selected factors. It is showed the strongest association (h^2 = 0.631) with CEB. The effect of respondent's current age remains also high after adjusting the effects of all other predictors used in the model (b^2=0.589). The respondents whose ages are 30-49 (3.53) and 20-29 category (2.01) tend to have higher fertility than the average, followed by the age <20 (1.21). Similarly, their education also plays a core role in reducing the mean number of CEB.

Therefore, an effective policies and recommendations are needed to create awareness among mothers living not only in slum areas of RCC but also other regions in Bangladesh. The specific recommendations are as follows:

- The slogan "One child is enough if two, not more" should be well accepted and early marriage of women (before age 18) should be discouraged to all by creating awareness about its negative impact on reproductive health and fertility. To do this, the law relating to it should be uniformly enforced all over the country.

- Specific strategy should be taken to educate the inhabitants of slum areas especially the women living in slum.
- Pregnancy related complications are more acute (even if the life may be lost) in higher ages. This should be strongly informed to slum areas through by information, education and communication (IEC) campaigns such as various mass media (radio, TV, billboard etc.).

References

Anderson, R.L. and T.A. Bancraft (1952), Statistical Theory in Research, New York, Mcgraw Hill.

Amin, N.R. and A.G. Marian (1993), Son Preference in Bangladesh: An Emerging Barrier to Fertility Regulation. *Journal of Biosocial Science*, Vol. 19, P. 221-228.

Bangladesh Bureau of Statistics (BBS) (1998), Statistical Year Book of Bangladesh, 1997-1998 Dhaka: Statistical Division, Governments of the People's Republic of Bangladesh.

Caldwell et al. (1999), Bangladesh Fertility Decline: An Interpretation. Population Development Review (New York), Vol. 25, P. 67-68.

Coale, A.J. (1973), The Demographic Transition. In the Population Debate-Dimension and Perspectives. Vol. 1, UN.

Population Reference Bureau (PRB) (2006), World Population Data Sheet.1875 Connecticut Ave, NW, Washington, DC 20009 USA. E-mail: popref@prb.org.

Population Census (2001), Bangladesh Bureau of Statistics, Planning Division, Ministry of Planning, Governments of the People's Republic of Bangladesh. July 2003.

United Nations (1989), Adolescent Reproductive Behavior. Evidence from Developing Countries, Population Studies, Vol. II, No. 109.

United Nations (1973), Women's Employment and Fertility: Comparative Analysis of World Fertility Survey Results for 38 Developing countries, Population Studies Series No. 96, New York.

United Nations (1979), World Population, United Nations Population Division, Department of Economic and Social Affairs, New York, U.S.A.

United Nations (1991), Adolescent Reproductive Behaviour: Evidence from Developing Countries, Population Studies, Vol. II, No. 109.

Yates, F. (1934), The Analysis of Variance with Unequal Numbers in the Different Classes, *Journal of American Statistical Association*, Vol. 29, pp.51-66.

6

Child Labour – A Case Study

Tapan Kumar Shandilya

Child labour is a burning issue of global concern. Child labour is a universal phenomenon and it is a by-product of socio-economic structure of the society. Children are an asset for any society as well as to nation. They are the blooming flowers of the society therefore; it is a duty of the society to protect these flowers so as to have a meaningful contribution through them in the future. It is a well-known fact that the future of a society or a nation or world depends upon the sound growth of the children. Due to certain forces and circumstances, children are compelled to work in the early stages of their childhood, which harm to the children and ultimately, the society. Hence, child labour is considered as an economic and social problem. The most horrifying myth about child labour is that they have very little say in choosing their occupation. They have no right as workers and they cannot join labour unions to raise their voice against exploitation. The Supreme Court, in one of the cases related to child labour, has observed: if there be no proper growth of children today, the future of the country will be in dark. It is the obligation of every generation to bring up children who will be citizens of tomorrow in a proper way. Today's children will be leaders of tomorrow who will hold the country's banner high and maintain the prestige of the nation. If the government of India commits itself towards combating the problem of child labour, then it is sure that the children of India who at present have engaged themselves in long hours of work could be freed and enabled to breathe joy of freedom. But today, working condition of child labour is a horrible child has to work more than 15 hours a day or till their masters are satisfied, without rest which is a complete violation of the Child Labour (P & R) Act, 1986. The child labours employed by private contractors were paid meagre wages and were living like animals in overcrowded slums.

Child labour in Bihar is found to exist in different fields Thousands of children are working in Hotels and Restaurants, Tea-Stalls, etc. I visited many hotels in search of child labour in Patna town. The researcher observed that long and arduous work had affected the children's nerves. During interview, the children betrayed extreme nervousness. In general, children are required to work beyond their physical capacity for a mere pittance. They do not get enough rest and recreation and are exposed to various pollutants and chemicals. In some cases, by the time children reach adulthood they are so debilitated that they cannot find gainful employment as adults. In hotels and restaurants they have to work from morning till the last customer leaves at night. Not only long hours of work and low wages, children also have to face many occupational problems. What are the motives with which these children have taken up work at such an early age? What factors have compelled them to go to work? In order to find solution to these questions the present study has been undertaken.

Objective of the Study

The main objectives of this study are mentioned below:

(a) To study the causes of child labour in hotel establishments in Patna.

(b) To study the demographic characteristics of the sample population.

(c). To study the working conditions and wage structure.

(d) To study the consequences of child labour on the socio-economic condition of the sample population.

(e) To assess the workload on the children and facilities provided to them and their employees.

(f) To evaluate effectiveness of the operation of child labour welfare legislations at the hands of government agencies.

(g) To suggest possible remedies for this social evil.

Hypothesis of the Study

- This is a socio-economic problem. So welfare legislations would not be sufficient to check this evil.
- The working condition of the child labour in Hotels, Tea stalls, Sweet-shops, Dhabas are far from satisfaction when compared to the spirit of child labour welfare legislations.
- That despite adequate safeguard and member of legislations the problems of child labour is increasing day-by-day for want of poor execution of these welfare legislations.

Methodology of the Study

The data for the study have been collected through a questionnaire. The questionnaire contained questions relating to personal details of the child labourers, income and educational level of the parents and reasons for taking up job. Convenience sampling method has been followed in choosing a sample of 184 child labourers working in hotels situated in Patna town.

Universe of the Study

The area of the present study is Patna town, which is capital of Bihar State. The town is spread over 99.45 sq kms. The town has various trades preferred by people in unorganized sector including Transport, Hotels, Construction work, Dairy farming, Poultry, Motor servicing, Bakeries and other many small manufacturing units which have employed a considerable chunk of population as labourers in them. A sizable population of the town mostly depends upon trade commerce, various service occupations and manufacturing units. The present study is confined to the Tea Stalls, Sweet Shops, Hotels and Line-Hotels located at the Patna town. We have selected a few pockets of these establishments to analyze the working conditions of child labourers. We have selected 70 establishments because it is not possible for us to conduct a comprehensive study of the entire Tea-stalls, Sweet shops and Hotels located in the town. Therefore, a few pockets have been chosen for the study. All there are mainly located in *Rajendra Nagar, Kankar Bagh, Kadam Kuan, Railway Station, Bus Stand, Gandhi Maidan, Boaring Road, Mushallapur Hat, Patna city, Raja Bazar, Mahendru, Sultanganj*. We have tried to cover almost all the workers of this establishment with a view to knowing the real number of child labourers in this establishment. Much attempt has been made to highlight all aspects of the child labour of the town.

Profile of Patna Town

Patna, the headquarters of the district as well as the capital of the state, is the largest city in Bihar, having a population of million plus (more than 10 lakhs) as per the provisional population figures of 2001 Census. The position of Patna among the cities of India, so far as population is concerned, is quite low. The city has glorious past and can boast of a very rich cultural heritage. In the early nineteenth century Buchanan Hamilton (1807-14) estimated its population at 3,12,000. As per the census of 1872, however, the population actually returned was 158,900 only. It seems that there were large omissions at this census and the actual number was perhaps more. As per the next census (1881) also, the population returned was 170,654 only. Between 1881 and 1921 the population of Patna was almost continuously on the decline mainly due to decrease in the river borne trade and, perhaps, due to repeated epidemics of plague. The population recorded during the census of 1911 was 136,153 which marked a slight increase over the 1901 population of 134,785. But the 1901 figure was admittedly low because of the virulent plague, which was raging at the time of census. A recount made six months later disclosed the population of this town at 153,739. In 1921 the population of Patna was 'at its lowest (119,976). It continued to fall in the decade 1911-21 in spite of the fact that the New Capital area had been set-up consequent upon designation of the city as the capital of the newly created Bihar Province. Perhaps the figures of 1921 were, to some extent, affected by the Non-Cooperation Movement also. Since 1921, however, the city has witnessed a steady growth. In 1931 its population stood at 159,690, an increase of over 33 percent, attributable mainly to the rapid development of the New Capital area and Bankipur area, extension of the University and large influx of immigrants. In the following decade (1931-41) also, the increase continued uninterrupted but at a slower pace (23 percent). High decadal increase occurred in 1941-51 when the population increased by 44.33 percent. This naturally reflected the rapid expansion of several Government departments and Semi-Government agencies no less than the beginnings of a developing urban economy and persons from West Punjab and East Bengal must have contributed substantially to the high rate of increase. In the decade 1951-61, the trend had been maintained though the rate of percentage increase had gone down to 28.61. In absolute number, however, the increase in the decade 1951-61 was not much less than in 1941-51 (Source: General Report, Bihar, 1961 Census). However, the decade 1971-81 had shown highest decadal increase in the 20th Century when population of Patna City increased by 64.14 percent. This reflected the rapid extension of the Municipal jurisdiction as many rural areas got merged in the city area. The percentage decadal variation during 1981-91 was significantly low. That the rate was not higher is presumably due to the fact that Patna owed it importance mainly to its being an administrative and educational town. It can hardly boast of any significant development in industrial or commercial sector during the decade.

During the present decade, i.e. in 1991-2001, the city of Patna has again shown comparatively higher decadal growth rate (50.12%). In 1911, the geographical area of Patna was mentioned as only 23.04 km while it has increased to 99.45 km in 2001 Census.

Findings of this Study

Child labour is a widespread phenomenon. There are several factors, which are responsible for the early entry of children in the labour force, but all of them cannot be quantified. The consequences of child labour are innumerable; some of them leave their impact on the child alone, whereas, others influence the society as a whole. There exists a certain relationship between the causes and effects of child labour, which is responsible for the continuance of this social evil. This section is aimed at finding the likely determinants and consequences of child labour and establishing a relationship between them.

Background Characteristics of Children

As mentioned earlier, the study surveyed 184 children who are currently working. All these children were males. Some background characteristics collected included their religion, age and level of education.

Religion/Caste

As observed from Table 1, data on religion-wise distribution shows that majority (95 percent) of the children are Hindus. Remaining 5 percent belong to Muslim religion. Further, caste wise distribution of the same indicates that two-thirds (66 percent) of the children belong to other backward caste, whereas around a quarter of them (24 percent) are scheduled caste. Children belonging to scheduled tribe constituted 7 percent and 4 percent belonged to general caste. Data clearly indicates that it is generally the children of the low social group who usually are economically poor, are the ones who are working as child labourers.

Age

Data on age-wise distribution indicates that the age of the surveyed children ranged between six years to 14 years. The number of children in each year varied and there is no particular pattern as such. Maximum (38 percent) number of children is reported in the age group of 12 to 13 years, followed by 28 percent in 8 to 9 years. Thirteen and fourteen

Table 1
Background Characteristics of the Children

Particulars	*Percent*
Religion	
Hindu	94.6
Muslim	5.4
Caste	
Scheduled caste	23.9
Scheduled tribe	6.5
Other backward castes	66.1
General castes	
Age (in years)	3.5
6-7	14.3
8-9	28.2
10-11	13.0
12-13	38.0
14 and above	6.5
Mean Age of Child (in yrs)	10.4
Number of Children	184

Source: Primary Data Collection

Thirteen and fourteen percent of the children are aged 6 to 7 years and 10 to 11 years respectively. Only 7 percent of the total children reported aged 14 years. Thus the overall mean age of the children interviewed is reported to be around 10 years.

Education Level

Children were further asked if they had either taken any formal education or could at least read and write. As seen from the analyses, almost three out of four (78 percent) children could not even read and write. Only 22 percent of them could read and write. Further probing was done from these children to understand the class upto which they had studied. Apparently the percentage of children decreases with the increase in the level of schooling. Little more than half of the children (55 percent) had studied upto class 2, 30 percent had reporting of class 3 to 4th, while only 10 and 5 percent had studied upto class 5 to 6 and 7th and above level of education respectively.

Currently none of the children are attending any formal or informal type of schooling. Hence, reasons for both discontinuing and/or never attending school are collected from the surveyed children. The most common reason cited by the children includes 'financial constrain' of the family (63 percent) that prevented them from attending school. Thirty two percent of the children reported that they 'dislike studies' and hence they did not go to any school. Some of the other reasons mentioned for never attending/discontinuing the studies include 'teacher is very rude' (16 percent), 'due to household chores' (8 percent) and 'school is far away' (5 percent). Thus, to a large extent it is the family background which inhibits the child from attending school, but at the same time the school also plays an important role in building environment. The attitude of the teachers towards these children can be made more cordial, as a result children could also be drained into studies and continue studying.

Given the fact that all these children are now working, attempt is made to assess their sensibility to attending school if given an opportunity for the same. Data indicates that more than half (59 percent) of the respondents did respond favorably, that is they would go back to school if they got the chance for the same. At the same time these children were further asked if their employer would allow them to do so. But only around three out of ten children mentioned that their employer would encourage them to do so, while the remaining was of the reverse opinion.

Background Characteristics of the Children's Family

Along with the child's characteristics some basic information about the child's family was also collected, namely, in terms of the number of family members staying in the household, level of education of the parents and their working status. Monthly income of the family was also collected as all this could have an implication on the work in status of the child.

As Table 2 shows that the average number of family members in the child's family is on the higher side at 7 members as compared to a general household size, which has 6.1 members in the state of Bihar (NFHS-2, 2001). Only 10 percent of the child's family had less than four members in their family. In yet another 12 percent, the number of members in the family was more than 11.

Level of literacy of the children's parents was also looked into, as this has a bearing on children's education and their care. Data shows that both mother and father of almost seven out of ten children cannot read and write. Only in case of one percent of the children both mother and father could read and write. In the case of 22 percent children only father could read and write and in case of 7 percent children only mother could read and write.

Table 2
Characteristics of Parents

Particulars	*Percent*
Number of family members	
< 4	9.8
5-7	47.8
8-10	
30.4	
11-13	9.8
14 and above	2.2
Mean family size	7.3
Literacy level of parentsCan read and write	
Both father/mother	1.1
Only father	21.7
Only mother	
6.5	
Cannot read and write	70.7
Working status of parentsDaily labour	
Both mother and father are working as daily labour	62.0

Source: Primary Data Collection.

Duration and Shifting of Work

Mobility of the children working in the hotel industry could be mainly in two ways. A shift from one hotel to the other but being involved in the same nature of work or shifting from one type of work to another type for different reasons. This would also indirectly indicate how long children below 14 years with the skills available with them continue working at one site.

Among the total 184 children interviewed at their current work place for the study, for 38 of them this was their first experience at the job. Almost six out of ten children were working at the respective hotel site for more than a year. Only 22 percent of the children had started working within five months prior to the survey. The average duration of months children are currently working at the total is around 14 months. Among the 146 children who have worked earlier, 92 (50 percent) were working in the same type of job earlier, while 54 children (29 percent) were working in another type of job. The average length of months children had worked in these jobs was 10 months and 5 months respectively.

Work

At the time of the survey all the children were working in the hotel. An attempt is made to understand the nature of work in which the children were involved. Analysis of the data indicates that around a little more than one-third of the children were involved either in 'carrying the used plates/ dishes' or in 'washing of used plates/dishes'. Around 19 percent of the children were involved in 'serving food/ tea' to the customers, while 8 percent were also involved in cooking. Four percent of the children had to attend to work outside the hotel premises, as they were involved in buying of products from the market.

These children were also asked the reason for their working. Nine out of ten children reported that it was the poor economic condition of their family that compelled them to work. This also corroborates with the findings discussed earlier on the family characteristics of the surveyed children. Some of the other reasons mentioned included 'parents did not fulfill their needs' (9 percent), ' parents cannot work' (8 percent), etc. Overall, the reasons elicited do indicate that it is the poor economic condition of the child's family that compels him to work.

Table 3
Shift in the Pattern of Work

Particulars	*Percent*
Current job is first time work	20.6
Total children	184
Duration of Job in Other Place	
Upto 2 months	43.5
2 to 5 months	13
5 months to 1 year	10.9
1 to 1.5 years	6.5
1.5 to 2 years	2.2
2 to more years	23.9
Mean Months Worked	9.7
Number of children who earlier worked in same type of work	92
Other job in Other Place	
Upto 2 months	40
2 to 5 months	20
5 months to 1 year	30
1 to 1.5 year	10

Source: Primary Data Collection

Table 4
Working Status of Children

Particulars	*Percentage*
Nature of Work"	
Carry dirty plates/dishes	38.9
Wash dirty plates/dishes	37
Cooking food tea	8.3
Serve food tea	19
Work in market	3.7
Reasons for Working"	
Poor economic condition	90.2
Parents did not fulfill all needs	8.7
Parents cannot work	7.6
Elders' responsibility	5.4
To pay debt of owner/employer	1.1
Others	5.4
Number of Children	184

"Multiple responses
Source: Primary Data Collection.

Analyses of the work by the age of children are also done to understand whether there is any variation in the type of work by variation in their age. The data should however be interpreted cautiously as the number of cases in each row is small. As seen in Table 5, it is observed that the younger children that are those aged six to eight years are more involved in collecting and washing of used/dirty plates. As they grow older, they are involved in other activities in the hotel too.

Further, the children were also asked if they liked the job and if so the reasons for the same. All the 184 children opined that they liked the job. Among which about 43 percent of the children liked it because they had a relative who was also working in the same hotel. Another one third of the children found the work interesting. Some of the other reasons expressed included 'get more money in this work' (12 percent), 'get good food' (5 percent), etc. A small percentage (5 percent) of the children was not able to decide whether they liked the job or not, while another five percent mentioned that they needed the job and there was no other alternative for them. Three percent of the children also mentioned that the income received from the job was necessary for their family. In other words the economic pressure of these children did not give them any choice to mention whether they liked the job or not.

Table 5
Distribution of Children's Work by Their Age

(Percentage)

Particulars	*Collect Dirty Plates*	*Wash Dirty Plates*	*Engaged in Other Work*	*Number of Children*
Age of Children (in year)				
6	66.7	33.3		6
7	40	50	10	20
8	40	40	20	30
9	25.5	67	7.5	22
10	57.1	14.3	28.6	14
11	20	60	20	10
12	40	33.3	26.7	30
13	40	25	35	40
14	33.3	16.7	50	12
Number of Children				184

Source: Primary Data Collection

In addition to liking the work, children were probed about any problems if they faced at the work place. Only ten children out of the total 184 did not have any problem. Among the remaining children some of them have more than one problem. The most common problem mentioned was 'employer usually scolds' (71 percent). A little more than a quarter of the children also said that they 'often get hurt' (26 percent), 'very long hours of work' (29 percent) and 'not adequately /regularly paid' (29 percent). Four children each also mentioned that they could not take leave and they did not have time for reading. The data very clearly shows that the children are in a very vulnerable position due to their age, compulsion to work and as they usually stay within the premises, they are utilized to work for long hours. The children are misused by their employers further by not paying them regularly and getting work from them for which they are not equipped.

Table 6
Reasons for Liking the Current Job

*Reasons**	*Percent*
Relative working here	43.3
Interesting	33.3
Pay more money	12.0
No alternative/needs jobs	5.4
Provide good food	5.0
For learning	4.3
It is good job from past work	3.3
Necessary for family income/foods	3.3
Don't know	5.5
Number of Children	184

*Multiple responses.
Source: Primary Data Collection.

Table 7
Problems in Work Place

*Type of Problems**	*Percent*
No problem	5.4
Employers usually scold	71.1
Very long hours of work	28.9

Contd.

*Type of Problems**	*Percent*
Often get hurt	26.3
Not regularly paid	18.4
Not adequately paid	
10.5	
Cannot take leave	2.6
No time for reading	2.2
Number of children	184

*Multiple responses.
Source: Primary Data Collection

Motivation to Change Work

Given both the advantages and disadvantages associated with the present work site, all the children were asked if now there was any possibility of their changing the job. Only 30 percent of the children confirmed that they would like to change their job, but majority (70 percent) thought they would be continuing with the same. Those children who had the desire to change the job were further probed into the reasons for the same. Around one-third of the children (32%) did have the desire to earn more money while 36 percent desired to get a better job. Eleven percent of the children also mentioned that they would shift to a job where it would be comfortable to work and it also involves technical education respectively. Another eleven percent of the children wanted to take an initiative in setting up their own business.

Table 8
Motive Toward Other Job Shifting

Particulars	*Percent*
Percent of children like to change the job	30.4
Number of children	184
*Reasons for motive job shifting in different area**	
Good work	35.7
More earn money	32.2
Comfortable work	10.7
Technical education	10.7
Self-business	10.7
Number of children	56

*Multiple responses.
Source: Primary Data Collection.

Health Status

Given the situation in which the children are living and working, it is necessary to understand the sickness pattern of these children too, some of which could be due to the general health problems while others could be work/place related. For this purpose, all the children were asked if they had experienced any type of sickness in the last six months. The data show that among all only 70 children (38 percent) had not experienced any sickness in the last six months, while the remaining 114 children in fact also reported multiple problems. Most commonly reported general health problem among these children included fever (55 percent), followed by headache/stomach problem (47 percent), cold/cough (37 percent), dysentery (18 percent) and malaria (7 percent). The other health problems reported by the children are obviously either due to work they are involved in or due to the poor hygienic condition at the site. This includes cut/burn problem (19 percent), scabies (9 percent), swelling in scrotum (7 percent), etc.

At the time of data collection among all the children interviewed, fourteen percent of the children had an open wound either on their hands or legs. This is both hazardous to the child as well as an easy mode of transmission of infections unknowingly.

Table 9
Pattern of Illness in Past 6 Months

Particulars	*Percent*
No illness in past 6 months	38
*Type of Illness**	
Fever	55.4
Headache and stomach problem	47.4
Cold/cough	36.8
Cut/burn problem	19.3
Dysentery	17.5
Weeping wound on hands/legs	14
Scabies	8.8
Malaria	7
Swelling in scrotum	7
Piles	7
Pain in leg	7
Number of Children	114

*Multiple responses.
Source: Primary Data Collection.

Duration of Work

Data was elicited from the respondents on their working pattern in terms of the number of hours and days they worked in a week. Regarding the number of working days in a week, as the data indicates, nearly 9 out of ten children were working for all the seven days in a week. Another 8 percent were working for 6 days in a week. Data on length of hours they worked in a day shows that obviously children were working for long hours that is around 14 hours, which is much more than the standard normative hours of work (8 hours) for adults. Only 7 percent of the children reported working up to 8 hours. On the other hand, about 4 out of 10 children were putting in more than 15 hours of work daily. Apparently, the data does indicate that the children were working almost on all the days of the week as only 10 percent of them received leave once a week. The data clearly indicates that the surveyed children were over utilized and made to work for long hours much against the standard working norms.

Table 10
Number of Days/Hours Children Worked

Particulars	*Percent*
Number of Days Working	
< 4 days	1.1
5 days	2.2
6 days	7.6
7 days	89.1
Mean Days Working	7
Number of Working Hours	
Upto 8	6.5
9-10	3.3
11-12	21.7
13-14	26.1
15-16	29.4
17 or more	13
Mean Hours Working	13.4
Percent of children get leave in a week	9.8
Number of Children	184

Source: Primary Data Collection.

Monthly Income of the Children

The study also made an attempt to estimate the monthly income earned by these children. Data indicates that the average income earned per month is only around Rs. 309. The amount varied anywhere between Rs. 300 and less than Rs. 900. The percentage of children earning income between Rs. 500 to Rs. 900 was below 10. The amount mentioned is obviously much less than what is set for minimum daily wage.

Table 11
Monthly Income of Children

Particulars	*Percent*
Monthly Income (in Rs.)	
Upto 300	41.3
301-400	34.8
401-500	14.1
501-600	5.4
601-700	2.2
701-800	1.1
801-900	1.1
Mean Income (Rs.)	309
Number of Children	184

Source: Primary Data Collection.

Eating Habit of Children

Given the long working hours and the amount that these children receive, an attempt is made to understand their nutritional level, by the number of times they receive food to eat, its preparation status and adequacy. Giving the information on the number of times children eat food in a day, a quarter (26 percent) of them received food only twice, another 55 percent reported eating food three times a day, while only 18 percent had the opportunity of eating food for four times a day. Given the set-up where these children are working, the status of the food consumed in terms of whether it is fresh preparation or the food consumed is stale food has also been collected. Majority (91 percent) of the children did report that they consumed fresh food, 8 percent mentioned that they ate both fresh and stale food, while one percent received only stale food to eat. Given the fact that the children are working in hotels where food is basically prepared and served, it is observed that only four percent of the children were satisfied with the amount of food they consumed. In other words, the above data indicates that the respondents are not receiving adequate quantity of food required for their age and labour that they are putting in.

Table 12
Frequency of Food Consumption and Its Status

Particulars	*Percent*
Number of times eat food in a day	
Twice	26.4
Thrice	55.4
Four times	18.2
Preparation status of food consumed	
Fresh	91.3
Stale	1.1
Both	7.6
Percent satisfied with quantity of food consumed	4.4
Number of children	184

Source: Primary Data Collection.

Resting Place

Sleeping pattern of the children was also looked into, as this is also an essential component for their well-being. Almost two out of three children were working at the work place only,

Table I 3
Place of Sleeping at Night and the Number of Persons Sharing the Room

Particulars	*Percent*
Place	
At home	12
At hotel	18.5
In hotel in group	66.2
With friends/relatives	1.1
Others	2.2
Number of persons who share the room for sleeping	
<2	10.9
2-3	18.5

Contd.

Particulars	*Percent*
4-5	40.2
6-7	18.5
8-9	7.6
10-11	3.2
12+	1.1
Number of Children	184

Source: Primary Data Collection.

that is, in the hotel where they were sleeping in a group along with the others. Only 12 percent of the children had a home to return to for sleeping purpose. Number of persons sharing the room for warning shows that only 11 percent and 19 percent had the opportunity to sleep in rooms with less than two or two to three persons respectively. Forty percent of the children were sharing a room with almost four to five persons, while 4 percent of the children were sharing the room with ten or more persons.

Leisure Activities

Given the situation and the long working hours, attempt was also made to understand from the children what they did in the leisure time if available. Six out of ten children mentioned that they chatted with their friends, 13 percent mentioned that they went out to play out door games, while another 14 percent mentioned that they utilized the time in sleeping. Only 50 percent of the children had the facility of watching television.

Table 14
Activities of Children

Particulars	*Percentage*
*Leisure activities**	
Chat with friend	50.6
Play out door games	12.9
Go to movies	5.5
Sleeping	13.8
Others	13.8
Percentage who watch television	50
Number of children	184

Source: Primary Data Collection

Summary of Findings

This section is based on the primary data collected by interviewing 184 working children engaged in Hotel, Restaurants, Tea Stalls, Dhabas, etc. of the Patna town. The findings of study are, hundred percent of the juvenile workers were male who had the freedom to enter into this activity whereas the girls have to restrict themselves to physical-security.

The study data shows that most of child worker belong to Hindu religion. Further, caste-wise distribution of the same indicates that two-thirds' of the children belong to other backward caste. Data clearly indicates that it is generally the children of the low social group, who usually are economically poor, are the ones who are working as child labourers. Data on age-wise distribution indicates that the age of the surveyed children ranged between six years to fourteen years. The number of children in each year varied and there is no particular pattern as such.

The interrogations confirmed that there was wide- spread illiteracy among the working children. Almost three out of four (78.1%) children could not even read and write. Further probing was done from these children to understand the class upto, which they had studied. Apparently, the percentage of children decreases with the increase in the level of schooling. A substantial proportion of those who were not going to school reported that financial constrain of the family prevented them from attending school. Thirty-two percent of the children reported that they disliked studies and hence they did not go to any school. The other reasons given by children for not studying were the fear of punishment given by class teachers, ill treatment by classmates, failure in studies, frequent shifts in the place of stay, etc. There are several factors which play an important role in determining the child labour, the education level of parent, family size, income of parents and working status of parents. umber of family members in the child's family is on the higher side at 8 members as compared to a general household size, which has 6.1 members in the state. Another level of literacy of the children's parents was also looked into, as this has a bearing on children's education and their care. The parents who have a higher level of literacy give priority to the education of their children, whereas, illiterate parents do not understand the importance of schooling in improving the lot of their children. Data shows that both mother and father of almost seven out of ten children cannot read and write. Working status of parents also died in the early age of working child. Data shows that 62.0 percent parents were working as daily labourers. Orphanage is another factor, which plays an important role in pushing children in the labour force at an early age. An orphan child lives at the mercy of others, who instead of providing him protection, try to exploit him in every possible way. Obviously, poverty is the main cause for the early employment of children. Analysis of family income indicates that the average income per family was approximately Rs. 1696, which is below the poverty level. Percentage-wise, around 45 percent of the children's family income ranged between Rs. 1001 to Rs. 2500. Mobility of the children working in the Hotel industry could be mainly in two ways. A shift from one hotel to the other but being involved in the same nature of work or shifting from one type of work to another type for different reasons. Almost six out of ten children were working .at the respective hotels site for more than a year. The average length of months children had worked in these jobs, was 10 months and 5 months respectively.

The survey data indicates that around a little more than one-third of the children were involved either in 'carrying the used plates/dishes' or in washing of used plates/dishes. Obviously, poverty is the main cause for the early employment of children. Nine out of ten children reported that it was the poor economic condition of their family that compelled them to work. Analysis of the work by the age of children is also done to understand whether there is any variation in the type of work by variation in their age. Further, the children were also asked if they liked the job and if so, the reasons for the same. Total sample to explain interviewed of children opined that they liked the job out of which about 43 percent of the children liked it because they had a relative who was also working in the same hotel. In addition to liking the work, children were probed about any problems they faced at the work place. The most common problep1 mentioned was scolding by the employer (71%). The survey results, therefore, show that the mandate of section 8 of the Child Labour (P & R) Act, 1986, is not at all obeyed by the owners of Tea-Stalls, Sweet shops and Hotels, located in the town. Despite their hard labour for prolonged hours children are not provided medical facilities in case of their illness, most of the employers are indifferent to them or they are provided nominal help. The data shows that 62 percent children had experienced multiple problems. Most commonly reported general health problems among these children were fever, headache, cold/cough, etc. On the observation it was found that seven percent of the children had open wound either on their hands or legs. This is both hazardous to the child as well as an easy mode of transmission of infections unknowingly. The survey results, therefore, show that the mandate of section 8 of the Child Labour (P&R) Act, 1986, is not at all obeyed by the Hotel establishments.

Data was elicited from the respondents on their working pattern in terms of the number of hours and days they worked in a week. Though most of the children worked up to 13 hours, the data clearly indicates that the surveyed children were over utilized and made to work for long hours much against the laws made to regulate the hours of work as prescribed under the Act 1986. It has been observed that the daily working hours of children vary between 8 to 17 hours, as against 6 hours, prescribed under section 7, clause (3) of the Child Labour (P & R) Act, 1986. The data reveals that the child workers are not allowed any rest during the whole course of their work in a day and week.. Almost all the children (90.2 percent) stated that there is no specific period/ day given to them for leave. This practice is open violation of section 7(3) of the Child Labour (P & R) Act, 1986, according to which every employer is under statutory obligation to arrange the period of work on each day in such a manner that no period shall exceed three hours and no child shall work for more han 3 hours before he had interval for rest for at least one hour.

A wide variation was observed in the income distribution of child worker. Data indicates that the average income earned per month is only around Rs. 309. The amount varied anywhere between Rs. 300 and less to Rs. 900. The study, therefore, discloses that the poor child workers are not paid even the minimum wages by their employer, which is in contravention to the decision of the Supreme Court given in M.C. Mehta Vs. State of Tamil Nadu (Air 1991 SC 417). The Hon'ble Court in this case has held that the child workers must get at least minimum wages which comes to 60 percent of prescribed minimum wage for adult employees doing the same job.

Data indicate that the child workers are not receiving adequate quantity of food required for their age and labour that they are putting in majority (91 percent) the child workers did report that they consumed fresh food, 8 percent mentioned that they ate both fresh and stale food, while one percent received only stale food to eat. Giving the information on the number of times children eat food in a day, a quarter of them responded they eat only twice, another 55 percent reporting eating food three times a day.

Sleeping pattern of child labour is essential component for their well-being. Almost two out of three children were sleeping at the work place only, that is, in the hotel where they were sleeping in a group along with the others. Almost 50 percent of the child workers stated that there was no recreation facility, they chatted with friends during leisure- time. Only few percent (15%) mentioned that they went out to play out-door games. This practice is open violation of section 7(3) of the Child Labour (P & R) Act, 1986. Some statistical exercises were performed to find out the effect of different factors on the employment of children. It was ascertained that there was an association between age of children and family size. In other words, we can say that there is a higher proportion of child workers comes from larger family. Another significant correlation is found between income of parents and age at employment, meaning thereby poverty is major cause of the wide prevalence of child labour.

Recommendations to Solve the Problem

Child labour is a many-faceted socio-economic problem, which needs multi-pronged programme embracing Acts relating to child labour, rehabilitation of child labour, strengthening primary education, improvements of parents' incomes, etc. After thorough investigation of the sample study of child labour in Patna town, the following measures are suggested for reduction in the incidence of child labour and for their betterment:

- An effective approach to eliminating and preventing child labour is compulsory. Primary education, which is provided for in the constitution and State legislations should be enforced for all children below the age of 14 years.
- The study shows a major chunk of child labour is attributable to poverty. So it is suggested that poverty alleviation programmes like IRDP, JGSY, PEEY, CMEY, etc. be strictly implemented to reach the poorest of the poor. It is also suggested that programmes be monitored to fetch good results.
- It is suggested that the government should implement suitable family welfare schemes and, if possible, adopt suitable population policy to restrict the family to one child.
- It is suggested that the government should take steps to reduce inequality of income and wealth.
- It is suggested that the government should strictly implement the laws enacted against child labour of Hotel and other establishments, which will reduce the extent of child labour.
- It is suggested that the government initiate some programmes like job guarantee scheme, etc. which give relief to parents.
- It is suggested that wide publicity be given to the evils of child labour and the parents be made aware of the problem of child labour.

We hope that these measures would bring some good results. Child labour could not be weeded out despite several welfare legislations enacted by the government for time to time. It needs a change in our social attitude. Social awareness is also needed to discourage the practice of child labour. Besides this, the tightening of laws and activating enforcement machinery is needed badly to weed out the child labour in its true perspective. Besides, the government and NGOs will have to play very effective role in implementing the government schemes for children's welfare.

References

A.N. Sharma (1979), "Child Labour in Patna".

Shandilya, Tapan Kumar (2003), "Child Labour: A Global Challenge", Deep & Deep Publications, New Delhi.

ORG Baroda Report on "Working Children in India", p. 33.

Kaur, Amandeep and Kaur, Kuldip, "Child Labour in India: Causes and Implications", article published in ed. volume of Sen, RK. and Dasgupta, Asis, entitled "Problem of Child Labour in India", Deep & Deep Publications, New Delhi, pp. 5-7.

Jain, Mahaveer, "Child Labour in India: A Select Bibliography, National Labour Institute", NOIDA, pp. 13-15.

Sachdeva, S. Arvindu, Malhotra, Rajeev and Murthy, S.V. Ramana (2001), "Child Labour in India: Nature, Strategies and Policy Options", IDPAD International Conference on Child Labour in South Asia, New Delhi.

Committee Appointed by Govt. of India (1979), Report of the Committee on Child Labour, Government of India, Ministry of Labour and Labour Bureau, 1979.

ORG Baroda, Report on "Working Children in India", pp. 19 to 22. Rodgers, G. Standing, G. (1981), 'The Economic Roles of Children: Issues for Analysis in Child Work, Poverty and Under-development", (Eds.), LL.O. Geneva.

SECTION – II

CHILD LABOUR – PROBLEMS AND STRATEGIES

7

Child Labour: A Bolt on Society

Syed Eqbal Afzal and Nibha Kumari

Introduction

Child labour is a concrete manifestation of violations of a range of children's rights and is recognised as a serious and enormously complex social problem in India. Working children are denied their rights to survival and development, education, leisure and play, and adequate standard of living, opportunities to developing their personality, talents, mental and physical abilities, and protection from abuse and neglect. Notwithstanding the increase in the enrolment of children in elementary schools and increase in literacy rates since 1980s, child labour continues to be a significant phenomenon in India.

The phenomenon of child labour is significant because the Child Labour (Prohibition and Regulation) Act, 1986 is a legislation to address hazardous industrial child labour in a limited way as the purview of the Act covers only the organized sectors of production. As it is inbuilt in the law, this Act has excluded a vast section of toiling children in the unorganized sectors, as over 90 percent of the labour force in India is accounted for by the unorganised sectors of production. The political weight behind the initiatives towards government, legal interventions have been very dissimilar across states of India. Generally under the era of globalization and liberalization policies, the underlying attitude of the government is not to strictly impose labour laws that will disturb the production process. With regard to other forms of intervention, the flagship programme of the Government of India is the National Child Labour Project (NCLP). The NCLP Scheme started in 1988, has so far covered 400,200 working children. About 3.08 lakh children have been mainstreamed into formal education system so far. The scheme is running in 250 districts in 14 states. Even after discounting for the inherent problems in the NCLP scheme, the coverage is very low compared to the magnitude of the problem (12 million according to 2001 population census) even by the official statistics. In fact, the magnitude of child labour has increased in absolute terms by about one million between 1991 and 2001.

Concept of Child Labour

The term 'child labour' is generally used to refer 'any work by children that interferes with them in their full physical development, the opportunities for a desirable minimum of education and of their needed recreation' (Stein and Davis, 1940). Children aged between four to fourteen years doing work on family farms or in occupations without wage or in factories, farms outside home for wages constitute child labour. Now-a-days child labour is a widespread phenomenon. It is not only confined to work on family farms or in traditional family jobs and occupations but it has also extended to other fields. They work in agriculture and allied activities, unorganized small sector and even in organized industries (Shandilya, 2006).

Child Labour - Some Arguments

Majority of the case studies identify poverty and paternal illiteracy as causes of child labour.

Poverty Argument

Poverty is overwhelmingly accepted as the primary cause of child labour. The argument is that if a family can afford schooling, children need not work rather can attend school.

Poor children are compelled to undertake wage labour outside or to perform to unpaid household job to support their families. There are number of studies at macro and micro level to establish this poverty argument (Bequele and Boyden 1988, CACL 1993, Jain 1994). Analysis of household survey date also reveals a negative effect of low income on schooling (Levy 1985, Buragohain 1997, Sing and Santiago 1997). Many surveys on child workers indicate that poverty is always the first reason offered by households (CPSS, 1995, APARD 2000) Prevalence of child labour in higher magnitude in relatively backward countries, in poor regions within a country and poor households in a locality testified the crucial role of poverty perpetuating it. But the relation between poverty and child labour is not always consistent as is evident in the correlation between per capita income and incidence of child labour among Indian states. Poorest among the states (Bihar) has almost same incidence of child labour as Punjab as the richest State in India has as per 1991 census. Andhra Pradesh and West Bengal have same level of per capita income but child labour largely differs, 10 per cent for the former and around 4 per cent for the latter. Evidence of Kerala as remarkable exception casts doubt on poverty argument. It is, therefore, increasingly considered that poverty is one of the major reasons for child labour not the exclusive reason. Even empirical works show inconsistent effects of household income on children's work and schooling. (Psacharopolous, 1997, Bhalotra and Heady, Dreze and Kingdom, 1999) Ravallion Wodon 2000). The weak foundation of poverty argument is exposed in many studies. For example CACL (1993) admits that stoppage of the inflow of children's income would push the families further down the poverty line, but it can not be ascertained to what extent those families would dip down. There is no guarantee that alleviation of poverty would reduce child labour (Anker and Melkas, 1996).

Parental Illiteracy Argument

The next important factor after household poverty is thought to be adult illiteracy which leads to lack of demand for education (Winer 1991, Bhalla 1995). It has been widely accepted that adult literacy and parental exposure to education has a positive effect on children's schooling. The strong effect has come into light in many econometric studies (Rosenzweig and Evenson 1977, Kanbargi and Kulkani 1991). Female literacy particularly mothers education contribute to child welfare specially education (World Bank 1980, UNICEF 1990, Colclough 1993). The fundamental postulate is that parents having schooling experience understands the value of education and therefore tends to send their children to school.

In India, parental illiteracy is compounded by obnoxious caste system where the tradition of education has been an exclusive privilege of the upper castes. Post-independent India saw government's initiative in imparting public education across the country. Still now low caste people such as dalits and tribal community face many barriers to schooling; inherent apathy is one of them. Upper caste and higher class people hinder the setting up of school for lower caste. They fear that education of lower caste children will stop the supply of cheap labour (Burra, 1995). Higher caste people oppose education of lower caste and even lower caste people do not ascribe much importance to education (Dreze and Sharma, 1998). Thus, an association between low income, illiteracy and caste is established to explain the prevalence of child labour. Some studies have shown independent effect of income (Rosenzwing and Evenson, 1997, Singh and Santiago 1997). But these studies have included parental education as quantifiable variable in the explanatory factor without considering the value of education the parents conceive. The exclusion of such paternal value in the context of child schooling is driven by the notion that illiterate parents never appreciate the value of education. This notion was found to be unfounded in many studies on parental view on education. UNICEF survey data finds that nearly half of the parents without any educational background express the importance of education.

Education system of a country can influence the supply of child labour, Bonnet (1993) asserts that defective education system in Africa has molded the mindset of many African parents to view work as better option than education.

Education does not bestow a child the required entry card to join the modern sector job. In an economic setting where informal sector work sustain and support the majority of people, many parents think it is wise to withdraw their children from school and engage them in any work. As one African scholar opines: 'Education broadens your mind but it does not teach you how to survive', Government can influence the household's behaviour with respect to child labour. A study in Malaysia has proved this efficacy. Malaysian government in a bid to encourage schooling of ethnic Malays introduced scholarship and other subsidies for them. The result was outstanding as no negative effect of household size on schooling of Malays children was observed. By comparison, in the cases of Chinese and Indian groups, where no stipends or subsidies were doled out, negative effect of large family size on the schooling of children was observed.

Marked wage rate of parents can influence the supply of child labour. A study on India (Rosenzwing, 1977) finds that cross-wage elasticity of child labour supply with the labour supply of mothers was found to be negative. It means that an increase in wages for mothers is likely to reduce the supply of child labour especially girl children. The effect has been found to be strongest for younger children. Evidence from Egypt finds that a 10 per cent decrease in women's market wages would lead to a 15 per cent decline in the labour of children aged 12 to 14 year and 27 per cent decrease in child labour for children between 6 to 11 years. In India, a 10 per cent increase in women's wage rates would decrease girls labour force participation by 9 per cent but it has no effect on boy's labour participation. The opposite happens in case of father's wage increase. An Increase of father's wage rate would reduce labour participation of boys but not of girls.

Discourse on Determinants: Supply Side and Demand Side Factors

Households supply child labour. Thus, fertility behaviour of parents is an important determinant of this supply. Number of child labour from a family unit naturally depends on the number of children. Another factor that influences the potential supply of child labour is the risk management in households, how labour power is understood to be used as risk management strategy of poor households. On the demand side, the two main determinations are nature of labour market and the prevalent production technology. Both supply side and demand side shape the degree of labour use of children.

Household Size, Fertility and Time Allocation

A child time is divided in two ways–leisure and non-leisure time. Non-leisure time may be devoted to schooling, domestic work or income earning activity in the market. Household allocate children's time and this allocation is driven by many factors: household size and its structure, productive potential of child and its parents in home and market work and the degree of labour substitution between the child and adults. Allocation of children's time within the existing labour market condition depends on the potential income from child labour and the potential determines desired family size. Households expect from children not only labour income but also support during old age of parents.

Larger household size reduces children's educational participation, attainment of learning and reduces parental investment in schooling. The natural corollary of these linkages is that the probability of children's work is influenced by household size. However, the magnitude of this effect is also determined by four factors: (1) The level of socio-economic development as the effect of household size is intense in urban area (2) The level of social sector spending by the state as the effect is neutralized by higher state spending on social overheads, (3) Family culture, where the effect is feeble in case of extended family system, (4) The phase of demographic transition. Thus, the effect of household's size on child labour substantially varies from context to context depending on the combination of aforesaid factors. An econometric study conducted in Philippines found dissimilar effect of household size on house work and on market work, rather the effects is determined by the sex and birth order of the child. The study observed that the presence of older siblings reduces the probability of market work by a child when both are of same sex. It indicates an arrangement of substitution is absent in case of domestic work. Gender roles in child are prominent; boys and girls are most likely to join market work and domestic work respectively.

The effect of household size on child labour has also been found to depend on cultural factors. A study in Malaysia finds that ethnic Chinese girls in larger households are disadvantaged while their brothers are not. Families in urban slums of Tamil Nadu provide private tuition to their boys to the utter neglect providing less expensive public education (Basu 1998). Land holdings are also a factor that affects the relationship among fertility, household size and child labour. Children in landless and in marginal farm families undertake wage labour in agriculture. But children in large holding families participate in family farm. The extent of child labour tends to rise with farm size because land and labour are complementary inputs.

Supply Side Factor: Responses to Risk of the Households

Poor households engage their children in income earning activities not only to augment the meagre household income but also to manage future exigency of income shortfall. Child labour can be an art of a strategy to minimize the risk of interruption of a household's income stream and hence to reduce the potential impact of job loss by a family, of a failed harvest, etc. (Cain and Majumdar, 1980). The impact of such a loss in more severe for poor households were the level of income is very low any interruption can be life threatening particularly in the absence of savings, liquid asset or ability to borrow. The Child labour is a self insurance strategy adopted by poor households. It has come to light that variability and uncertainty of household income reduces school attendance of children. Small households suffer more from income shocks because they are less able to insure themselves. The risk perception of households can frustrate any child labour programme, particularly any ban or compulsory schooling. Out-and out ban or coercive legislation could threaten the survival of poor households. The only way out is the provision of insurance to face the risk, for example, short term interest free credit without collateral.

Demand Side Factors: Labour Market Structure

The most important factor in demand side structure or the pull side is the profit motive. The nimble figure arguments are offered as a reason for employment of children in certain industries. Children are docile, punctual, pliable, dexterous and productive at least in certain jobs. But are those advantages really substantial? Studies conduct by ILO does not establish irreplaceability and dexterity of child labour:

"In the industries where argument is being used for example in carpet industry, diamond polishing and sport goods stitching, adults and children work side by side when some of the tasks are performed exclusively by children, the skill required are so nominal that child labour is clearly replaceable by male or female adult labour, profit margin would drop marginally if child labour were to be replaced by adult labour. In the carpet and bangle industry, the difference in production cost between adult labour and cheaper child labour has been calculated to be lower than 5 per cent (Chandrashekhar, 1997)."

The structure of the labour market determines the level of wages. In a competitive market where wages are flexible, children can substitute adults in the market place. If wages are at a floor level, may be because of legislation or collective action, the employer would prefer adult worker, assuming the productivity of adult worker is higher than that of children. Thus, effective minimum wage, as a demand side intervention can deter child labour. Although in practice one must ask whether minimum wage legislation is more likely to be effectively enforced than is legislation banning child labour (Grootarert and Kanpur –1995).

Many studies have brought to light wage rate differential and discrimination against children. In a review of case studies Bequele and Boyden (1988) concluded that children's earning are consistently lower than those of adults, even where the two groups are engaged in the same tasks. It has been confirmed on the basis of case studies conducted in Malaysia. Monoposonistic market condition i.e. single buyer in the labour market brings down the children's wage rate. Monoposonistic conditions occur often in developing countries labour markets and can be result of concentrated ownership of land, credit and product monopolies, share cropping arrangements, natural restrictions on labour mobility or a lack of alternative employment possibilities (Cain and Majumdar, 1980). Segmented labour market, the tiny formal sector and an expensive informal sector in the economy are major determinants of demand for child labour. The evidence suggests that extent of child labour in formal sector is insignificant with exception in the case of plantation (Bonnet, 1993). However, formal sector is gradually sinking in many countries by informalization of production process. Formal enterprises are splitting in to smaller units and in many case subcontracting to households or informal units is on the rise only to escape many legislations and taxes. In such production chain, demand for child labour would certainly go up.

Production Technology as a Demand factor

In specific works, adults can not replace children. For example, in mines boys are employed because the tunnels are too narrow for adults to crawl in. The same is the reason for engaging boys for sweeping chimneys. Girls labour is used exclusively for weeding and picking of cotton. Weaving of carpets is easier for children as they can tie the smaller knots very fast. Thus, change in technology can replace the aforesaid work of children and can reduce the demands for child labour. In the industrial revolution, the mechanization of spinning and weaving led to reduction in the demand for child labour. The green revolution in India led to reduced demand for child labour and increased school attendance. The mechanization of Egyptian agriculture and the resultant extensive use of tractors and irrigation pumps reduce the demand for child labour and increased school attendance. The mechanization of Egyptian agriculture and the resultant extensive use of tractors and irrigation pumps reduce the demand for child labour in tasks such as picking cotton, driving animals to power water wheel or haul freight. Introduction of electricity in some habitations in Philippines reduced the market labour of children. In addition to that, electricity connection at home significantly reduced home work of children. In the quarries of Bagota, the introduction of wheel barrows displaced children who previously carried rocks pieces by pieces on the other hand, introduction of new technology sometime can enhance the demand for labour. For example, the assembly line production of modern electronics and electrical appliances may again demand for nimble finger. In garment production, the inexpensive multi function sewing machines can encourage home production and sub-contracting arrangement. Girls at home may be drawn to this kind of work.

Push and Pull, Converging Supply and Demand Factors

Most of the research studies on the causes of child labour tend to focus on supply side factors or push factors. In addition to poverty factor, common in all explanatory exercises, the conditions that surround children's life are also considered. These include paternal literacy, mothers work, number of children, number of dependents, birth order, gender, children schooling and so on.

'The onus for child labour in this frame of mind rests with the family, not with the employers. The various studies relate to the way parents react to the opportunities and the challenges. They are players in the game and the regression exercises are meant to calculate how they will play the game (Lieten, 2004)'.

This understanding of supply side factors find its extreme form in the theory that poor people beget large number of children in expectation of income they would earn by participating in labour market. Therefore, poor parents opt for "quantity" rather than "quality". This axiom has received quick and wide acceptance withcut waiting for evidence to testify. Weiner (1991) has asserted this axiom as well know fact.

'It is well known that poor parents bear children in order to enhance family income. As economists say, children are viewed as economic assets, not as economic liabilities. Indian policy makers accept as the basis for policy the fact that child bearing for low income Indian as part of their strategy for family survival and well being.'

The assumption in this explanation is that fertility rate among poor parents causes child labour rather than child labour causing high fertility. Children work because people have children, rather than people have children because children work. Mere survival compels some parents to send their children to work. This is push factor in poverty ridden families. But poverty itself can not place a child in the labour market if pull factor is altogether absent. There is external force that pulls children, for example, to furnace, to brick kilns, to gem polishing, to carpet weaving, to child domestics and even to prostitution. A more sustained focus on pull factor is necessary to isolate and identify the factors that cause child labour (ILO 1996) puts it as:

Research on the causes of child labour tends to concentrate on the supply factors both because of justifiable pre-occupation with the victims and because of the commonly shared view that poverty is the driving force. But the demand for child labour plays a critical role in determining the involvement of children in labour.

Magnitude of Child Labour

According to Census of India, 2001, there were 12.26 million working children in the age group of 5-14 years as compared to 11.3 million in 1991 revealing an increasing trend in absolute numbers though the work participation rates of children (5-14) has come down from 5.4 percent during 1991 to 5 percent during 2001. The recent round of the National Sample Survey Organisation (NSSO) estimates suggests that the child labour in the country is around 8.9 million in 2004/2005 with a workforce participation rate of 3.4 per cent (NSSO 2004/05). Due to definitional problems, as discussed is this paper, a substantial proportion of child labour may remain uncounted.

Census data shows that there is a decline in the absolute number as well the percentage of main workers of children (5-14 to total population in that age group, from 4.3 percent in 1991 to 2.3 percent in 2001. But there was a substantial increase in marginal workers in every category of worker irrespective of sex and residence. As a result, despite the number of main workers declining from 9.08 million in 1991 to 5.78 million in 2001, the total number of children in the workforce increased. A large part of the increase was accounted for by the increase in marginal workers, which increased from 2.2 million in 1991 to 6.89 million in 2001. Main and marginal workers put together, the work participation rate (WPR) of children in the 5-14 age group has declined from 5.4 percent during 1991 to 5 percent in 2001. The trends between 1991 and 2001 of declining main child workers along with increasing marginal workers may indicate the changing nature of work done by children. There is a general trend of marginalization of labour force in the country and this is also reflected in the Census figures. This is to be seen in the context of decelerating employment growth in general in the economy during the last decade that is characterized as an era of globalization.

Table 1
Changes in Work Participation (Main and Marginal) Rate of Children in Different Age Groups

	1991			*2001*		
All India	*Boys*	*Girls*	*All Children*	*Boys*	*Girls*	*All Children*
5 to 9	0.9	0.9	0.9	1.5	1.4	1.4
10 to 14	10.9	9.9	10.4	8.8	8.5	8.7
5 to 14	5.7	5.1	5.4	5.1	4.9	5.0

Source: Census of India, 2001.

Age Group Wise Work Participation Rate (WPR)

However, if we look at the WPR for different age groups among children, the trend is different. The WPR for children in 5 to 9 age group has marginally increased from less than 1 percent during 1991 to 1.4 percent during 2001. In the case of 10-14 years age group children, the decline is only marginal i.e., from

10.4 percent during 1991 to 8.7 percent during 2001. This indicates that a substantial number of children in the 10 to 14 age group are in the labour force despite the decline in the proportion of children in the total population. Latest available estimates on WPR children are from the 61st Round of NSSO (2004-05).

Table 2
Magnitude of Child Labour and Children Out of School

Distribution of Children	*2001 Population Census*	*2006 Population Projection and Estimates*	*% of Children to Population* 2001	*% of Children to Population* 2006
Population				
Male	132367710	125485000		
Female	120795938	116274000		
Total	253163648	241759000		
Child Labour (10-14)				
Male	6804336	4276744	8.8	6.7
Female	5862041	3894131	8.5	6.3
Total	12666377	8082954	8.7	6.6
Children out of School				
Male	36428634	19199205	27.5	15.3
Female	45878836	24184992	38.0	20.8
Total	87126075	43274861	34.4	17.9

* Census of India, 2001

* Population of children in 2006 is based on the projections of the Report of the technical group on population projections constituted by the National Commission on Population, Population Projections for India and States 2001-2026 (Revised December 2006), Office of the Registrar General & Census Commissioner, India. Estimates for working children and out of school children are based on NSSO 61st Round, Report Number 515 (61/10/1), "Employment and Unemployment Situation in India" 2004-05, Part I, Table (19): Per 1000 distribution of persons by usual activity category taking also into consideration the subsidiary economic status of persons categorized 'not working' in the principal status for each age group.

According to NSSO estimates, WPR for children in the 5-9 age group is negligible and for children in the age group of

10-14, it still continues to be significant though declining (Table 2). NSSO data being based on a sample survey reflects the current economic situation with regard to general employment in the economy. Decline in child labour has to be seen in the context of general decline in employment growth. The current economic process has rendered many more children vulnerable to labour related exploitation, though many of them are classified as out of school children but not in work.

Magnitude of Child Labour Across Major States in India

As per the census data, the trend on the magnitude of child labour is not uniform across the country. There is across the board decline in the incidence of child labour in the southern and western Indian states and union territories between 1991 and 2001. However, there has been an increasing trend in the eastern and north Indian states and union territories (Table 3). There is an increase in the absolute magnitude of child labour between 1991 and 2001 in the states of Uttar Pradesh, Bihar, Rajasthan, Punjab, Haryana, Himachal Pradesh and Madhya Pradesh. If we combine the bifurcated states from Madhya Pradesh, Uttar Pradesh and Bihar the increase in magnitude is much more than what is seen in the divided states (Table 3). While the stories of Kerala and Tamil Nadu are well known, it is heartening to see that the state of Andhra Pradesh that had a dubious distinction of having the largest child labour force in the country, shows reduction in magnitude of child labour and work participation rates along with a dramatic increase in the enrollment of children in school. However, Andhra Pradesh is the second largest state in terms of magnitude by 2001 Census.

As for as the percentage share of child labour across the states, Uttar Pradesh account for a larger share of about 15 percent child workforce in India followed by Andhra Pradesh with 10.8 percent. Rajasthan, Madhya Pradesh, Bihar garnered 10, 8.8 and 8 percent respectively of India's child employment. The share of Uttar Pradesh has shot up from less than 13 per cent during 1991 to 15.2 per cent in 2001, which is a cause for

Table 3
Change in the Magnitude of Child Labour and WPR between 1991 and 2001 (Children in the Age Group of 5-14)

States	*Child Workers 1991*	*Child Workers 2001*	*Work Participation Rates 1991*	*Work Participation Rates 2001*	*Percentage Share of Child Labour in the State 1991*	*Percentage Share of Child Labour in the State 2001*
Andhra Pradesh	1661940	1363339	9.98	7.7	14.7	10.8
Arunachal Pradesh	12395	18482	5.65	6.06	0.1	0.1
Assam	327598	351416	5.46	5.07	2.9	2.8
Bihar	942245	1117500	3.99	4.68	8.3	8.8
Chattisgarh (New)		364572		6.96	0.0	2.9
Delhi	27351	41899	1.27	1.35	0.2	0.3
Goa	4656	4138	1.95	1.82	0.0	0.0
Gujarat	523585	485530	5.26	4.28	4.6	3.8
Haryana	109691	253491	2.55	4.78	1.0	2.0
Himachal Pradesh	56438	107774	4.55	8.14	0.5	0.9
Jammu & Kashmir		175630		6.62	0.0	1.4
Jharkhand (New)		407200		5.47	0.0	3.2
Karnataka	976247	822665	8.81	6.91	8.7	6.5
Kerela	34800	26156	0.58	0.47	0.3	0.2
Madhya Pradesh	1352563	1065259	8.08	6.71	12.0	8.4
Maharashtra	1068418	764075	5.73	3.54	9.5	6.0
Orissa	452394	377594	5.87	4.37	4.0	3.0
Punjab	142868	177268	3.04	3.23	1.3	1.4
Rajasthan	774199	1262570	6.46	8.25	6.9	10.0
Sikkim	5598	16457	5.18	12.04	0.0	0.1
Tamil Nadu	578889	418801	4.83	3.61	5.1	3.3
Tripura	16478	21756	2.29	2.79	0.1	0.2
Uttar Pradesh	1410086	1927997	3.81	4.04	12.5	15.2
Uttranchal (New)		70183		3.24	0.0	0.6
West Bengal	711691	857087	4.16	4.5	6.3	6.8
India	11285349	12666377	5.37	5.0	100.0	100.0

Source: Compiled from census of India 1991 and 2001

serious concern (Table 4). Over 53 percent of the child labour in India was accounted for by the five states namely; Uttar Pradesh, Andhra Pradesh, Rajasthan, Madhya Pradesh and Bihar during 2001. Karnataka, Maharashtra and West Bengal together had about 20 percent of the child labourers in India during 2001. It is also to be noted here that there is a general increasing trend in the magnitude of child labour in the north east region of the country. Surprising is the case of Himachal Pradesh, which has shown significant increase in school attendance and in literacy level. However, there is a dramatic increase in the percentage of children in the age-group 5-14 years who are classified as workers, both main and marginal. In Himachal Pradesh, the percentage of child workers has gone up from 5.5 percent in 1991 to 8.6 percent in 2001. This is a reflection of the emerging crisis of poorer segments of the population in many other states.

Child Labour and Eleventh Plan

The Eleventh Plan emphasises on gender equality and arresting the decline in the child sex ratio. Nutrition Programme for Adolescent Girl, Kishore Shakati Yojana, Balika Samriddhi Yojana are the current schemes catering to the girl child. Though, the schemes are definitely not health and family welfare oriented issues, they require be treating and viewing as protection issues.

Child trafficking and sexual exploitation are problems that the society is increasingly being confronted with. The Eleventh Plan proposes to ensure that this vulnerable group is protected from further abuse. Children affected by HIV / AIDs, Children in Conflict with Law, Children in Distressed Circumstances, Children with Disabilities are going to be addressed and treated as Critical Target Groups.

Through an Act of Parliament, the Government of NCT Delhi has set up Delhi Commission for Protection of Child Rights (DCPCR). The Commission is meant to protect and fulfill the various rights for children enumerated under UN's Convention on Rights of Child (UNCRC) for their survival, protection, development and participation. The creation of Delhi Commission for Protection of Child Rights by the Delhi Government is a historic and pioneering initiative. The children are reported to be extremely deprived, marginalized and poor and suffer multiple forms of abuse and exploitation. A large number of them are legally defined as "Children a Need of

Care and Protection" under Juvenile Justice Act 2000. The Commission is committed to convert these children into "Supreme Assets", which they are actually meant to be the interventions and programmes recommended for the 11th Plan Period should include improving the reach and quality of existing programmes and formulating new schemes to address hitherto un-addressed areas and issues based on National Policy for Children, 1974. National Charter for Children, 2004, which makes special mention of the importance of protecting the rights and dignity of girl children; National Common Minimum Programme and the National Plan of Action for Children 2005.

The Eleventh Plan marks a big step forward in the area of Child Rights. It is entrenched in a Rights Framework that views children as agents and not as recipients. It recognizes and acknowledges multiple discriminations wherein the children are trapped in. This acceptance of the situation of the children can alone safeguard their rights and ensure better outcomes for children.

The recent trend in the global system is to evaluate the development of any country, not in terms of their military or economic strength or the splendour of their capital cities and public buildings, but also in terms of human development or the well-being of its people. Against this backdrop the existence and perpetuation of child labour has been one of the main limiting factors in the way of human development in almost all the third world countries including India. The issue of child labour is major human rights issue and at the same time it is highly emotive one, these emotions tend to be coupled with very strong views both on what the child labour problem is and on what ought to be done for its elimination. Although the predominance of child labour has to be quite pronounced in all the developing and under developed countries, it is a global phenomenon which exists in almost all the countries of the world the difference, if any, is of degree only. The concept and practice of child labour being economically unsound, psychologically wrong and socially disastrous has posed a big threat to peace and overall world development. Therefore, the gravity of the situation and pervasive nature of the problem has attracted the urgent attention of all social, political organisations, social scientists, activist groups and governments of the world including India. The term 'Child Labour' is generally used to refer "any work by children that interferes with them in their full physical development, the opportunities for a desirable minimum of education and their needed recreation."

Children aged between four to fourteen years are doing work on family farms or in occupations with or without payment or in factories; farms outside home for wages constitute child labour. Of late, child labour has become a widespread phenomenon. It is not only confined to work on family farms or in traditional family jobs and occupations but it has also extended to other fields. They work in agricultural and allied activities, unorganized small scale sectors and even in organised industries.

Conclusion

The practice of child labour in India or in any other country of the world is an age old phenomenon. In pre-industrial agricultural society of India, children worked as helpers and learners in hereditarily determined family occupations under the benign supervision of adult family members. The work place was an extension of the home and work was characterised by personal informal relationships. The task and technology that work involved were simple and non-hazardous.

Radical changes, however, occurred on social economic front with the advent of industrialisation and urbanisation under the impact of the newly generated centrifugal and centripetal forces, there was unbroken stream of the rural people migrating to urban centres in search of livelihood. As a result, the children were in a situation where they had to earn for themselves as well as for the families. Family-based economy was destroyed and work now exposed the child to unhealthy environment. The child's ability to grow and to develop into a mentally and physically sound adult was severely restricted. No doubt, the elimination of child labour is a big challenge for the country. A progressive as well as integrated approach has been adopted by the Government in order to resolve this intense socio-economic problem.

References

Stein, E. and J. Davis (eds.), (1940), Labour Problem in America, Farrance and Richer, New York.

Anker, R. and H. Melkas (1996), 'Economic Incentives for Children and Families to Eliminate or Reduce Child Labour', International Labour Office, Geneva.

Bequele, A. and J. Boyden (1988), 'Combating Child Labour', ILO, Geneva.

CACL, (1993), Child Labour in India: A Dossier Campaign Against Child Labour, Sponsored by UNICEF.

Jain, M. (1994), "Perspective on Child Labour in India", Awards Digest Journal of Labour Legislation, Special Issue, Child Labour, 20(7).

Buragohani, T. (1997), "Differential in Literacy Rate by Social Group", Margin, Vol.29, No. 3.

Singh, R.D. and M. Santiago (1997), "Farm Earnings, Educational Attainments and Role of Public Policy", Some Evidence from Mexico, World Development, Vol. 29, No. 3.

CPSS (1995), 'Child Labour in Hazardous Industries', Department of Labour, Centre for Public Studies, Hyderabad, Andhra Pradesh.

APARD, (2000), "Child Labour in Agriculture: Study of Hyderabad", Academy of Rural Development for UNICEF, Andhra Pradesh

Bhalotra, S. and C. Heady, (1988), 'Child Labour in Pakistan and Ghana', Department of Economics, University of Bristol

Dreze, J. and Kingdom, G.G. (1999), School Participation in Rural India, Delhi School of Economics, New Delhi.

Ravallion, M. and Wodon, Q. (2000), "Does Child Labour Displace Schooling? Evidence on Behavioural to an Enrolment Subsidy", The Economic Journal, Vol. 110, No. 402.

Winer, M. (1991), "The Child and the State in India: Child Labour and Education Policy in Comparative Perspective", Princeton University Press.

Bhalla, A.S. (1995), "Uneven Development in Third World: A Study of India and China", St. Martin Press, London

Rosenzweig, M.R. and Evensong (1977), 'Fertility Schooling and the Economic Contribution of Children in Rural India: An Econometric Analysis', Economterica, Vol. 45, No. 5.

Kanbargi and Kulkani (1991), Child Work, Schooling and Fertility in Rural Karnataka in Kanbargi, R. (ed.), Child Labour in Indian Sub-continent: Dimension and Implication, Sage Publications, New Delhi.

World Bank (1980), World Development Report, Oxford University Press.

UNICEF (1990), The State of the World Children, Oxford University Press.

Colclough, C. (1993), "Human Development: Towards a More Integrated Framework for Planning in the 1990s", Institute of Development Studies, Paper No. 323.

Burra, N. (1995), Born to Work: Child Labour in Rural India, Oxford University Press, New Delhi.

Dreze, J. and Sharma (1998), 'Palanpur, Population, Society, Economy' in Lanjouw, P. and Stern, N., "Economic Development in Palanpur Over Five Decades", Clarendon Press, Oxford.

Bonnet, M. (1993), 'Child Labour in Africa', International Labour Review, 132(3).

Cain and Majumdar (1980), 'Labour Market Structure, Child Employment and Reproductive Behaviour in Rural South Asia, World Employment Programme Research, ILO, Geneva.

Stegeman, Ingrid (2004), "Child Labour in Context of Globalisation" in G.K. Lieten (ed.) Working Children Around the World, Child Rights and Child Realities, IREWOC Foundation, Amsterdam.

Chandrashekhar, C.P. (1997), 'The Economic Consequences of Abolition of Child Labour – An Indian Case Study', Journal of Peasant Studies, 24(3).

Basu, K. and P.H. Van (1998), "The Economics of Child Labour", A.E.R. 88(3).

Grootaert, C. and R. Kanpur (1995), "Child Labour: An Economic Perspective", International Labour Review, (134).

Shandilya, T.K., Nayan Kumar and Navin Kumar (2006), Child Labour Eradication, Deep and Deep Publications Pvt. Ltd., New Delhi.

Kulshreshtra, J.C. (1978), Child Labour in India, Ashish Publishing House, New Delhi.

Mehta, P.L and Jaiswal S.S. (1996), Child Labour and the Law, Deep & Deep Publications, New Delhi.

Mustafa, Mohd. And Sharma, Onkar (1977), Child Labour in India: A Bitter Truth, Deep & Deep Publications, New Delhi.

Singh, Bhagwan Prasad and Mohanthy Shukla (1993), Children at Work-Problems and Policy Options, B.R. Publishing Corporation, New Delhi.

8

Child Labour—Disgrace to Mankind

Mithilesh Kumar Sinha

Children are the future citizens of our country. So it is our duty to look after them, protect them and provide them better care for their physical, mental and psychological growth. In a welfare state it also becomes the duty of the government to protect children, have welfare programmes for them through different schemes and policies, so that they are not exposed to any sort of hazards which may damage their growth in any respect which ultimately damages the political, social as well as economic growth of society.

Concept of Child Labour

The practice of child labour is as old as the history of mankind. It has continued from ancient period and is contrary to the values of modern society. The child labour is a chronic problem prevalent in the developing economies of the world. This is more so in India wherein multi-class social structure exists and a complex of traditional and pre-capitalistic production relations are operative. Indeed, child labour is a disgrace to mankind. It is mostly prevalent in developing countries including India. Child labour constitutes the most deprived section of society, which has been forced to earn a pittance or to contribute to family work, sacrificing development at prime age for want of opportunity. Poverty occupied with ignorance and increasing dependency load are behind the grim incidence of children's employment in the villages and towns of developing countries.

Homer Folks, Chairman of the United Nations, Child Labour Commission, defined child labour as "any work by children that interferes with their full physical development and their opportunities for a desirable minimum level of education or their needed recreation" (Labour Investigation Committee Main Report, 1946).

According to the International Labour Organization, "Child Labour includes children permanently leading adult lives, working long hours for low wages under conditions damaging to their health and to their physical and mental development, sometimes separated from their families, frequently deprived of meaningful educational and training opportunity that could open up for them a better future."

According to Sri V.V. Giri, former President of India, the term child labour is commonly interpreted in two different ways- as an economic practice and secondly as social evil. In the first context, it signifies employment of children in gainful occupation with a view to adding the income of children in the family. It is in the second context that the term child labour is generally used. It is necessary to take into account the character of the job in which children are engaged, the Danger to which they are exposed and opportunities of development which they have been denied

Forms of Child Labour

Children are working in all the three sectors of the economy- the agrarian, Industrial and Service sectors and each has its own peculiar features which basically are in the form of migrant labour, bonded labour, wage based labour, self-employed labour, invisible labour.

Magnitude of Child Labour

According to ILO, in 1995 at least 120 million of the world's children between 5-14 years did full time pay work (ILO, 1996).

When child labour includes part-time workers, the number more than doubles (Basu: 1999).

Magnitude of child labour may be ascertained by (a) considering the number of child labourers, (b) the percentage of children who work as labourers (i.e., the participation rate) and (c) the child participation rate as percentage of over-all participation rate. According to the criterion mentioned in (c), if an area, the participation rate of children as percentage of general participation rate is higher, the relative prevalence of child labour may be considered to be higher there.

Let us now briefly compare the incidence of child labour in India with that in the world, Asia and China; the incidence of child labour is here measured by the participation rates for children, 10-14 years (Table-1) over a period ranging from 1950 to 2010 (as projected).

Table 1
Participation Rates for Children (10-14 Years)

Region	*1950*	*1960*	*1970*	*1980*	*1990*	*1995*	*2000*	*2010*
World	27.57	24.81	22.30	19.91	14.65	13.02	11.32	8.44
Asia	36.06	32.26	28.35	23.42	15.19	12.77	10.18	5.60
China	47.85	43.17	39.03	30.48	15.24	11.55	7.86	0.00
India	35.43	30.07	25.46	21.44	16.68	14.37	12.07	7.46

Source: Economically Active Population: Estimates and Projections, 1950-2010, Geneva; ILO, quoted in Basu (1999).

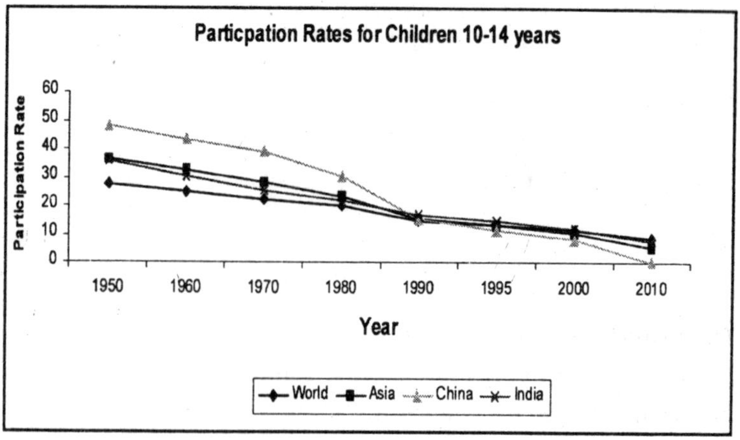

Up to 1990, the participation rate of children was higher in Asia compared to the aggregate world figure; thereafter the Asian rate has fallen below the world rate. The Chinese rate was higher than Asian rate up to 1990. Thereafter, China has experienced a sharp fall in the rate, and China is expected to be free from child labour by 2010. The participation rate for children was much lower in India than in China in 1950. The occurrence rate of child labour in China continued to be higher than that of India up to 1980. Thereafter, the fall in child participation rate has been much slower in India compared to China. The Indian rate exceeded the Chinese rate by 1990, by 2010, it is expected that the participation rate of children would be around 7.46 in India (Chatterjee & Nandi: 2000).

Incidence of Child Labour in States

We are made to accept that in all states there is 'a strong inverse correlation between rural literacy rates and the incidence of child labour', and that 'a strengthening of rural literacy programmes would lead to nearly a 50 per cent decline in the incidence of child labour' (V.V. Giri National Labour Institute, 2000). These correlations, in a statistical sense, may indeed exist, but a quick look at the cases selected in Table 2, informs us that there are significant differences, within states and particularly between states.

There is obviously an observable (and calculable) correlation. For example, Jhabua (Madhya Pradesh) has a child labour incidence of 25.5 per cent and total literacy rate of 13.4 per cent. The figure for Durg, on the other hand, is 5.5 per cent and 50.4 per cent respectively. But some districts have a high child labour incidence under conditions that are not necessarily worse than conditions in other districts and in other states. Why should Mahboobnagar and Kurnool (Andhra Pradesh) have a child labour incidence of 14.6 per cent and 14.1 per cent respectively? They have a total literacy rate of 25.3 per cent and 33.3 per cent respectively? Why should Saharsa (Bihar) have a child labour incidence of only 5.9 per cent (while its rural literacy rate is 26.9 per cent) whereas Kalahandi in Orissa has a comparable literacy rate and a much higher incidence of child labour. Periyar (Tamil Nadu), on the other hand, has a child labour ratio that is comparable to Dumka in Bihar but it has almost double the rural literacy levels of the latter. In respect to the variables, 'agricultural orientation' and 'overall development', similar 'anomalies' can also be found.

Table 2
Example of Child Labour-Prone Districts

Districts	*Incidence of Child Labour*	*% Total Rural Literacy Rate*	*% Workers in Agriculture*	*Rural Development Index (RID)*
Jhabua (Madhya Pradesh)	25.2	13.4	90.4	84
Surguja (Madhya Pradesh)	11.1	24.98	4.3	46
Durg (Madhya Pradesh)	5.5	50.4	70.0	80
Kurnool (Andhra Pradesh)	14.1	33.3	75.2	83
Mahboobnagar (Andhra Pradesh)	14.6	25.3	83.4	53
Saharsa (Bihar)	6.0	26.9	91.0	24
Dumka (Jharkhand)	7.9	31.5	85.5	32
Kalahandi (Orissa)	12.5	27.9	85.6	51
Koraput (Orissa)	12.7	17.4	84.7	54
Periyar (Tamil Nadu)	8.5	53.8	75.4	128
Kamarajar (Tamil Nadu)	8.9	55.7	52.7	115
Dharampuri (Tamil Nadu)	8.1	43.3	80.8	79

Note: RID is derived from a weighted combination of various indicators such as the importance of Industry, the spread of bank services, literacy, etc.

Source: V.V. Giri National Institute, 2000 (Various Booklets).

The incidence of child labour can be witnessed through Table 3 which represents state wise incidence of child labour.

The Table 3 shows that female work participation has a strong influence on the prevalence of child labour. In general, one observes a positive correlation between the two indicators. The two outliers are Maharashtra and Gujarat. The state with the lowest child labour incidence, are also states with reasonably low female work participation. Kerala, Haryana, Assam, Bihar and Punjab, despite showing stark differences in other variables, also have a low child labour incidence. The inference is in the line with the theory of labour market segmentation and complementarily, under conditions of high demand for labour in the lower segments of the labour market, poor families will be tapped for additional labour power; after the adult male and adult female labour power, the child labour will be pulled into employment.

Table 3
Child Labour, Literacy, Income and Work Participation Across Selected States

State	*Child Labour*	*Per Capita Domestic Product*	*Female Literacy*	*Work Participation*	
				All	*Female*
Andhra Pradesh	17.8	7006	24.8	81.0	72.4
Karnataka	13.9	7242	34.6	74.9	61.3
Himachal Pradesh	13.6	6896	51.5	79.9	72.9
Rajasthan	12.2	5315	15.0	77.6	67.2
Tamil Nadu	10.4	8051	42.8	74.8	64.7
Madhya Pradesh	8.7	5516	22.1	76.5	63.0
Orissa	7.4	4662	30.5	65.3	45.7
Maharashtra	6.5	12010	39.7	77.7	70.5
West Bengal	5.1	6247	40.7	58.9	28.5
Uttar Pradesh	5.0	4794	22.9	61.9	34.7
Gujarat	4.1	9054	36.1	73.2	57.9
Bihar	3.7	3417	19.7	56.6	26.9
Punjab	2.7	12934	43.9	58.7	32.4
Assam	2.6	5520	52.1	54.5	23.9
Haryana	2.6	12934	43.9	58.7	32.4
Kerala	0.8	6524	81.7	53.4	32.5

Note: Domestic Product in Rs. the other column in Percentages.
Source: NSS 50th Round in Dev and Ravi, 2002.

A separate study for incidence of rural-urban child labour may be made with the help of Table 4. Child labour incidence is high in Southern states like Andhra Pradesh, Karnataka and Tamil Nadu and low in poorer states like Bihar and Uttar Pradesh. There are significant regional disparities in the incidence of child labour. Table 4 provides the percentages of child labour across states from three sources (Census, NSS and NCAER).

NSS provides two types of estimates: one based on principal status and the other based on principal and subsidiary status. The work participation rates for children are

Table 4
Incidence of Child Labour across Selected Indian States (5-14 Age Group)

	Rural				Urban		
	Census	NSS		NCAER	Census	NSS	
	1991	1993-94		1994	1991	1993-94	
State		PSS	PS			PSS	PS
Andhra Pradesh	12.5	17.8	15.3	9.0	3.1	6.8	5.7
Assam	-	2.6	1.7	2.6	-	3.8	3.6
Bihar	4.4	3.7	3.2	3.9	1.6	1.3	1.2
Gujarat	7.1	4.1	2.8	6.2	1.7	2.0	1.4
Haryana	3.0	2.6	1.3	1.9	1.1	2.4	1.9
Himachal Pradesh	4.8	13.2	3.2	0.8	1.3	2.4	1.5
Jammu & Kashmir	-	5.6	3.3	-	-	1.1	0.8
Karnataka	11.0	13.7	10.7	7.4	3.5	4.3	4.0
Kerala	0.6	0.8	0.5	0.4	0.5	0.6	0.5
Madhya Pradesh	9.9	8.4	6.4	3.5	1.8	1.5	1.1
Maharashtra	8.1	6.5	5.3	8.0	1.6	2.1	1.8
Orissa	6.5	7.4	5.5	5.1	1.9	2.8	2.2
Punjab	3.6	2.7	2.1	3.4	1.6	1.7	1.4
Rajasthan	7.8	12.2	11.4	1.2	1.7	3.2	2.6
Tamil Nadu	5.9	10.4	9.3	5.6	2.6	5.2	4.6
Uttar Pradesh	4.2	5.0	3.4	1.5	2.3	3.2	2.2
West Bengal	4.9	5.1	3.5	6.7	1.9	3.8	2.9
All India	6.4	7.2	5.8	4.3	2.0	3.1	2.5
CV Across States (%)	49.0	65.0	76.0	63.0	39.0	55.0	60.0

Source: 1. Census 1991, 2. NSS 50th Round on Employment and Unemployment, 3. Duraisamy, M. (2000) for NCAER Data.

high for the latter category. The NSS principal and subsidiary numbers for rural areas show that it was the highest in Andhra Pradesh (17.8 per cent) and lowest in Kerala (0.76 per cent). These two states have same ranks for urban areas also. The regional disparities are much higher for rural areas as compared to urban areas. The coefficient of variation given in Table-4 shows the regional disparities in the incidence of child labour are much higher for NSS data as compared to that of Census data. The CV is 76 per cent for principal status workers while Census data shows that it was 49 per cent in rural areas. It is interesting to note that poorer states like Bihar, Uttar Pradesh, M.P. and Orissa have lower incidence as compared to Southern states. The NSS data for Himachal Pradesh needs some explanation. If we take principal and subsidiary status, Himachal Pradesh showed one of the highest incidences in rural areas (13.6%). On the other hand, if we take principal status, the participation rate was low (3.2%) in the state. One of the reasons could be that many children might be working in a subsidiary status apart from attending school. In the case of Rajasthan it is not clear why the NCAER data shows a very low level of incidence (1.2%) as compared to NSS and Census data. On the other hand, Gujarat has lower incidence under NSS as compared to that for Census and NCAER. Madhya Pradesh has lower incidence while West Bengal has higher incidence under NCAER source as compared to other source.

II

Causes of Child Labour

Child labour is a universal phenomenon. Child labour remains widespread throughout the world. Their exploitation is an abuse of human rights. Millions of children are made to sacrifice their health and tender emotions by forcing them to work in hazardous industries and other occupations. Those who should be in schools are working at various jobs in the most unhygienic conditions for a pittance. The main causes of child labour are the following:

1. *Poverty:* The foremost reason of child labour is acute poverty which exists in developing countries. In cities, a large number of child labours is seen who come in search of employment as a household servant, or servant on shops, dhabas and hotels.
2. *Low Income of the Bread Earner of the Family:* The inadequacy of wage of the adult earning members of the family compels them to send their children to work and supplement the family income.
3. Unemployment: Children seek work because of their unemployed parents or adult relations in the family which is sometimes due to under-employment of the adults.
4. *Large Family:* In most cases, child workers belong to a large family with a low income. Therefore, their parents send them to work for more income.
5. *Child Labour Is Cheaply Available:* Employers like to get more production with cheap labour cost which they get easily by employing child labour rather than adults which ensures greater margin of profits. Poverty is a blessing to these employers as they get the poor children more easily in the labour market.
6. *Illiteracy and Ignorance:* Most of the children belong to the communities who live below the poverty line. Children and parents of these communities show little interest towards school education. The illiterate, ignorant parents do not think of the future but the present, and hence they do not send their children to school which they take as unnecessary wastage of time and money.
7. *Absence of Social Security Measures:* This compels some children to work consequent upon the death of their parents.

Adverse Effects of Child Labour on the Child and Society

Mankind owes to the children special attention, care and safeguards for the good of the society. But by engaging the children as labourers we deprive them of certain basic physiological, psychological, biological and social needs which are disgrace to mankind. Child labours are deprived of:

- Full and harmonious development.
- An atmosphere of affection and love.
- Moral and material security.
- Education.
- Culture.
- Opportunity to develop to their abilities.
- Opportunity to develop a sense of moral and social responsibility.
- Legitimate right to childhood.
- The assurance to develop into productive adults and to take their legitimate place in the society.
- Putting children to work may be temporarily beneficial to family, but costs heavily to the child as an individual, its family and the society at large. Unhappy and disturbed childhood does not offer sound foundation for their future growth and development.

Poor children are generally malnourished but their work increases their energy requirement and leads to calories deficit. If they suffer from anemia, fatigue and inadequate rest and slip, they become more susceptible to infectious diseases. Generally children at work suffer from physical health hazards, body injury and postural deformities.

Working children are easily exposed to biological disorder, unclean, unhealthy working conditions prevailing in unorganized manufacturing units, contaminated drinking and polluted air cost immune competency in the working children due to premature and under developed biology.

Virus, bacteria and parasite easily enter into tender and premature body system, affect digestive system and cause disease like diarrhea, typhoid, malaria, jaundice etc., and jeopardize biological growth of children resulting in functional disorder in the organism thus reducing life span.

Children working in a hazardous occupation exposed to toxic gases, vapours, fume, dust, smoke, resulting in impairment of lungs, respiratory system, throat, ear, eyes and skin. By the time working children reach adulthood, they suffer from chronic diseases like T. B., Asthma, Anemia and diseases of nerves. Exposure to loud noise at tender age impairs children's hearing, affects blood vessel, nervousness and psychiatric illness in childhood.

Child labour practice means greater loss to the society in the form of diminishing contribution of adults whose health, education and energies have been sacrificed during their childhood. Many children particularly girl children become victims of sex abuse infected with HIV, S.T.D., AIDS and spread sexually transmitted diseases in society.

III

Abolition/Elimination of Child Labour

It may be recalled here that the Constitution of India in its chapter on "Directive Principles of State Policy" (Art. 14) declares that "no child below the age of 14 years shall be employed in any factory or mine or engaged in any other hazardous employment". However, actually the problem of child labour began to receive some serious attention only after the U.N.O. declaration of 1979 as the International Year of the Child. It is surprising that while the Indian Constitution was adopted as far back as in 1950, it was only in 1986 that the Child Labour (Prohibition and Regulation) Act was promulgated. Despite the constitutional vow and the enactment of the 1986 Act, a large multitude of children in India continue to be involved in various hazardous and non-remunerative occupations.

Abolition of child labour in our country is not an easy job and mere enactments of child labour abolition laws will not guarantee the attainment of the desired goal. There are hosts of factors that can easily render the existing laws blunt and ineffective. A fundamental problem relates to the definitional aspect of child labour. On the other hand, the poor parents, having no other assets, themselves treat their children as assets rather than liabilities. Rather than sending their wards to schools, they prefer to associate their children in whatever income-earning activities that may be available before them. In most cases, these activities turn out to be petty income earning and/or niggardly paid activities. Often the rate of payment is not the parent's concern; the absolute income earned by the children is the major deciding factor.

Of late, both the Central and the various State Governments have woken up to the problems of child labour in the country. Various NGOs are especially waging a battle in favour of child labour abolition. Even at the global level, some developed nations have hardened their stance on this issue- these developed countries are threatening to ban exports from developing countries, which rely on utilization of cheap child labour. These countries are trying to stick to the clause that some particular exports from developing countries must come with a certified declaration from the appropriate authority that the products have no child labour content.

At the national level, apart from passing relevant Acts, the Central and state Governments have attempted to lure children from work places to schools by making primary education free and introducing mid-day meal scheme at the schools. In the states like West Bengal, along with free primary education, books etc. are being distributed free of cost at the primary school level. A large part of credit for forcing and inducing the governments in initiating steps against widespread use of child labour is due to some NGOs. In recent years, a number of NGOs has undertaken a crusade against the evils of child labour and have been largely responsible for spreading campaign on the issue among the masses.

The pertinent questions on this issue are: (1) can and should child labour be stopped altogether, and, if so, (2) how can it be stopped? The first of these two involves some normative considerations. Obviously, the first best and ideal world is the situation where the phenomenon of child labour is totally absent. But the existing socio-economic condition in India, mainly that of the rural masses and of the vast low-income population, first best solution overnight is ruled out. A more pragmatic approach would be to strive to mitigate the plight of the child labourers in the immediate short run and to get rid of the vice in the long run, if not possible in the near future. For this, however, it is imperative to set a deadline- say 8-10 year horizon from now on- and work sincerely towards attaining a child-labour free society.

Simply passing of laws and making education free, obviously, cannot ensure the emancipation of child labour. In fact, we have observed that what is truly lacking is presence of quality education at primary level. Because of this, families are forced to seek private tuitions for their children, which 6they cannot afford. Naturally, free primary education scheme fails to serve any meaningful purpose. The entire question needs to be addressed in a general equilibrium framework and within the ambit of present socio-economic parameters. It can safely be presumed that the current parametric configuration is not conducive to improved well being of the child workers simply based on legal intervention. The economic condition of the poor families needs to be improved, coupled with the general awareness- about the long term benefits of education as well as of family planning- among the low income people. Economic condition of the poor families can not just be improved by some stop-gap, ad hoc measures and measures like minimum wage laws. It is interesting and ironical too, to learn that Kausik Basu in a recent work has even come up with the piquant situation where adult minimum wage laws actually encourage, while inducing their wards to work longer.

It will perhaps be worthwhile to contemplate an India free from the vice of child labour by the year 2010. A specific deadline like this must be adhered to, which the Governments - Central and State, various agencies, NGOs, and all other must accept as unalterable. Unless and until a rigid time frame is adopted, the total abolition of child labour may well remain an elusive goal. If we can undertake such programmes like 'Polio-free India', 'Drinking water for all' etc. (set to be achieved within a given time), then why cannot we achieve the same thing in case of child labour? A few things, however, must be borne in mind. First, given the present dimension of the problem, the initiatives on the part of the Central and State Governments along with a vigorous media campaign, alone would not suffice; what is needed is active involvement of various NGOs in making people aware of the ill-effects of child labour. The NGOs possibly will be able to act as watchdog as well as to monitor the progress towards a child labour free society. The NGOs should, therefore, be armed with adequate legal powers so that they are able to play a much more effective role in arresting, if not eliminating, the growth of population of working children. The existence of large, unorganized and scattered nature of child labourers in the country, there will always be problems arising out of asymmetric information. In other words, even of any government tightens its child labour laws and attempts to plug the existence lacunae in the laws; it will still be extremely costly to successfully implement these laws. The NGOs usually work at grass root level and, accordingly, they possess much more and reliable information on the uses and abuses of child labour. Second, the political leadership at the grass root level also needs to be thoroughly motivated in seriously taking up the challenge of abolition of child labour (Das & others: 2000).

However, it is an undeniable fact that the long run solution of the problem requires radical reforms in property relations. This issue is now all the more important because the current phase of economic reforms has been pushing a large majority of population, who mostly reside in rural areas, on to the brink. Encouraging free market forces, coupled with globalization and open-door policy, and/or elimination of subsidies in many key-sectors are going to hurt these people severely. This is likely to accentuate the problem of the child labour since the poor parents or families will be forced to rely more on child labour than before. On the other hand, if the child labour related laws are made more stringent, the children of the poor families may well be forced to earn their livelihood from underground and undesirable activities, like drug-trafficking, child-proposition etc. (e.g. drug-Mafiosi often finds it easier to rely on children as 'carriers' as they may be usually unsuspecting). Therefore, creating ample opportunities for gainful employment among the masses is extremely urgent. Serious and honest land reforms along with sufficient provision of credit and other infrastructure facilities are very much essential. In other words, the total effacement of child labour phenomenon in India in the long run can be possible under a comprehensive policy package, and not simply by enactment of laws (i.e. reforms in property relations, reforms in primary education, reforms in legal structure etc.).

Concluding Observations

Our analysis in this paper has shown that a multi-pronged strategy is needed for eradication of child labour. It depends on improvements in quality of schooling, economic growth, adult wages, poverty reduction etc. Child labour is a complex issue and therefore requires complementary strategies and the involvement of all sections of civil society, i.e. NGOs, human right activists, lawyers, media, trade unions, employer's organizations, academicians and so on.

We conclude the paper with a few suggestions for further research. There are at least three areas where research will be useful in the case of child labour. One area is to have micro studies in different occupations to examine the impact of globalization on child labour. Second area is on determinants of child labour. In the literature economic growth and reduction in poverty are considered as main determinants for reducing child labour. The researchers should examine the issue whether economic growth or poverty reduction alone can reduce child labour.

The third area that is related to the second is the issue of education and schooling on child labour. It is useful to quote Amartya Sen's recent lecture at ILO, Geneva. Sen (1999) says, "it is often claimed that the abolition of child labour will harm the interests of the children themselves, since they may end up starving because of lack of family income and also because of increased neglect. It is certainly right that the fact of family poverty must be considered in dealing with this issue. There is no escape from that. But it is not at all clear why it must be presumed that the abolition of child labour will lead only to a reduction of family income and further neglect of children, without any other economic analysis and ethical examination is very strong in all these cases." Therefore, one area for research would be the impact of educational adjustment on child labour (Dev: 2000).

References

Basu, Kaushik (1999), "Child Labour: Cause, Consequence and Care with remarks on International Labour Standards", Journal of Economic Literature, Vol. XXXVII, September, pp.1083-1119.

Chatterjee, P.K. and Nandi, Arun K. (2000), "Child Labour: Inter-State Variations in Rural", IEA Conference Volume, 2000, p.442

Das, Swagata, Ghosh, Santanu, Chattopadhyay, Samit and Daniari, Nandini (2000), "Child Labour in the Cotton Handloom Industry: A Case Study of Two West Bengal Districts", IEA Conference Volume, 2000, pp.532-543.

Dev, S. Mahendra (2000), "Child Labour in India: Dimensions, Determinants and Policies", IEA Conference Volume 2000, p.437

9

Child Labour: The Shame of A Nation

Md. Reyazuddin and Shahnaz Mirza

Poor children in India begin working at a very young and tender age. Many children have to work to help their families and some families expect their children to continue the family business at a young age. It is useful to quote **Amartya Sen's** lecture at ILO Geneva. Sen (1999) says, "It is often claimed that the abolition of child labour will harm the interests of the children themselves, since they may end up starving because of lack of family income and also because of increased neglect. It is certainly right that the fact of family poverty must be considered in dealing with this issue. There is no escape from that. But it is not at all clear why it must be presumed that the abolition of child labour will lead only to a reduction of family income and further neglect of children, without any other economic or social or educational adjustment. The case for a broader and more inclusive economic analysis and ethical examination is very strong in all these cases."

The government has failed to eliminate this dehumanization of childhood. It has also failed to launch compulsory education and 100 million child are still at work instead of going to school and around 10 million are working in hazardous industries. India has the biggest child population of 380 million in the world, plus the largest number of children who are forced to earn a living. Is the Indian State fulfilling its constitutional obligations when the nation's children are sacrificing their childhood, unable to lead carefree, secure, happy and healthy life, which is their basic right?

According to the UN Convention on Child Right (CRC), which was adopted on September 2, 1990, "Every child by reason of his physical and mental immaturity needs special safeguard and care, including legal protection, before as well as after birth." India ratified CRC in December 1992 and is obliged to guarantee every child primary education and a healthy childhood. However, there seems to be little progress in this direction.

We have many laws that ban child labour in hazardous industries. According to the Child Labour (Prohibition and Regulation) Act, 1986, the employment of children (below the age of 14) in hazardous occupations has been strictly banned. But each state has different rules regarding the minimum age of employment; this makes implementation of these laws difficult.

Also, there is no ban on child labour in non-hazardous occupations. The act applies to the organized or factory sector and not to the unorganized or informal sector where most children find employment as cleaners, servants, porters and waiters among other forms of unskilled work. Thus, child labour continues because the implementation of the existing laws is lax.

There are industries, which have a 'special' demand for child labour because of their nimble fingers, high level of concentration and capacity to work hard at abysmally low wages. The carpet industry in Uttar Pradesh and Kashmir employs children to make hand knotted carpets; there are 80,000 child workers in Jammu & Kashmir alone. In Kashmir, because of the political unrest, children are forced to work while many schools are shut. Industries like gem cutting and polishing, pottery and glass want to remain competitive by employing children.

The truth is that it is poverty, which is pushing children into the brutish labour market. We have 200 million people below the poverty line in India; a large number of them are women. Poor, vulnerable parents, especially women-headed families, have no option but to push their little ones in this hard life in hostile conditions with no human or labour rights.

There is a lobby which argues that there is nothing wrong with children working as long as the environment for work is conducive for learning new skills. But studies have shown that children are made to do boring, repetitive and tedious jobs and are not taught new skills, as they grow older. In these hellholes, like the sweetshops of old, there is no hope.

Children working in hazardous industries are prone to debilitating diseases, which can cripple them for life. By sitting in cramped, damp, unhygienic spaces, their limbs become deformed for life. Inside matchstick, fireworks and glass industries, they are victims of bronchial diseases and TB. Their mental and physical development is permanently impaired by long hours of work. Once trapped, they can't get out of the vicious circle of poverty. They remain uneducated and powerless. Finally, in later years, they too are compelled to send their own children to work. Child labour perpetuates its own nightmare.

If the government were at all serious about granting children their rights, an intensive effort ought to have been made to implement the Supreme Court's directive of 1997, which laid down punitive action against employers of child labour (Rs. 20,000 per child to be paid by offending employers). The compulsory primary education amendment should have been working by now; the bill is stuck in the Rajya Sabha. There should have been faster poverty reduction programmes and more employment for women in rural areas. But all we have is stagnation and insensitivity.

In the absence of faster growth, the role of the civil society and NGOs to free bonded child labour is crucial. The trade unions need to be more sensitive because by employing children, the general level of wages gets depressed and there is a sharp rise in un-employment among adult workers.

If 380 million children are given a better life and elementary education, India's human capital would be greatly enhanced. But that needs, as the then President Abdul Kalam said, a "Second Vision". Can our political establishment see beyond the haze of shallow real politic?

Child labour is associated with literacy. Where the level of literacy is lower, the greater is the extent of child labour; Bihar is at the lowest rank of the literacy ladder. According to 1991 census, percentage of literates is 38.64% of the total population. This seems to indicate that children are not attracted to school system this backed by poverty forces the majority of children to take up wage employment at an early age, adding to the already existing child labour force. So far a systematic survey to estimate the child work force in the state has not been undertaken either by the government or by any NGO. The only figures available are those based on census reports. Child labour is widely prevalent in the State of Bihar. Table–1 provides data on the incidence of child labour in the State of Bihar, Kerala and Punjab. The performance of Bihar can neither be considered to be favourable in this regard nor is there any indication that the incidence of child labour is reducing in Bihar as the census data for the period from 1971 to 2001 shows.

Table 1
Child Labour as Per Census (1971-2001)

States	*1971*	*1981*	*1991*	*2001*
Bihar	1059359	1101764	942245	1117500
Kerala	111801	92854	34800	26156
Punjab	232774	216939	142868	177268
All India	107539895	13640870	11285349	12666377

Source: Economic Survey, 2007-08. Govt. of Bihar

Causes of Child Labour

The issue of child labour is a major human rights issue and at the same time it is highly emotive one, these emotions tend to be coupled with very strong views both on what the child labour problem is and on what ought to be done for its elimination. Although the predominance of child labour has to be quite pronounced in all the developing and under-developed countries, it is a global phenomenon, which exists in almost all the countries of the world. The concept and practice of child labour being economically unsound, psychologically wrong and socially disastrous has posed a big threat to peace and overall world development. Therefore, the gravity of the situation and pervasive nature of the problem has attracted the urgent attention of all-social and political organizations, social scientists, activist groups and governments of the world including India. The term 'Child Labour' is generally used to refer to "any work by children that interferes with them in their fully physical development, the opportunities for a desirable minimum of education and their needed recreation."

Children aged between four to fourteen years of age doing work in family, farms or occupations with or without payment in factories, outside home for wages constitute child labour. Of late, child labour has become a widespread phenomenon. It is not only confined to work on family farms or in traditional family jobs and occupations but it has also extended to other fields. Children work in agricultural and allied activities, unorganized small-scale sectors and even in organized industries. The phenomenon of child labour is a symptom of disease and is consequence of exploitative system, operating at the national and international levels, lopsided development, uneven resource ownership, correlating of large-scale unemployment and abject poverty among the nations.

The practice of child labour in India or in any other country of the world is an age-old phenomenon. In pre--industrial agricultural society of India, children worked as helpers and learners in hereditarily determined family occupations under the benign supervision of adult family members. The work place was an extension of the home and work was characterized by personal informal relationships. The task and technology that work involved were simple and non-hazardous.

Radical changes, however, occurred on social economic front with the advent of industrialization and urbanization under the impact of the newly generated centrifugal and centripetal forces; there was unbroken stream of the rural people migrating to urban centres in search of livelihood. As a result, the children were in a situation where they had to earn for themselves as well as for the families. Family based economy was destroyed and work now exposed the child to unhealthy environment. The child's ability to grow and to develop into a mentally and physically sound adult was severely restricted.

The existence and perpetuation of child labour is a blot on the conscience of Modern day civilized society. The child is born free and equal but often finds an uncertain future and becomes prey to exploitative set-up of the society. Children are put to work at so tender an age, which requires care and affection the most and education to equip them and provide better opportunities to grow and become able citizens. Unfortunately, they are denied these opportunities and are untimely subjected to enter the work force. In India, we are faced with an ever rising child labour growth curve. Their number is swelling unabatedly and the problem has acquired dangerous dimensions.

Children are the future hope of society and are destined to play important role in shaping the destiny of the nation. But unfortunately they are a suffering lot subjected to toilsome work without having opportunities to grow. The remark sums up the sad plight of child labour "It is really sad to note that children in most of the developing countries are living miserable, cheerless lives, toiling endlessly to ward off starvation totally deprived of all comforts and opportunities for self-growth and development.

The phenomenon of child labour robs the child of his youthful life, restricts the prospects of education, which can enable him to reach a higher level at a later stage of life, and, ultimately, it harms the progress and prosperity of the nation. It has been correctly stated: "Starve a child of food, of affection, of freedom, of education and you produce an adult who is stunted as an individual and holds back progress towards development rather than accelerate it." This is exactly happening in our country when put to work at a tender age, it reduces physical growth of children, lowers their efficiency, scale of intellectual growth and ultimately their ability and thereby nation's growth in future. Thus, child labour is economically unsound, psychologically disastrous and physically as well as morally dangerous and harmful. It is inefficient utilization of labour power at a lowest productivity level, which precludes full development of children's potentialities and ultimately harms economic development.

Poverty is undeniably a major factor leading to child labour because children from poverty-stricken families are compelled to join labour force but equally important is the exploitative nature of the system. Due to poverty 'parental authority' is misused. In this context Marx said: "It was not the misuse of parental authority that created the capitalistic exploitation of children's labour but on the contrary, it was the capitalist mode of exploitation which by sweeping away the economic basis of parental authority made its exercise degenerate into a mischievous misuse of power." There are many who view problem in this way and link it with exploitative capitalist mode of production and working of capitalist system. It has been opined: "Child labour, more truly, mirrors the character of the society and policy, including the nature of transition, than any other set of indicators." Thus the exploitative capitalist order perpetuates the problem.

The roots of the problem lie in the exploitative systems prevailing not only at the national level but also at the international level. At the national level the lopsided development process in the background of socio-economic structure results in marginalisation of the poor, who are left with no option but use child labour as a survival strategy. And at the international level, the need for foreign exchange, on the one hand, and stiff competition for markets in the developed world, encourage the producers of export industries in the third world to use cheap and vulnerable child labour. Also, powerful multinational corporations use child labour directly or indirectly, to minimize cost of production and to maximize profits.

Experiences of European countries analyzed by Klaus Voll, Ester Kostal et. al. show that child labour has been an integral part of the early stages of the development of the capitalist mode of production, and for a considerable extent its incidence depends on socio-cultural and religion-based values of the society. Indira Hirway regards the phenomena of child labour as both a consequence as well as cause. The existence of child labour reduces the level of employment of adults, which has a dampening effect on their wage rate. The resulting poverty, in turn, encourages parents to send their children out to work for the survival of the family. The vicious circle is further strengthened through the limited access of the poor to nutrition, health, education and skill. The poor access reduces the productivity as well as wages of adults, which again forces them to use their children's work for survival. The child labour system is thus used as a tool by the vested interests to strengthen their own position further and to maintain and sustain the poverty of the poor. Thus, the child labour problem has a complex dynamics having its dimension within the precinct of national boundary extending up to international level. The exploitative system both within and outside sustains and supports this child labour exploitation.

Rodgers and Standing employ useful categories to classify child labour. These are: (a) domestic work; (b) non-domestic and non-monetary work; (c) bonded labour, and (d) wage labour. In the first category are included household work like those of maid servants, domestic servants, etc. Children are employed in the time consuming activities such as child care, cooking, cleaning, washing, etc. The examples of second category are commonly found in the form of grazing of cow, goat, pigs, etc. where child of five to six and especially female child have to bear the burden. These children may be engaged in family activity or may be a type of self-employment. In spite of ban on bonded labour in the country-side, examples are not uncommon where parents pledge their children to employ both in rural agricultural and urban unorganized sectors against loans taken. The children so pledged have to work for a pittance. Children are also employed as wage labour, though their wages are often very low. Thus, they perform as unpaid worker in home or on their own fields as helpers and as paid labour on other's fields or in factories.

The concentration of child labour is to be seen in agriculture as cultivators and agricultural labourers: Children work as helpers in different agricultural operations such as sowing, weeding, harvesting and threshing. They are also engaged in road construction, digging of wells and house building. A large number of them are employed in plantations. We see their concentration in agriculture and unorganized sector due to lack of enforcement of child protection laws there and partly due to the legal restrictions put on employing them in organized sector. Children are found commonly in wayside restaurants, small hotels and dhabas, tea stall and sweets shop.

They are engaged in casual work where there is no provision of holidays, social security or other permissible allowances are completely absent and they have to work in hazardous, adverse working conditions affecting their health and efficiency. As they start work at a very young age, they are deprived of education, training (vocational or otherwise) which ultimately limits their earnings and restricts upward mobility.

Besides, child labour creates many social and psychological problems. Due to their misuse for illegal, immoral works, viz. smuggling, prostitution, etc. their personality development is impaired. They grow as stunted ill-mannered citizens. This psychological deprivation (due to lack of care-free life and freedoms) harms millions of children and so not only individual or family suffers but ultimately society loses, leading to .so many adverse impacts and social problems.

Here, it is very saddening to note that India has the largest number of world's working children. According to the World Bank Report, published in the first week of January, 2000, has revealed that there are six crore working children in India including the one and a half crore bonded working children. No doubt, the elimination of child labour is a big challenge for the country. A progressive as well as integrated approach has been adopted by the Government in order to resolve this intense socio-economic problem.

With the heralding of the new millennium, the problem of child labour stands as one of the most important global challenges. Millions of children in the world today turned into child labour due to various socio-economic problems. Provisions have been laid down in the Constitution prohibiting employment of children in factories. Under Article 24, it has been stated no child below the age of fourteen years shall be employed in any factory or mines or other hazardous occupation or work. Similarly, Article 31 provides that the State shall endeavour to provide in its policy specially to ensure that youthful age of the children is not abused and they are not forced to accept an employment detrimental to their age and physical ability owing to any economic compulsion. Article 45 provides for free and compulsory education for children under the schedule of the Child Labour (Prohibition and Regulation) Act, 1986 and employment of the children is prohibited in 12 occupations and 51 hazardous processes. Our Government formulated the National Child Labour Policy in 1987 to tackle the child labour problem. An action plan has also been made under this policy, which includes a statutory action plan for benefiting the working children. Focus has been laid towards launching a project-based action plan in child labour endemic areas where children are engaged in paid and under-paid occupations. Similarly, the government's approach towards the child labour problem has been described in the National Agenda for Governance (1998).

In view of the magnitude of the problem, an international programme for the elimination of child labour has also been implemented in India by the International Labour Organisation. Under this programme; financial assistance, awareness, creation, rehabilitation and education, etc. are provided for the elimination of this social menace. Even in the International Labour Conferences held during the year 1998-99, effective efforts were made by India for presenting a resolution on child labour. Apart from these numbers of child labour study groups and committees, i.e., Harbans Singh Committee, Gurupadswami Committee, Sanad Mehta Committee, Singhvi Committee, etc. have given their respective valuable suggestions. As per 1981 census, the country had 1.36 crore child labours which has come down to 1.13 crore in 1991 census. These statistics relating to working children are taken at the time of figures collected during census. In fact, the number of working children in India could be even more. This higher side figure could be because the maximum numbers of working children are in disguised form. These children work in agricultural farms, conventional industrial occupations. Many are engaged with their poor parents as companies' helpers. Andhra Pradesh constitutes the largest number of working children in the country where there were 17 lakh of working children as per 1991 census. More than 90 percent of these children are engaged in rural sectors, i.e., agriculture and its allied activities like harvesting, farming, animal husbandry, forestry and fishing. Presently, the child labourers are concentrated mainly in the industries of Sivakasi (Match and Fire Works), Firozabad (Glass Industry), Khurja (Pottery), Srinagar, Mirzapur, Bhadoi (Carpet), Muradabad (Brassware), Aligarh (Lock-making), Jaipur (Jems and Jewellary), Sagar (Biri), Mandsaur (Slate Industry), etc.

The phenomenon of child labour is deep-rooted in socio-economic stratification, mass poverty, illiteracy and unemployment particularly in rural India. Although the child labours system in India is an age-old phenomenon but its evil effects got prominence only after the industrial revolution in England. Despite several legislations to prohibit child labour, it is still rampant in our country. Therefore, the burgeoning problem of child labour requires appropriate solution. There is an urgent need to evolve development schemes for the economic upliftment of the parents of children involved in various occupations. Greater amount of public awareness is to be created and rights of children must be protected to prevent the destruction of this valuable human resource.

The sincere, massive and joint efforts by concerning organizations and international agencies like ILO, UNESCO, WHO, NGOs and world community can mitigate the persistence of this sub-human practice and finally eliminate this menace from the entire world. It is the high time for all to be very serious towards it to ensure better social and economic lives to all, at least in the interest of human dignity in the new millennium. There are several causes for continuation of child labour in India. But main causes are poor economic condition, traditional authority of father, high fertility rate, lack of status of the child in the society, low level of adult and child literacy, lack of social security and cheapness of human labour. And at the same time the lack of vigilance of the society to see that all the laws enacted for betterment of the children are really enforced properly is not less responsible for continuation of child labour in India. The responsible factors have been collected and discussed broadly under the following sub-headings such as poverty, low educational attainment, low inspirational level and defective plans and programmes of development.

Strategy for Elimination of Child Labour

The problem of child labour continues to pose a challenge before the nation. Government has been taking various pro-active measures to tackle this problem. However, considering the magnitude and extent of the problem and that it is essentially a socio-economic problem inextricably linked to poverty and illiteracy, it requires concerted efforts from all sections of the society to make a dent in the problem.

Way back in 1979, Government formed the first committee called Gurupadswamy Committee to study the issue of child labour and to suggest measures to tackle it. The Committee examined the problem in detail and made some far-reaching recommendations. It observed that as long as poverty continued, it would be difficult to totally eliminate child labour and hence, any attempt to abolish it through legal recourse would not be a practical proposition. The Committee felt that in the circumstances, the only alternative left was to ban child labour in hazardous areas and to regulate and ameliorate the conditions of work in other areas. It recommended that a multiple policy approach was required in dealing with the problems of working children.

Based on the recommendations of Gurupadaswamy Committee, the Child Labour (Prohibition & Regulation) Act was enacted in 1986. The Act prohibits employment of children in certain specified hazardous occupations and processes and regulates the working conditions in others. The list of hazardous occupations and processes is progressively being expanded on the recommendation of Child Labour Technical Advisory Committee constituted under the Act.

In consonance with the above approach, a National Policy on Child Labour was formulated in 1987. The Policy seeks to adopt a gradual and sequential approach with a focus on rehabilitation of children working in hazardous occupations and processes in the first instance. The Action Plan outlined in the Policy for tackling this problem is as follows:

- *Legislative Action Plan* for strict enforcement of Child Labour Act and other labour laws to ensure that children are not employed in hazardous employments and that the working conditions of children working in non-hazardous areas are regulated in accordance with the provisions of the Child Labour Act. It also entails further identification of additional occupations and processes, which are detrimental to the health and safety of the children.
- *Focusing of General Developmental Programmes for Benefiting Child Labour* - As poverty is the root cause of child labour, the action plan emphasizes the need to cover these children and their families also under various poverty alleviation and employment generation schemes of the Government.
- *Project Based Plan of Action* envisages starting of projects in areas of high concentration of child labour. Pursuant to this, in 1988, the *National Child Labour Project (NCLP)* Scheme was launched in 9 districts of high child labour endemicity in the country. The Scheme envisages running of special schools for child labour withdrawn from work. In the special schools, these children are provided formal/non-formal

education along with vocational training, a stipend of Rs.100 per month; supplementary nutrition and regular health check ups so as to prepare them to join regular mainstream schools. Under the Scheme, funds are given to the District Collectors for running special schools for child labour. Most of these schools are run by the NGOs in the district.

Government has accordingly been taking proactive steps to tackle this problem through strict enforcement of legislative provisions along with simultaneous rehabilitative measures. State Governments, which are the appropriate implementing authorities, have been conducting regular inspections and raids to detect cases of violations. Since poverty is the root cause of this problem and enforcement alone cannot help solve it, Government has been laying a lot of emphasis on the rehabilitation of these children and on improving the economic conditions of their families.

An evaluation of the Scheme was carried out by independent agencies in coordination with V. V. Giri National Labour Institute in 2001. Based on the recommendations of the evaluation and experience of implementing the scheme since 1988, the strategy for implementing the scheme during the 10th Plan was devised. It aimed at greater convergence with the other developmental schemes and bringing qualitative changes in the Scheme. Some of the salient points of the 10th Plan Strategy are as follows:

- Focused and reinforced action to eliminate child labour in the hazardous occupations by the end of the Plan period.
- Expansion of National Child Labour Projects to additional 150 districts.
- Linking the child labour elimination efforts with the Scheme of Sarva Shiksha Abhiyan of Ministry of Human Resource Development to ensure that children in the age group of 5-8 years get directly admitted to regular schools and that the older working children are mainstreamed to the formal education system

through special schools functioning under the NCLP Scheme.

- Convergence with other schemes of the Departments of Education, Rural Development, Health and Women and Child Development for the ultimate attainment of the objective in a time bound manner.

The Government and the Ministry of Labour and Employment in particular are rather serious in their efforts to fight and succeed in this direction. The number of districts covered under the NCLP Scheme has been increased from 100 to 250, as mentioned above in this note. In addition, 21 districts have been covered under INDUS, a similar scheme for rehabilitation of child labour in cooperation with US Department of Labour. Implementation of this Project was recently reviewed during the visit of Mr. Steven Law, Deputy Secretary of State, from the USA. For the Districts not covered under these two schemes, Government is also providing funds directly to the NGOs under the Ministry's Grants-in-aid Scheme for running Special Schools for rehabilitation of child labour, thereby providing for a greater role and cooperation of the civil society in combating this menace.

Elimination of child labour is the single largest programme in this ministry's activities. Apart from a major increase in the number of districts covered under the scheme, the priority of the Government in this direction is evident in the quantum jump in budgetary allocation during the 10th Plan. Government has allocated Rs. 602 crores for the Scheme during the 10th Plan, as against an expenditure of Rs. 178 crores in the 9th Plan. The resources set aside for combating this evil in the Ministry is around 50 per cent of its total annual budget.

The implementation of NCLP and INDUS Schemes is being closely monitored through periodical reports, frequent visits and meetings with the district and state government officials. The Government's commitment to achieve tangible results in this direction in a time bound manner is also evident from the fact that in the recent Regional Level Conferences of District Collectors held in Hyderabad, Pune, Mussoorie and Kolkata district-wise review of the scheme was conducted at the level of Secretary. These conferences provided an excellent opportunity to have one-to-one interaction with the collectors, who play a pivotal role in the implementation of these schemes in the district. Besides, these conferences also helped in a big way in early operationalisation of scheme in the newly selected 150 districts.

The Government is committed to eliminate child labour in all its forms and is moving in this direction in a targeted manner. The multipronged strategy being followed by the Government to achieve this objective also found its echo during the recent discussions held in the Parliament on the Private Member's Bill tabled by Shri Iqbal Ahmed Saradgi. It was unanimously recognized therein that the problem of child labour, being inextricably linked with poverty and illiteracy, cannot be solved by legislation alone and that a holistic, multipronged and concerted effort to tackle this problem will bring in the desired results.

Child Labour and Constitutional Provisions

Article 21 A

Right to Education: The State shall provide free and compulsory education to all children of the age of 6 to 14 years in such manner as the State, by law, may determine.

Article 24

Prohibition of Employment of Children in Factories, etc.: No child below the age fourteen years shall be employed in work in any factory or mine or engaged in any other hazardous employment.

Article 39

The State shall, in particular, direct its policy towards securing the health and strength of workers, men and women and the tender age of children are not abused and that citizens are not forced by economic necessity to enter avocations unsuited to their age or strength.

Legislative Provisions Prohibiting and Regulating Employment of Children

- As per the Child Labour (Prohibition & Regulation) Act, 1986 "child" means a person who has not completed his 14th year of age.
- The Act prohibits employment of children in 13 occupations and 57 processes contained in Part A & B of the Schedule to the Act (Section 3).
- Under the Act, a Technical Advisory Committee is constituted to advice for inclusion of further occupations and processes in the Schedule.
- The Act regulates the condition of employments in all occupations and processes not prohibited under the Act (Part III).
- Any person who employs any child in contravention of the provisions of section 3 of the Act is liable for punishment with imprisonment for a term which shall not be less than three months but which may extend to one year or with fine which shall not be less than Rs 10,000 but which may extend to Rs 20,000 or both. (Section 14).
- The Central and the State Governments enforce the provisions of the Act in their respective

Main Features of the Directions of Supreme Court in their Judgment dated 10.12.1996

On 10th December 1996 in Writ Petition (Civil) No.465/1986, the Supreme Court of India gave certain directions on the issue of elimination of child labour. The main features of judgment are as follows:

- Survey for identification of working children;
- Withdrawal of children working in hazardous industry and ensuring their education in appropriate institutions;
- Contribution @ Rs.20,000/- per child to be paid by the offending employers of children to a welfare fund to be established for this purpose;

- Employment to one adult member of the family of the child so withdrawn from work and if that is not possible, a contribution of Rs.5,000/- to the welfare fund to be made by the State Government;
- Financial assistance to the families of the children so withdrawn to be paid-out of the interest earnings on the corpus of Rs.20,000/25,000 deposited in the welfare fund as long as the child is actually sent to the schools;
- Regulating hours of work for children working in non-hazardous occupations so that their working hours do not exceed six hours per day and education for at least two hours is ensured. The entire expenditure on education is to be borne by the concerned employer.
- The implementation of the direction of the Hon'ble Supreme Court is being monitored by the Ministry of Labour and compliance of the directions have been reported in the form of Affidavits on 05.12.1997, 21.12.1999, 04.12.2000, 04.07.2001 and 04-12-2003 to the Hon'ble Court on the basis of the information received from the State/UT Governments.

To Sum Up

Child labour cannot be approached as an isolated problem. It is a complex socio-economic-demographic phenomenon, which can be reduced and eliminated by a multiplicity of actions both by government and public, at social as well as individual levels. The aim of the social policies should be to reduce the intensity of child labour and improve the quality of working conditions for children in the short term and finally, eradicate the child labour in long term planning.

There is an urgent need for attitudinal change, social awareness and aggressive campaign against the scourge of child labour. It becomes our national obligation to ensure physical and mental development of these young ones with measures for regulating and humanizing child labour along with attack on poverty. We hope, there would be gradual elimination of this problem. The eradication of the problem is a long process, which requires intensive efforts on many fronts and also creation of general social awareness and needs co-operation of different sections. The basic strategy concerning child labour should be to reduce gradually and eliminate it through improving and enforcing legislation, promoting school enrolment and raising public awareness. Prof. Amartya Sen also advocated that compulsory education is essential for eradication of child labour in our country.

References

Anna Davin; "Child Labour the Working Class Family and Domestic Ideology in 19th Century Britain", in Gerry Rodgers & Guy Standing (eds.), Child Work, Poverty and Underdevelopment, ILO, Geneva, p. 641.

Child in Third World; 1981, Report and Tables based on 5, percent Sample Data, Part II-Special, Series-I, India, Part II, Tables, pp. 2-3.

Gerry Rodgers and Guy Standing; "The Economic Roles of Children: Issues for Analysis", p. 32.

Gupta Manju (1997), "Child Labour in India", p. 2.

J.C. Kulshrestha (1978), Child Labour in India, Ashish Publishing House, New Delhi, pp. 46-47.

Kamla Mankekar (1982), "Who Exploits Children?" The Illustrated Weekly of India, April 18, p. 27.

Leela Dube (1981), "The Economic Roles of Children in India: Methodological Issues", in Gerry Rodgers and Guy Standing (eds.), Child Work, Poverty and Underdevelopment, ILO, Geneva, pp. 189-194.

M.E. Khan (1980), Sociological Aspects of Child Development: A Study of Rural Karnataka, Concept Publication Company, New Delhi, p. 171.

Madhur Chaturvedi (1980), "Child Labour; The Shame of a Nation", The Illustrated Weekly of India, Vol. C129, July 20-26, p. 12.

Mihaly Simai (1979), "Situation of Children in New Global Realities in the Year 2,000" New Perspectives: Journal of the World Peace Council, Vol. 9, 6/p.34.

Ministry of Labour (1979), Report of the Committee on Child Labour, Government of India, Dec. p. 17.

Musafir Singh, V.D. Kaura and S.A. Khan (1980), Working Children in Bombay-A Study NIPCCD, New Delhi, pp. 152-155.

Padmini Sengupta (1975), "Children Work to Live", Social Welfare, April, p. 11.

Pati, R.N.: Rehabilitation of Child Labour in India, p. 144.

Sandilya, Tapan Kumar, Child Labour: A Global Challenge, Deep and Deep Publication Private Limited, New Delhi.

Shandilya Tapan Kumar, Nayan Kumar and Navin Kumar (2006), "Child Labour Eradication", Deep & Deep Publication, New Delhi.

Singh, Bhagwan and Shukla Mohanty (1993), Child Labour at Work, B.R. Publishing Corporation, Delhi and Indian Society of Labour Economics, Patna.

10

Child Labour: Socio-Economic Evil and Its Consequences

Pushpa Sinha

Introduction

Although the percentage of children in the labour force may be lower than it is in many developing countries the hard truth is that India has the largest number of child labourers in the world. Near about 1.40 crore child labour are here. Child labour is a colossal problem in India. The child work participation rates are also higher in India than in other developing countries. This problem is a great hurdle of any economy and its growth. Child labour is concerned with all the children working below 14 years of age. This activity hampers the growth of the child.

Causes of Child Labour

There are several problems and causes of child labour in India.

- Child labour is a source of income for poor families. A study conducted by the 'ILO' Bureau of Statistics found that "Children's work was considered essential to maintaining the economic level of house holds chores in order to free adult household members for economic activity elsewhere" (Mehra-Kerpleman 1996,8). In some cases, the study found that a child's income accounted for between 34 and 37 percent of the total household income. This study concludes that a child labourer's income is important to the livelihood of a poor family. The questionable aspect of this study was conducted in the form of a survey, and the responses were given by the parents of the child labourers. I found the parents biased into being compelled to support their decision to send their children to work, by saying it is essential. They are probably right because for most poor families in India, alternative sources of income are close to non-existent.

- The percentage of the population of India living in poverty is high. In 1990, 37% of the urban population and 39% of the rural population was living in poverty. Poverty has an obvious relationship with child labour, and studies have "revealed a positive correlation in some instances a strong one-between child labour and such factors as poverty" (Mehra-Kerpelman, 1996,8). Families need money to survive, and children are a source of additional income. Poverty it-self has underlying determinants, one such determinant being caste. When analyzing the caste composition of child laburers Nangia (1987) observes that, "if these figures are compared with the caste structure of the country, it would be realised that a comparatively higher proportion of scheduled caste children work at a younger age of their own and their families: economic support". I observed that scheduled caste children tend to be pushed into child labour because of their family's poverty. In the study, 63.74% of child labourers said that poverty was the reason they worked.
- The combination of poverty and the lack of a social security network from the basis of the even harsher type of child labour bonded child labour. For the poor,

there are few sources of bank loans, governmental loans or other credit sources, and even if there are sources available, few Indians living in poverty qualify. Here enters the local money lender; for an average of two thousand rupees, parents exchange their child's labour to local money-lenders. Since the earnings of bonded child labourers are less than the interest on their loans these bonded children are forced to work, while interest on their loans accumulates. A bonded child can only be released after his /her parent makes a lump sum payment, which is extremely difficult for the poor. Even if they are released, "the same conditions of poverty that caused the initial debt can cause people to slip back into bondage" (International Labour Organization 193,12).

- Even though poverty is cited as the major cause of child labour, it is not the only determinant. Inadequate schools, a lack of schools, or even the expense of schooling leaves some children with little else to do but work. The attitudes of the parents also contribute to child labour; some parents feel that children should work in order to develop skills useful in the job market, instead of taking advantage of a formal education.

So, these were some important and crucial causes of child labour in India. We cannot deny these problems at any cost. To remove or to avoid child labour, we have to give importance to these causes.

It is difficult to cite a current figure for the number of children engaged in child labour. This difficulty is attributed to the fact that the Indian government "has been negligent in its refusal to collect and analyze current and relevant data regarding the incidence of child labour. As of 1996, official figures continue to be based on 1981 census figures" (Human rights Watch 1996,122). The 1981 census reports that there were 13.6 million child labourers in India. According to the 2001 census 1.25 crore children in the age group 5-14 years are indulge in hazardous and non-hazardous occupation. But NGOs state this data only includes the children in organized sector not in unorganised sector

UNICEF "cites figures ranging from seventy five to ninety million child labourers under the age of fourteen" (Human Rights Watch 1996,122). A universal difficulty in obtaining accurate data may be that individuals fail to report child labour participation during surveys, for fear of persecution.

Although, the figure for the number of child labourers varies, they are all significantly high when considering that the Child Economic Activity rate for 1980-1991 was 13.5% for males and 10.3% for females (International Labour Organizations, 1995,113).

In comparison, other developing countries such as Sri Lanka and Malaysia (where data is available), have lower activity rates: 5.3% for males and 4.6% for females in Sri Lanka, and 8.8% for males and 6.5% for females in Malaysia (ILO, 1995, 113). Historical census data shows an overall child work participation rate of 12.69% in 1961 and 7.13% in 1977 (Census of India 1971 cited in Devi 1985, 50). This data is misleading because the definitions of child labour are different in the two censuses because unpaid workers are not included in the 1971 census, thus a comparison cannot be completely valid. The data shows that in a span of twenty years (1961-1981), the proportion of children who are working has not changed significantly.

The present figure of the child labourers is around six crore under the age of fifteen. According to the World Bank Report published in the first week of January 2000. It is very saddening to note that India has the largest number of world's working children. Child labour is a social evil. Child slavery is a national curse. It is a grave problem in India. The phenomenon is multi-dimensional and multi-layered. It is a by-product of socio-economic structure of the society. Problem of child labour is not confined to the third world countries only. It has been more or less a global problem. The difference, if any, is only of degree.

The issue of child labour is a major human rights issue and at the same time it is highly emotive one, these emotions tend to be coupled with very strong views both on what the child labour problem is and on what ought to be done for its elimination. Although the predominance of child labour has to be quite pronounced in all the developing and under developed countries, it is a global phenomenon, which exists in almost all the countries of the world. The concept and practice of child labour being economically unsound, psychologically wrong and socially disastrous has posed a big threat to peace and overall world development. Therefore, the gravity of the situation and pervasive nature of the problem has attracted the urgent attention of all-social and political organisations, social scientists, activist groups and governments of the world including India.

The term 'child labour' is generally used to refer to "any work by children that interferes with them in their fully physical development, the opportunities for a desirable minimum of education and their needed recreation."

Children aged between four to fourteen doing work on family farms or in occupations with or without payment or in factories, farms outside home for wages constitute child labour. Of late, child labour has become a widespread phenomenon. It is not only confined to work on family farms or in traditional family jobs and occupations but it has also extended to other fields. Children work in agricultural and allied activities, unorganized small-scale sectors and even in organized industries.

The phenomenon of child labour is a symptom of disease and is consequence of exploitative system, operating at the national and international levels, lopsided development, uneven resource ownership, correlating of large-scale unemployment and abject poverty among the nations.

The practice of child labour in India or in any other country of the world is an age-old phenomenon. In pre-industrial agricultural society of India, children worked as helpers and learners in hereditarily determined family occupations under the benign supervision of adult family members. The work place was an extension of the home and work was characterized by personal informal relationships. The task and technology that work involved were simple and non-hazardous.

Radical changes, however, occurred on social economic front with the advent of industrialization and urbanization under the impact of the newly generated centrifugal and centripetal forces; there was unbroken stream of the rural people migrating to urban centres in search of livelihood. As a result, the children were in a situation where they had to earn for themselves as well as for the families. Family based economy was destroyed and work now exposed the child to unhealthy environment. The child's ability to grow and to develop into a mentally and physically sound adult was severely restricted.

The child is born free and equal but often finds an uncertain future and becomes prey to exploitative set-up of the society. Children are put to work at so tender an age, which requires care and affection the most, and education to equip them and provide better opportunities to grow and become able citizens. Unfortunately, they are denied these opportunities and are untimely subjected to enter the work force. In India, we are faced with an ever rising, child labour growth curve. Their number is swelling unabatedly and the problem has acquired dangerous dimensions.

Children are the future hope of society and are destined to play important role in shaping the destiny of the nation. But unfortunately they are a suffering lot subjected to toilsome work without having opportunities to grow. The remark sums up the sad plight of child labour. "It is really sad to note that children in most of the developing countries are living miserable, cheerless lives, toiling endlessly towards starvation, totally deprived of all comforts and opportunities for self-growth and development."

Poverty is undeniably a major factor leading to child labour because children form poverty-stricken families are compelled to join labour force but equally important is the exploitative nature of the system. Due to poverty 'parental authority' is misused. It has been opined: "Child labour more truly mirrors the character of the society and policy, including the nature of transition, than any other set of indicators." Thus the exploitative capitalist order perpetuates the problem. Indira Hirway regards the phenomena of child labour as both a consequence as well as cause. The existence of child labour reduces the level of employment of adults which has a dampening effect on their wage rate. The resulting poverty, in turn, encourages parents to send their children out to work for the survival of the family. The vicious circle is further strengthened through the limited access of the poor to nutrition, health, education and skill. The poor access reduces the productivity as well as wages of adults, which again forces them to use their children's work for survival. The child labour system is thus used as a tool by the vested interests to strengthen their own position further, and to maintain and sustain the poverty of the poor. Thus, the child labour problem has a complex dynamics having its dimension within the precinct of national boundary extending upto international level. The exploitative system both within and outside sustains and supports this child labour exploitation.

The concentration of child labour is to be seen in agriculture as cultivators and agricultural labourers. Children work as helpers in different agricultural operations such as sowing, weeding, harvesting and threshing. They are also engaged in road construction, digging of wells and house building. A large number of them are employed in plantations. We see their concentration in agriculture and unorganized sector due to lack of enforcement of child protection laws there and, partly due to the legal restrictions put on employing them in organized sector. Children are found commonly in wayside restaurants, small hotels and *dhabas,* tea stall and sweets shop. They are engaged in casual work where there is no provision of holidays, social security or other permissible allowances are completely absent and they have to work in hazardous, adverse working conditions affecting their health and efficiency. As they start work at a very young age, they are deprived of education, training (vocational or otherwise) which ultimately limits their earnings and restricts upward mobility.

Besides, child labour creates many social and psychological problems. Due to their misuse for illegal, immoral works, viz. smuggling, prostitution, etc. their personality development is impaired. They grow as stunted ill-mannered citizens. This psychological deprivation (due to lack of care-free life and freedoms) harms millions of children, and, so not only individual or family suffers, but, ultimately society loses, leading to so many adverse impacts and social problems.

Here it is very saddening to note that India has the largest number of world's working children. According to the World Bank Report, published in the first week of January, 2000, has revealed that there are six crore working children in India including the one and a half crore bonded working children in. No doubt, the elimination of child labour is big challenge for the country. A progressive as well as integrated approach has been adopted by the Government in order to resolve this intense socio-economic problem.

With the heralding of the new millennium, the problem of child labour stands as one of the most important global challenges. Millions of children in the world today turned into child labour due to various socio-economic problems. Provisions have been laid down in the Constitution prohibiting employment of children in factories. Under Article 24, it has been stated no child below the age of fourteen years shall be employed in any factory or mine or other hazardous occupation or work. Similarly, Article 31 provides that the State shall endeavour to provide in its policy specially to ensure that youthful age of the children is not abused and they are not forced to accept an employment detrimental to their age and physical ability owing to any economic compulsion. Article 45 provides for free and compulsory education for children under the schedule of the Child Labour (Prohibition and Regulation) Act, 1986, and employment of the children is prohibited in 12 occupations and 51 hazardous processes. Our Government formulated the National Child Labour Policy in 1987 to tackle the child labour problem. An action plan has also been made under this policy, which includes a statutory action plan for benefiting the working children. Focus has been laid towards launching a project-based action plan in child labour endemic areas where children are engaged in paid and under-paid occupations. Similarly, the government's approach towards the child labour problem has been described in the National Agenda for Governance (1998). In view of the magnitude of the problem, an international programme for the elimination of child labour has also been implemented in India by the International Labour Organisation.

Some Important Facts of Child Labour in India

As I went through this subject, I came to know several aspects of child labour. The result of the observation was that there are different facts for the emergence of child labour in India. Child labour in India is not based on industrialisation or capitalism. In India children do not work in large scale industries as used to be happened in 19th century in England and America. But they are popular most in small seals Industries, cottage industries, Handicrafts, house-holds work, agricultural, Mechanical, etc.

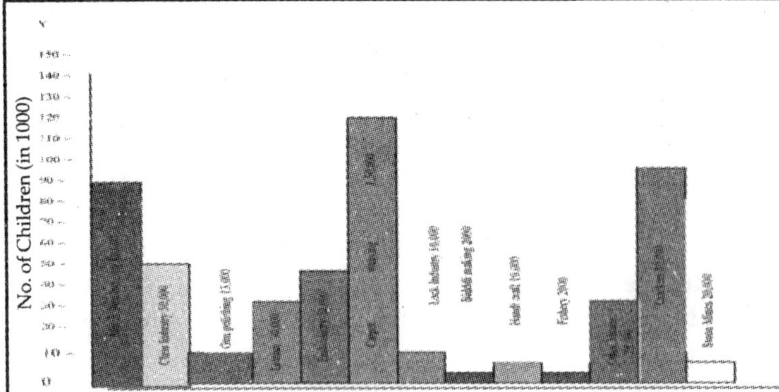

Child Labour in Different Sectors
Source: Pratiyogita Darpan, October, 2004

Child Labour in Different Sector's in India

The western countries in 19th and 20th century children used to finish at least their education till the age of 6 to 9 years, whereas, India has uneducated or illiterate children to the maximum of this age. Or they are forced to leave or dropout the school in std-IV or V. Most of them have never seen the school only. Because of no compulsion in studies, children start working in early age only. In India, children start working in small scale industries, cottage industries and the house-hold work at the age of 5 years only. Compared to villages with town, children start learning different profession than their parents in town. In Auto-mechanic workshops, children learn or work in groups. The work which they can learn further, they are learning in their childhood only.

The work taken by the owners (bosses) or government employees says that children are fast and quick to understand or learn to do the work. They do it with full devotion. This makes them to exploit fully the small and innocent children.

The child labour does not give the guarantee of getting the work in the future. They are not asked the questions that were they used to work in the childhood. The wages are not based on their experience. In fact, due to early stage of working hampers the growth of the child in every case. They become weak in their young age which affect their working ability and shows the great difference between their incomes.

Due to restriction in working in the large scale industries, they get the freedom to work in small and cottage industries. So, they don't have proper union which gives full chances of exploitation of the children. Due to which children suffers a lot.

The parents do not understand the illiteracy problem of their children. It is not that the source of income rises because of children. But in some places they are bound to work because of the loans which their parents have taken for marriages or any other work. The unavailability of proper food, clothes, and medicines tends to increase in the number of child labourers. The low standard of living as well as thinking never allows them to come out of this problem. Because of low status they get involved in child work.

The biggest difference between the girl child and boy child also is a biggest cause of child labour. Parents believe that girls are born to work only. So, the ratio of child labour regarding male and female, the female is higher than the male. This difference never allows them to come over this problem. Their status effects their whole life. Even if they are literate, they don't get the jobs. So, they don't want to waste their time in studies but in the work. Due to mental block of the society, the poors are asked to utilize their hands not brains. The people think that education is made for special or particulars group of people but not for poors.

These are some important facts which I was compelled to think over it. These problems are genuine among the poor people because of different causes or reasons in their life. We should try to break these obstacles by doing good efforts in the favours of children involved in child labour. At the age of playing with toys or books they have to play with the machines and tools for their breads. The whole society should be blamed for this. They should open their minds and hearts for the development of the child who is the future of the country. We should try to help them to come out of this problem.

Socio-Economic Consequence of Child Labour

Society as such has never approved child labour. It is only the circumstances that make the society accept child labour, if it is to be considered evil. Child also temperamentally never likes to work, as strenuously as any adult would do. So these little adults if not kept employed then remain under constant threat of unemployment and thereby are at a loss of adequate food shelter and clothing for themselves. Being exposed to adult life, at an early age creates numerous problems for the child labour itself. As many of them are working for long hours even during night, with least protection from polluted environment at the place of work, and under constant mental and physical strain, their growth becomes somewhat stunted and some of them become useless for any other jobs in the adulthood than what they out of necessity do in their childhood. The work lays them open to the risk of exploitation. Those who are working for wage earning are the most vulnerable to exploitation. In few cases those working for wage are also equally exploited.

As stated above the children in their tender age, if given very odd jobs such as carrying heavy loads, working in constant chemical polluted plants, performing acts of various nature unhygienic conditions, etc., then their physical and mental development becomes abnormal. This situation later affects the society at large, keeping their speech, infatuation for short lived and cheap things, and most importantly an inferiority complex. Depending upon the type of job and involvement in it, the child is also exposed to the infectious diseases or develops some deformity. Some of the impacts on health of child are known.

Now we will discuss the consequences of child labour on different heads.

Impact of Child Labour on Health

Poverty is a biggest problem for them. From the time of their birth only they are not paid attention regarding their health. This causes diseases and health rate increases. Lack of medical facilities, the death rate is higher than the birth rate. But the male-oriented society pays less attention on the girl child than the boy-child, which makes a great difference in the ratio. Because of poverty and rise in population the children are forced to work from their childhood. This affects their health a lot. Because of heavy load of work they became weak. They use to do very hard work in all the field to survive and are paid less. This may cause many types of diseases. But heavy work pressure and low income never allows them to concern on this health. High prices of medicines and high charges of doctors are not affordable by them. Lack of governmental dispensaries and medical shops hampers there health.

They do not get nutrious food to eat to be healthy. The environment also affect their health. Not only physical but it affects their mental states also. Some of the disease like T.B, Asthma, skin disease, Itching or Burning problems, which affect the health of the child labours working in different environment or field. This hampers the health of the child like slow poison which results in a bad way. This should be taken in consideration to check the problems affecting their health.

Impact of Child Labour on Education

Every child has right to education. But in the context of India, the different classes of the society, it makes a vast difference. Due to poverty, the poor people are unable to send them to school for studies. The mental block of "Education for them is of no use", stops them to do so. They think that the time spend on studies can be wastage for them. It's better for them to teach their children to work from their childhood which will help them in future. Actually, the making of the society is like that the society thinks. Education is for special group of people only. It is not for the poors. This difference creates a big gap between the rich and the poor.

Even if they are educated, they don't get proper jobs or work. The differentiation between the male and female also not allows to poor to study. They can teach the boys till 4th or 5th class. But the girls are not allowed to see the picture of the school also. This gender problem will never allow them to come over this mentality. They think girls are born to work at home only and they push or compel the females to work from their childhood. They use to work in the houses, factories, garbage collection, etc. Even if the child wants to study they are not allowed to do so because of the greatest need of the family i.e. food and clothes.

The education is very important for each and every child for awareness of political life, social, historical, health (including sex), legal, geographical and etc. But these children only studies about the working ability to earn money for their livelihood. Because of this, most of the intelligent and studious children who can do wonders disappear in zero.

Lack of education blocks the mind and mental condition and their development does not become proper. Lack of Education may create a big problem in more exploitation of children. The poor suffer from inferiority and sometimes jealousy which is not good for a child. This feeling may destruct their minds and they can do illegal things. The state of mind reflects the body also. Education is must for every child. The Government has tried several options or programmes for child education.

Due to lack of education there knowledge is limited. So, they are unable to judge right thing for themselves. This invites exploitation of the children. There is a low standard of living and narrow thinking people who are uneducated.

Education can make them feel better and make a difference between the right and the wrong. Compared to other countries, the literacy rate in India is very low. Even if the children goes to school; there is a higher percentage dropping out the school at a certain extent.

Education develops the mental growth and the personality of a child. It helps them to raise their status in the society. Without education no one is complete. Education will open their minds in all aspects like they can choose their leaders, they can understand their rights and duties and laws of their countries which they must know. Education can only lighten their lives to remove the darkness of their lives.

In the recent years, lot of literacy camps was organized for the children. Different Education programmes were announced and were active. This helped to a great extent. At-least they become literate. But most of the population is still suffering from illiteracy.

Impact of Child Labour on Personality Development

The involvement in the work from their childhood does not allow their personality to develop properly. They do not enjoy their childhood due to heavy pressures on work, earning, food, clothes etc. They totally concentrate on the source of income. So, children starts working from their childhood does not grow properly.

They don't get appropriate time to study or to play. They are unable to learn new things around them because they are not allowed to lift up their heads while working. Due to exploitation of the children, loose their mental balance and development. The lack of education does not allow their personality to grow to an extent. They become more mature than their age. Poverty only teaches them to live and work. Due to low standard of living, they are unable to talk properly or impressively. Their language is not good. The physical condition becomes bad because of lack of notorious food. (Notorious) Overall, their personalities are undeveloped and not so good. These all are due to the problem of child labour, poverty, food problem, education, surroundings, environment, circles and etc.

To develop their personality, it is necessary to educate them properly and they should make difference between the good and bad. The development of this sense will help to develop this personality specially the females, who are always under estimated by the society in every field.

Conclusion

Child labour is a universal phenomenon and it is a by-product. of socio-economic structure of the society. Children are an asset for any society as well as to nation. They are the blooming flowers of the society it is, therefore, a duty of the society to protect these flowers so as to have a meaningful contribution through them in the future. It is a well-known fact that the future of a society or a nation or world depends upon the sound growth of the children. Due to certain forces and circumstances children are compelled to work in the early states of their childhood, which does harm to the child and society. Hence child labour is considered as an economic and social problem. The most horrifying truth about child labour is that they have very little say in choosing their occupation. They have no right as workers and they cannot join labour unions to raise their voice against exploitation. The Supreme Court, in one of the cases related to child labour, has observed: if there be no proper growth of children today, the future of the country will be in dark. It is the obligation of every generation to bring up children who will be citizens of tomorrow in a proper way. Today's children will be leaders of tomorrow who will hold the country's banner high and maintain the prestige of the nation. If the government of India commits itself towards combating the problem of child labour, then it is sure that the children of India who at present have engaged themselves in long hours of work could be freed and enabled to breathe joy of freedom. But today, working condition of child labour is horrible. Children have to work more than 15 hours a day or till their masters are satisfied, without rest which is a complete violation of the Child Labour (P&R) Act, 1986. The child labours employed by private contractors were paid meager wages and were living like animals in overcrowded slums.

Child labour in Bihar is found to exist in different fields. It is estimated that in Bihar alone, around 6,43,233 children are working in different activities. Thousands of children are working in hotels and Restaurants, Tea-Stalls, etc.

Child labour cannot be weeded out despite several welfare legislations enacted by the Government from time to time. It needs a change in our social attitude. Social awareness is also needed to discourage the practice of child labour. Besides this, the tightening of laws and activating enforcement machinery is needed badly to weed out the child labour in its true perspective. Long-term and short-term measures are required to check this menace. This problem cannot be seen in isolation of other social changes also. Besides, the Government and NGOs will have to play very effective role in implementing the Government Schemes for children's welfare. After all, children are the blooming flowers of the garden of our society. Therefore, it is every one's responsibility to protect these flowers from the damaging effects of excessive exposure to heat, cold and rains. They should be put on the right track always, as they are the seeds of future national growth.

So, we can conclude that child labour is a significant problem in India. The prevalence of it is shown by the child work participation rates which are higher in India than in other developing countries.

The major determinant of child labour is poverty. Even though children are paid less than adults, whatever income they earn is of benefit to poor families. In addition to poverty, the lack of adequate and accessible sources of credit forces poor parents to engage their children in the has form of child labour, bonded child labour. Some parents also feel that a formal education is not beneficial, and that children learn work skills through labour at a young age. These views are narrow and do not take the long term developmental benefits of education into account. Another determinant is access to education. In some areas, I found that education is not affordable, or is found to be inadequate. With no other alternatives, children spend their time in working.

Child labour cannot be eliminated by focusing on one determinant, for example education or by brute enforcement of child labour laws. The government of India must ensure that the needs, of the poor are filled before attacking child labour. If poverty is addressed, the need for child labour will automatically diminish. Not matter how hard India tries, child labour always will exist until its need is removed. The development of India as a nation is being hampered by child labour. Children are growing up illiterate because they have been working and not attending school. A cycle of poverty is formed and the need for child labour is reborn after every generation. India needs to address the situation by tackling the underlying causes of child labour through governmental policies and the enforcement of these policies. Only then will India succeed in the fight against child labour affecting health, education, growth and personality development of the child.

References

Devi, R. (1985), Prevalence of Child Labour in India, A Secondary Data Analysis.

Human Rights Watch (1996), The Small Hands of Slavery Bonded Child Labour in India. New York: Human Rights Watch.

International Labour Organization (1992), World Labour Report Geneva.

International Labour Organization (1993), World Labour Report. Geneva.

International Labour Organization (1995), World Labour Report. Geneva.

Mehra-Kerpelman, K. (1996), Children at Work: How Many and Where? World of Work 15:8-9.

Nangia, P. (1987), Child Labour: Cause, Effect Syndrome, Janak Publishers, New Delhi: Subhrahmanya, R.K.A. (1987), Can the Child Labour Act of 1986 Effectively Control Child Labour? In

Young Hands at Work-Child Labour in India, edited by M.Gupta & K. Voll., Atma Ram & Sons, Delhi

Shandilya, T.K., Kumar Navin and Kumar Nayan (2006), Child Labour Eradication, Deep & Deep Publications, New Delhi.

Mishra Lakshmidhar – Child Labour in India.

Sen R.K. Dasgupta, A – Problems of Child Labour in India.

11

Child Labour—A Moral Conundrum

Mahesh Chandra Prasad

Introduction

The problem of child labour is a gigantic, complex and delicate one. This harsh reality is fostered by socio-economic factors such as grinding poverty, population growth and illiteracy. Redress of these factors is the only prerequisite for the elimination of child servitude from our society. Working children opt to work, aim to survive, improve their own life and that of their families. But their aims are not exactly achieved due to wage discrimination and other types of basic rights deprivations. These factors sometimes lead to conditions of absolute slavery.

The number of working children is increasing from year to year. Some reasons are economic situation of their family, lack of employment opportunities for the adult members and the preference of the employers to hire children to save on production costs. The child loses all the pleasures of life and potentials of growth and development.

There is worldwide awareness and laws have been enacted to prohibit children from being employed. Illegal recruitment of children still continues. There is also a great scope for exploitation and abuse of child. The social workers and activists from the trade unions are finding it difficult to help the child because of the existing legislations and other social factors. Such workers do not get proper empirically verified research data on the nature, causes and conditions of child labour on one side and feelings and aspirations of the children on the other.

It is recognized that the exploitation of child labour is a form of sale of children. Generally, when one considers the notion "child labour" per se, it is not necessarily detrimental to children. However, when it gives rise to exploitation, usually by another party who has power over the child, it may result in negative consequences for children, both with regard to their rights and their development. It also constitutes sale because the child becomes the object of a transaction in cash or in kind. It appears that in many parts of the world, children are sold into several types of employment, either by their parents, guardians or other intermediaries.

The International Labour Organisation (ILO) estimated that there were about 88 million working children between 10 and 14 years of age. Instances of exploitation are to be found in all regions of the world but Asia and South America figure high in the number of children in difficult circumstances. The worst forms of child labour exploitation often take place in the informal sector and small-scale industries.

Generally, the exploitation of child labour may arise from a variety of root causes including poverty, migration, gender discrimination and criminality. Much of the exploitation appears to be a consequence of the pervasive poverty in developing countries. Likewise, economic needs push children to undertake exploitative work in developed countries. As children are cheaper and easier to employ, adults are kept out of the labour market. According to the notion of "globalization", it appears that people have become more mobile, traveling easily to other countries. This mobility is also reflected in their search for jobs. As a result, it leads to the emergence of migrant labourers and immigrants, shedding new light on the old problem of child labour.

The Union Government banned in 2006 the employment of children below 14 years in restaurant, hotels, tea-stalls, eateries and in domestic help. According to child rights activists, there has been little improvement in the situation. Child labour is still rampant across the country. According to the 2001 census, there are over 61,000 children working in hotels, restaurants, tea-stalls and road side eateries. This figure is just a small fraction of over 12.6 million child labourers in India, the highest in the world.

Though law is a necessary step, it does not solve the problem. The ban does not work. Is it realistic? Will it be successful? Will the parents cooperate? Will the children give up their jobs so easily if they are earning some livelihood? When the US banned carpet exports in 1990s, Nepalese children turned to prostitution. When Bangladeshi garment industry suffered, children turned to stone crushing and similar hazardous work. In almost every case, children are forced into labour either by economic or social compulsions or due to absence of choices and opportunities. The parents of working children are either unemployed or do not get work for even 50-60 days in a year.

The policy makers must be aware of the harsh realities of society. If children are completely deprived of their employment and made to study in a school, they might have studied upto matriculation. But what is thereafter? Will they be assured of any job? In our country, it is not easy to get a job. Instead, if children are learning a craft, they should be encouraged. At the same time, appropriate provision must be made for their education. They can be made to learn while they earn. They must be given enough time to play. It is society's responsibility to provide all facilities to our children for their moral, emotional and physical development. Therefore, we have to look at it from a holistic angle.

Causes of Child Labour in India

The magnitude of child labour employment differs from region tc region and even in the same region, intensity of sex-wise distribution of child labour also differs.

A large number of studies had been undertaken in different parts of India on the problem of child labour. Most of them have paid enough attention to find out how many children are working and what proportion of total workers are represented by children. Few of the studies have been devoted to explore why in a country like India, where a large section of the adult population is unemployed or underemployed, a child has to work and earn. There are several causes for continuation of child labour in India. But main causes are poor economic condition, traditional authority of father, high fertility rate, lack of status of the child in the society, low level of adult and child literacy, lack of social security and cheap of human labour.

Poverty

It is a generally acceptable proposition that poverty is the main reason for which the children are forced to work. Chronic poverty is the largest factor responsible for the prevalence and perpetuation of child labour. Poverty forces parents to send their children to seek employment. Diseases and other contingencies may need extra-money and the employment of children is resorted to as an easily accessible method to bring in that money.

Thus, as long as the wages earned by the parents are below the poverty line, any talk of abolition of child labour is bound to remain on paper. Whenever a family is faced with the irreconcilable problem of ever increasing demand of the basic needs, such as, food, shelter, clothes, etc. one householder is compelled to augment the family income by pressing the children to work and earn wages.

Poverty of the households may be due to several factors: inadequate income of the family, due to unemployed adults, absence of schemes for family allowance, large family, etc. It has been found in some studies that parents force their children to take up employment because of their own earnings being very low. Further, in India, there is no provision for the poor families so that they are forced to send their children to the labour market.

Child labour actually creates and perpetuates poverty. It not only displaces adults from their jobs but also condemns the child to a life of unskilled, badly paid work. Ultimately this leads to the same impoverished, unemployed fate as their parents, with each generation of cheaper children undercutting wages. Children become part of the vicious circle of poverty from generation to generation. Migration is another cause of child labour.

Further, a large percentage of children start working because of being orphaned, dejected by parents or because of broken families and other domestic problems. Some experts are of the view that if children were eliminated from the labour market in India, employment opportunities for at least 20 million adult unemployed workers would be increased.

Low Educational Attainment

Education always plays a vital role in the socio-economic and cultural development of any society. Hence, there exists a high positive correlation between the level of educational attainment and the socio-economic standards of community life. Our education system perpetuates the domination of the privileged few over the entire society while the children of poor people continue to remain uneducated. It is commonly found that the level of the parents' education and aspiration are closely associated with child labour. Class membership which can be considered as proxy for the socio-economic status shows an important bearing on the work and schooling of children. Children from the higher class representing higher economic status, usually have a higher school attendance while those from the lower economic strata, have lowest schooling.

Due to illiteracy of the parents/guardians, the importance of education has not yet been realized and appreciated by them. The findings of several research studies that education plays significant role in the solution of child labour problems but our society lacks proper and adequate educational facilities, schools and well qualified teachers.

This low level of the ratio of children attending schools in the primary school going age group speaks loudly that if the children will not attend school where will they go? There can be basically three reasons behind their not going to school. Firstly, they do not have adequate number of teaching schools with adequate teaching infrastructure. Secondly, schools fail to attract the children of society and lastly, parents of the children do not let them to go to schools because of economic considerations. First two reasons are from the management, government side and only they can provide adequate teaching infrastructure in a welfare state of ours.

Defective Developmental Plans and Programmes

Due to defective and unsuitable plans and programmes of development particularly on educational policies, we find that the objectives are not met successfully. Most of the schemes, whether poverty elimination or literacy campaign do not fulfil the local needs of the people and the schemes meant for them being not fit for their socio-economic and cultural environment are not fruit bearing. Experiences show that a very negligible percentage of children (particularly tribal children) get admitted into primary schools and majority of them drop-out after continuing there for a year or two. During the seasons of agricultural operations, most of them remain absent.

At the international level also, we find that the pool of poor children that can be exploited in this way has increased because of international economic developments over the last decade and a half. Structural adjustment programmes imposed on the economies of developing countries by the World Bank and the International Monetary Fund (IMF) have meant cuts in social spending that have hit the poor disproportionately. In the countries experiencing economic hardship in the last decade, per capita spending on education has declined significantly. In all regions, spending per student for higher education fell during the 1980s and in Africa and Latin America, spending per pupil also fell for primary education.

Education is under funded and in decline. But the school system in most developing countries is blighted by more than just a lack of resources. Thus education has become part of the problem. It has to be reborn as part of the solution.

The Attitude of the Government and Employer

Though the Government is undertaking legislative measures to protest child labour in India, these are not effectively implemented. Moreover, there is need for strengthening the existing legislations aimed at protecting child labour to make it completely free from loop-holes.

The employers are also responsible for intensifying the problem of child labour in India. Though the employers' community prides itself in providing law bound welfare measures, this section is not whole-heartedly interested in implementing the spirit behind the legislative measures. The employer always wants to cash in on the loop-holes prevalent in the legislation. Hence, there is need for change in the attitude of the employers towards the upliftment of child labour. But, this humanism is mostly lacking in most of the employers.

Low Aspiration Level

Generally a man adopts suitable means in order to attain his goal in life. This is the philosophy of life in the case of every individual, may he be a tribal or a ruralist or a city-dweller. When the educational level is very low, economic conditions are adverse and exposure to modern materialistic civilization is almost negligible, it is but natural that socially backward people cannot aspire to a better standard of living. Moreover, the man who is confronted with the problem of starvation can never dream of a better future. For him the problem that needs immediate attention is the question of survival. Therefore, the immediate solution which offers itself to him is to get some work and earn for livelihood.

Perception about the Child

In our country, a child is brought to the world with the expectation that when the parents become old, the son or daughter will look after them in the old age. A child is taken as an insurance policy for them against any eventuality. In general, it is expected that a son will definitely look after the parents. The child is supposed to have a moral obligation to provide for the parents in their old age. But the parents, who are responsible for bringing a child to the world also have some sort of moral obligations to the child. The socio-economic compulsions of the parent/guardian are also responsible for making the institution of child labour survivable. Though an unmistakable under current of anxiety for the future of their children is seen in some of the parents/ guardians, this attitude hardly helps them to help their children in view of their poverty stricken lives.

Another direct cause of child employment is the situation at home. There may be tension and uncertainty, provoked or increased by poverty, the father may have left home, the father or the mother or both may fall ill or die. However, the argument that the children are obliged to work because of the disappearance of the bread-winner is often fallacious, because it is generally the head of the family himself who sees to it that his children go out to work.

Although child labour exists all over the world, it is more pronounced in the poor developing countries and less pronounced in rich developed countries. Further, both among the developed and developing countries, it is less prevalent among those countries which are more welfare-oriented. The pertinent case of point is that of the U.S.A. in relation to Sweden. Though U.S.A. has a higher per capita income than Sweden, it has a much higher incidence of child labour. Similarly, among the developing countries, though Brazil has six times higher per capita income than China, it has an equally higher incidence of child labour and so is the case with Thailand and India. The former has both higher income as well as incidence of child labour than the latter. Hence, child labour appears to be a case of underdevelopment

In every village, there are a number of poor parents sending their children to school while their better off counterparts are sending them to work. How does one explain that? Actually there is no 'poverty line' below which all parents are compelled to send their children to school. This is a pure myth. Parents' basic desire to ensure a better future for their children reduces the poverty threshold at which they must send their children to work to much lower levels than we imagine. It is only this that explains why many poor parents (though not as many as we would want) actually send children to school today. To understand the problem of child labour and education therefore, we must actually understand why children are in schools instead of why they are not.

Unfortunately because we believe in the Poverty Argument we also think every child who is working is doing so because of poverty. Actually there is very little correlation between the two and although there are plenty of examples to show, no one wants to accept it.

Then why are so many children out of school and working? We just have not tried to understand the basic causes.

- No one has bothered to tell the poor parents that the schools are for them and that the entire government machinery will support them in their endeavour to send their child to schools as if they mean it. No one has even told them that it is right for them to think it is wrong to send their child to work.
- A child comes to school for the first time. He is the first person in his family ever to attempt this. Are the teachers sensitive to this? Is the system sensitive to this?
- Worse still, a child is 10 years old. He has never been to school. He now wants to. Does the system have any solution than putting him along with the five year olds in class 1?

The fact is that we have never tried to make it easy for the parents to send their children to school. We simply decided (quite conveniently) that they do not want to.

The conscience of the upper and middle classes is not shaken whey they see children of 5 to 14 years of tender age working day and night in different activities ranging from agriculture to manufacturing and service sectors, losing out on their childhood. At first they do not even consider children working in agriculture as a form of child labour because in their views, agriculture is the 'given' or 'natural' culture and accustomed with their lives or because it is not considered hazardous to them. Similarly, they consider domestic child labour as non-hazardous and hence, it is to be continued. Further, they perceive that girls are meant for doing domestic chores and taking care of their siblings. But these are myths that need to be demystified and disorgonised.

Social and Intellectual Myths

- Childhood is part and parcel of every individual's personality and it is not separable from adulthood. This however, is an incorrect premise because childhood is not only a separate category but also the golden period for formation of personality and children are the future citizens of every society and is 'the father of the man'.
- Child labour is necessary for the socialization of children-learning the ins and outs of new expected roles and functions with positive effect. This too, is not wholly true because there is a distinction between socialization and exploitation and child labour is associated with the latter. Further, it deprives children of education and restricts them to the traditional and hereditary tasks only.
- Child labour is inevitable and irreplaceable. Such notion is blemished because many developed countries of Europe have eliminated child labour and even in Kerala (South India) the magnitude of child labour is extremely low.
- Child labour is essentially for learning new skills and techniques and childhood the appropriate age for learning. But actually there is no fixed age for learning; rather it is a life-long process. Learning skill as a child labour at a tender age results into educational deprivation and perpetuation of low-income job forever.
- Child labour cannot be eliminated till the income-poverty gap is totally eliminated. But this at the best, is a half-truth. For elimination of child labour, distribution and proper management of fund as well as good governance is more important than the total eradication of poverty in one go. Kerala is a suitable example in this regard.

- That inequality is given and inevitable and hence, child labour is essential for social cohesion, harmony and equilibrium. This is not true because inequality is more of a socio-economic and political creation that a natural one. Inequality actually leads to social tension and disharmony and child labour reflects such an inequality.

Hence, we tend to agree with a broad definition of child labour to include: "Children prematurely leading adult lives, working with or without wages, under conditions damaging their physical, social, emotional and spiritual development, denying them their basic rights to education, health and development. This includes children working in any sector, occupation or process, including the formal and non-formal, organized and unorganized, within or outside the family." Thus we believe that any child who is deprived of school education is an example of child labour even if he/she is not working outside the family.

While poverty may be the background within which children work, it can no longer be a justification for child labour in a country with 9% growth rates. Most children who work, come from the poorest areas of India such as UP, West Bengal and Bihar and from the poorest and most discriminated sections, such as lower castes and tribal areas. We also know that in the aftermath of natural disasters, such as floods or droughts many children are forced into work as their families lose everything-their homes, assets and livelihoods. Often children are taken by uncles or middlemen into cities for work, bonded for years.

Poor parents are ignorant of the law and often seduced by the promises that they are doing good for their child, that he/she will learn a trade and send home ever-higher pay cheques. They are also unaware of the various government poverty alleviation schemes (28 at last count) available to them.

Since the launch of the Sarva Shiksha Abhiyaan, the government has promised a school within a 1km radius and education for children between 6 to 14 years has been declared free and compulsory.

Employing Children

We also know that children are paid half what adults earn at best and in many cases, nothing at all. They are compelled to work long hours-sometimes 12-15 hours a day in unhealthy and unsafe conditions, subject to physical sexual abuse and being more vulnerable and powerless are exploited the full. Make no mistake, child labour is the cheapest and most exploitative labour. And these children and their families can be exploited in this way because of their own poverty and powerlessness. Increasing urbanisation and the demand for cheap labour has further pushed children into work.

Childhood Stolen

Research shows what is needed is a collective commitment to restoring children their right to childhood. Childhood should be a time for education, leisure and protection from harm, protection that we as adults have a responsibility to provide for children, rather than exploiting them. Political will and political commitment, backed by funding and a complete cultural un-acceptance of child labour is necessary.

Conclusion

As child labour is a complex problem occurring for a myriad of reasons, it will thus require a consistent, long-term effort with broad based strategies that ensure the long-term goal of eradication of child labour. Critically, eradicating child labour needs to be seen alongside the commitment to universalisation of education, so critical for the countries economic and social development.

The problem of child labour is a global phenomenon. Even today, it is not confined to the Third World Countries. It is more or less prevalent every where in the world, the difference if any, is only of degree or kind. It is saddening to note that India is the largest employer of child labour in the world and has earned a dubious distinction of exploiting this human resource. We have not yet been able to grapple with this shameful menace. Child labour is mostly in unorganised sector in multifarious occupations. A sizeable population of working children is engaged in health hazardous activities. Incidence of the child labour is higher in rural areas than the urban due to cheap labour supply. Magnitude of child labour varies from state to state due to variation in the levels of poverty, literacy and other such factors. It is the highest in Andhra Pradesh and the lowest in Kerala. Female child labour mostly found in unorganised sector is both male and female child labour belong to SC, ST and backward castes in 95 per cent of cases.

Child labour is the cause and consequence of exploitative system prevailing not only at the national level but also at the international level. Child labour practice causes unemployment for adult persons also. Insufficient utilisation of labour power at the lowest productivity level which precludes full development of children's potentialities and ultimately harm economic development of a nation. Since children are the future hope of society, they are destined to play important roles in shaping the destiny of the nation.

On the basis of the study, the following suggestions are placed for consideration by the Government, the economic planners and the administration:

- The problem of child labour is directly connected with the poverty and illiteracy of Indian mass. There should be every possible effort on the part of Government and NGO's.
- Poverty elimination programmes such as NREP, IRDP, DPAP, RLGEP, TRYSEM, EAS, JRY, etc. should be effectively worked out in rural areas.
- Unemployment allowance, old age pension and red-card scheme for supplying the grains at half price among the poor should be properly and fairly implemented. Benefit should reach genuine and needy people.
- Poverty alleviation programmes would be formulated and implemented in a decentralised manner with the participation of people at the grass-root level through village panchayats, panchayat samities, zilla parishads, etc.

- Ongoing schemes such as Special Rice Programme, Operation Flood II, Programmes for Handlooms and Agriculture, etc. should be given a specific direction towards the target group of the IRDP.
- Productivity may be augmented through land-based activities like minor-irrigation, dry farming, horticulture and even farm forestry
- What the poor need is a stake in the land they till; fair wages for their work, education, training and upgradation of skills; credit and infrastructural support for self-employment in primary, secondary and tertiary sectors. Above all, they need self-confidence and social recognition to come out of the poverty trap.
- The state has to recognise the problem of child labour with full responsibility and give the insurance of basic needs of the both to the parents and children.
- Laws on child labour and education should be consistent in purpose and implemented in a mutually supportive way.
- Top priority should be given to universalisation and elementary education for children between 6 to 14 years within a time frame not exceeding more than 5 years. The other important programme would be non-formal education to help children who are unable or unwilling to attend full time school. These facilities should be provided by NGO's.
- Adequate medical and recreation facilities should be provided to the deprived children for their emotional and psychological developments.
- The parameters of human development achievement in Kerala are at par with developed countries. Kerala Human Development is an outstanding testimony to the crucial role of female literacy in India; other states should also follow it.

Therefore, there is an urgent need for attitudinal change, social awareness and aggressive campaign against the source of child labour. It becomes our national obligation to ensure physical and mental development of these young ones. With measures for regulating and humanising child labour along with attack on poverty, we hope there would be gradual elimination of this problem. The eradication of the problem is a long process which requires intensive efforts on many fronts and also the creation of general social awareness and needs for co-operation from different sections of our society.

References

Census of India (2001), Office of the Registrar General and Census Commissioner, India, New Delhi

UNICEF–Patna (1997), Child Labour in India.

Gangrade and Gathia (1983), Women and Child Labour in India, Concept Publishing House, Delhi.

Gomango, S.P. (2001), Child Labour–A Precarious Future, Authors Press, New Delhi.

Jain, S.N. (1979), Law and Child in India, Indian Journal of Public Administration, New Delhi, Vol. XXV, No.3.

Kulshrestha, J.C. (1978), Child Labour in India, Ashish Publishing House, New Delhi.

Mehta, P.L. and Jaswal S.S. (1996), Child Labour and the Law, Deep & Deep Publications, New Delhi.

Miller, S. (2008), Child Labour–A Moral Conundrum, Yojna, May.

Pati, R.N. (1991), "Rehabilitation of Child Labour in India," Ashish Publishing House, New Delhi.

Shandilya, T.K. & Khan, S.A. (2003), Child Labour–A Global Challenge, Deep & Deep Publications (P) Ltd, New Delhi.

Sharma, S. (1995), Child Labour in India, Parkashan Sansthan, Delhi.

Sharma, S. and Mishra, D. (2008), Child Labour–Myth and Reality, Yojna, May.

Siddiqui, M.I. (2005), Child Labour, Anamika Publishers, New Delhi.

White, B. (ed.) (1982), Child Workers, Development and Change (Special Issue), New Delhi.

12

Child Labour in India: Causes, Magnitude and Policies

Anjali Prasad

The existence of child labour is a slur on a modern welfare state which seeks to promote the all round development of its citizens. Children are the future hope of the society. They are like buds, which need to be properly nursed and well, taken care of so that they bloom fully, grow into able human beings, and contribute their worth to the future development of the society. On the contrary, instead of being sent to schools and properly educated, they are made to word; it amounts to squeezing the bud before it blooms. In not only thwarts the development of children but of the society as well, since only able citizens make an efficient society. Hence child labour has been regarded as a evil in India since time immemorial. In ancient India, it was the duty of the king of educate very boy and girl and parents could be punished for not sending their children to schools, called Ashrams, which were really residential schools under a Guru (a learned sage). Child labour existed only in the form of child slaves who were purchased to do some low and dishonorable' work. Kautilya (4th Century B.C.) considered it degrading to make children work on such jobs and hence prohibited the purchase and sale of children below 8 years (Kautilya's Arthasastra). A number of legislative measures have been taken in independent India to control the evils of child labour. Article 24 of the Indian Constitution clearly states that "no child below the age of 14 years shall be employed to work in any factory or mine or engaged in other hazardous employment". Article 39 (e) states that the tender age of children should not be abused and citizens should be not be forced by economic necessity to enter avocations unsuited to their age or strength. Article 39 (f) states that children should be given opportunities and facilities to develop in a healthy manner and in conditions of freedom and dignity. Article 45 states that the state shall endeavour to provide within a period of ten years from the commencement of the constitution free and compulsory education for all children until they complete the age of fourteen years (the Constitution of India, p.26). Despite these, however, India is presently having the highest number of child labour in the world. And, the evil appears to be rising, in stead of declining, over time.

Child labour is a multi-dimensional problem. Poverty, caste, tradition, size of the family, labour scarcity, wage rates, illiteracy, ignorance, schooling facilities, etc., are the major factors for the occurrence of child labour. Parents are of opinion that more children mean more earnings and hence, they force their children to work. Poverty and child labour go together and tend to reinforce each other in poor families. Some studies show that in poor families children release women from household work to work outside home for wage. This results in higher Child Work Participation (CWP) in household work. Traditionally, children of the upper caste families begin their lives in schools according to their own culture whereas children of the lower caste start their lives in work according to their family culture. In rural areas young boys assist their parents in agricultural as well as non-agricultural activities. The girl children have to provide help to their mothers, along with agricultural activities, in looking after young siblings, sweeping house and cooking food, etc. in order to release their mothers for work. The girl child worker faces a lot of troubles compared to male child. Non-availability of school facility in village and unwillingness of the parents to send their children to neighboring villages to attend schools increase the number of child labour. Employees view the employment of children as advantageous on the ground of availability of cheap labour force. Moreover, they prefer child labour, as they do not form unions.

The magnitude of child labour is alarming. The developed countries which boast of the absence of the problem of child labour and advise the developing countries to take steps to solve the problem of child labour are not free from this problem according to the studies of UNICEF and the ILO.

It is not possible to have an exact estimate of child labour in India due to the informal and unorganized nature of the labour market. However, various agencies have given estimates of child labour in India, which vary from source to source.

Twenty-five million children in India are estimated to be outside the schools and engaged as labourers, including those children engaged in hazardous areas of work. This comes to about 4.80% of the total. child population and about 5% of the total labour population. Children working in agriculture and allied activities account for about 85% of the total child labour force. Child labour in hazardous occupations is estimated to be two million. On the basis of 1981 and 1991 Census data, it can be presumed that 14,217,588 children are employed on a full time basis. However, it is argued that this figure may not represent the true picture. The Operation Research Group (ORG) estimate it to be 4.40 crore. NGOs, however, put it at over six crore. If all the children who do not go to school are included the figure may be somewhere near eight crore. This wide variation in figures is primarily because child labourers work predominantly in unorganized sectors.

Apart from the above statistics, World Development Report published in the first week of January, 2000, states that globally 6 crore children were working children of which 1.15 crore were bonded labour. Presently, child labour in India is mostly concentrated in such industries as matches, glass, pottery, carpet, brassware, lock-making, gems and jewellery, beedies, slate, etc. This report also reveals that children in India are also forced to prostitute themselves or else join hazardous occupations. Child smuggling is flourishing in Bengal. This report emphasizes that lakhs of child labourers become permanently sick due to working conditions.

Most child labourers are employed in unskilled jobs. They are usually children from Scheduled Castes and Tribes, religious minorities, urban poor, victims of riots or natural disasters, and many of them are girls. Exploitation in various forms suffered by child labourers is a universal phenomenon. A UNICEF Report on the State of the World's Children, 1977 says that child labour in. hazardous occupation is a betrayal of every child's rights as a human being and is an offence against civilization.

Child labour has become a topic of hot discussion in India and abroad. Various organizations have joined the campaign to stop the exploitation of child workers and protect the rights of children. Attempts to eradicate child labour at the international level have also been made. Some European countries have banned the imports of goods in preparation of which child labour is being used. It is obvious that along with the legislations, effective administrative machinery is also needed to implement the Acts in the correct spirit. The Government should provide more funds for education. School facilities should be created in every village and the parents should be motivated to send their children to schools. Last but not the least, efforts for the eradication of poverty is to be vigorously implemented.

Across the globe, to a lesser or greater degree, visible or invisible, whether admitted or not, child labour exists. The future of a society of a nation or the world as such depends upon the sound growth of children. The forces and circumstances, which compel the child to work in its early stage of childhood, do more harm than good. Child labour is both an economic and social problem. It is a social evil resulting in moral degradation of the bulk of children. Child labour deprives him of education, training and skill, which are the requisites for earning power and economic development.

Child labour harms not only the present generation but the posterity of the nation as well. If one thinks of child labour, it brings before the eyes, the picture of exploitation of little, physically tender, illiterate and under-nourished children working in hazardous occupations and unhealthy conditions. Since the root of the problem of child labour is abject poverty and social backwardness, it cannot be simply legislated against for a quick solution. The use of child labour is, in fact regarded as social evil because of the abuse of child labour on a large scale.

Children are an asset for a nation and it is the nation's responsibility to nurture them through various stages of their development to enable them to realize their full human potential. However, the existence of millions of working children in India today is one of the tragic realities. It is also a grim reminder of the fact that a tremendous effort has to be made in order to overcome the pernicious practice of employment of child labour.

The 43rd Round of the National Sample Survey (1987-88) estimated about 17 million working children in India with

Table 1
Percentage of Child Labour to Total Population

States	*1981*	*1991*
Andhra Pradesh	3.28	2.50
Assam	1.60	1.46
Bihar	1.28	1.09
Gujarat	1.36	1.27
Haryana	1.10	0.67
Himachal Pradesh	1.41	1.08
Karnataka	2.60	2.17
Kerala	0.27	0.12
Madhya Pradesh	0.63	2.04
Maharashtra	2.01	1.35
Orissa	1.95	1.43
Punjab	1.07	0.70
Rajasthan	1.72	1.76
Tamil Nadu	1.80	1.04
Uttar Pradesh	1.14	1.01
West Bengal	0.96	1.04

Source: Census of India, 1981, Series –1, Part-III-A

projected 20 million working children by the year 2000. The Operations Research Group (ORG), Baroda, a research institute commissioned by the Ministry of Labour in 1980-81, put the figure of working children (5-14 years) at 44 million. The 1990-91 census put child labour population at 11.28 million. Different definitions of 'working child' and 'work' explain the wide variations in the number, since official figures, generally, omit children engaged in on-wage domestic work.

Causes of Child Labour

It is difficult to cite a current figure for the number of children engaged in child labour. This difficulty is attributed to the fact that the Indian Government has been negligent in its refusal to collect and analyze current and relevant data regarding the incidence of child labor. As of 1996, official figures continue to be based on 1981 census figures (Human Rights Watch 1996, 122). The 1981 Indian census reports that there were 13.6 million child labourers in India (Census of India 1981 cited in Weiner 1991, 20). Indian government extrapolations of this 1981 data place the current number of child labourers at between seventeen and twenty million (Human Rights Watch 1996, 122). This extrapolation seems highly unlikely as "The Official National Sample Survey of 1983 [of India] reports 17.4 million child labourers, while a study sponsored by the Labour Ministry, concluded that the child-labour force was 44 million" (Weiner 1991, 20-21). UNICEF "cites figures ranging from seventy-five to ninety million child laborers under the age of fourteen" (Human Rights Watch 1996, 122)

Child labour is a source of income for poor families. A study conducted by the ILO Bureau of Statistics found that "Children's work was considered essential to maintaining the economic level of households, either in the form of work for wages, or help in household enterprises or of household chores in order to free adult household members for economic activity elsewhere" (Mehra-Kerpelman 1996, 8). In some cases, the study found that a child's income accounted for between 34 and 37 percent of the total household income. This study concludes that a child labourer's income is important to the livelihood of a poor family. There is a questionable aspect of this study. It was conducted in the form of a survey, and the responses were given by the parents of the child labourers. Parents would be biased into being compelled to support their decision to send their children to work by saying that it is essential. They are probably right: for most poor families in India, alternative sources of income are close to non-existent.

The percentage of the population of India living in poverty is high. In 1990, 37% of the urban population and 39% of the rural population was living in poverty (International Labour Organization 1995, 107). Poverty has an obvious relationship with child labour, and studies have "revealed a positive correlation - in some instances a strong one - between child labour and such factors as poverty" (Mehra-Kerpelman 1996, 8). Families need money to survive and children are a source of additional income. Poverty itself has underlying determinants, one such determinant being caste. When analyzing the caste composition of child labourers Nangia (1987) observes that, "if these figures are compared with the caste structure of the country, it would be realised that a comparatively higher proportion of scheduled caste children work at a younger age for their own and their families' economic support" (p. 116). Scheduled caste (lower caste) children tend to be pushed into child labour because of their family's poverty. Nangia (1987) goes on to state that in his study 63.74% of child labourers said that poverty was the reason they worked (p. 174).

The combination of poverty and the lack of a social security network form the basis of the even harsher type of child labour—bonded child labour. For the poor, there are few sources of bank loans, governmental loans or other credit sources, and even if there are sources available, few Indians living in poverty qualify. Here enters the local moneylender; for an average of two thousand rupees, parents exchange their child's labour to local moneylenders (Human Rights Watch 1996, 17). Since the earnings of bonded child labourers are less than the interest on the loans, these bonded children are forced to work, while interest on their loans accumulates. A bonded child can only be released after his/her parent makes a lump sum payment, which is extremely difficult for the poor (Human Rights Watch 1996, 17). Even if bonded child labourers are released, "the same conditions of poverty that caused the initial debt can cause people to slip back into bondage" (International Labour Organization 1993, 12).

Even though poverty is cited as the major cause of child labour, it is not the only determinant. Inadequate schools, lack of schools, or even the expense of schooling leaves some children with little else to do but work. The attitudes of parents also contribute to child labour; some parents feel that children should work in order to develop skills useful in the job market, instead of taking advantage of a formal education.

The Magnitude of Child Labour

As per the Census of India, there were 10.75 million child workers in the age group 5 to 14 in 1971, 13.64 million in 1981 and 11.28 million in 1991. In absolute terms, there is no definite trend in the number of working children at the national level. This is only expected considering the period 1971-91 has recorded the highest decadal population growth in independent India. It is only in the 1990s that with a significant decline in the population growth rate along with improvement in over-all literacy rates, in general, and school enrolment/attendance in particular that one would expect a decline in the absolute number of child labour. This expected decline in the magnitude of child labour, narrowly defined, is already mirrored in the declining incidence of child labour.

Table 2 summarizes the incidence for Census years 1981 and 1991. In estimating the incidence of child labour from the Census data, a correction has been made by excluding the child population in the age group 0-4, for the year 1981, as it is obvious that there can be hardly any working children in that age group. Thus, the absolute number of working children is taken as a ratio of the child population in the age group 5 to 14. The incidence of child labour, accordingly estimated and on a comparable basis for the census years 1981 and 1991 has been presented in Table 2.

The picture on the incidence of child labour changes dramatically as one moves from the narrow definition of child labour to the more 'inclusive' broader definition for which a case has been made earlier in the paper. At the aggregate national level, the incidence of child labour increases from 7.6 percent to 60.5 percent in the year 1981, when the NWC are also included in the category of child labour. The corresponding figures for 1991 are 5.4 percent and 50.6 percent. What comes out clearly and on expected lines is that the composition of child labour in the two sets of estimates is different. In case of child labour narrowly defined the incidence of child labour for boys is higher than that for girls both in urban and rural areas, both in 1981 as well as in 1991. However, in case of child labour broadly defined the incidence of girl child labour (Le. Including NWC) is considerably higher than that of boys.

Table 2
Incidence of Child Labour in India

(Figures in Percent)

Child Labour	*1981*	*1991*
Rural Children	8.9	6.4
Boys	10.0	6.6
Girls	7.8	6.3
Urban Children	2.7	2.0
Boys	3.7	2.8
Girls	1.6	1.2
Combined Children	7.6	5.4
Boys	8.6	5.7
Girls	6.4	5.1

An analysis of the State-wise data indicates labour, both in larger states, Andhra Pradesh had the highest incidence of child labour, both in 1981 and 1991: the estimate being 13.8 percent and 10 percent respectively. The incidence of child labour was also high, in excess of 10 percent, in States like Jammu & Kashmir, Karnataka and Madhya Pradesh and above 8 percent in case of Orissa, Tamil Nadu, Rajasthan and Himachal Pradesh. In 1991, the States with proportion of child labour in excess of 8 percent were Madhya Pradesh and Karnataka. The incidence of child labour in the states of Orissa, Maharashtra, Assam and Gujarat was in excess of or close to the national average. The incidence of child labour was higher for boys in comparison to that of girls, and the difference being much larger in 1981 than in 1991. Himachal Pradesh, Maharashtra and some other small states were an exception to this trend in 1981. However, in 1991 the incidence of child labour among girls was higher than that of boys in Andhra Pradesh, Gujarat, Madhya Pradesh, Rajasthan and Tamil Nadu, apart from Himachal Pradesh, Maharashtra and some other smaller states.

Table 3
Incidence of Child Labour (including NWC) in India

(Figures in Percent)

Child Labour	*1981*	*1991*
Rural Children	65.0	55.7
Boys	58.0	48.8
Girls	72.8	63.4
Urban Children	44.0	34.2
Boys	40.8	31.8
Girls	47.4	36.9
Combined Children	60.5	50.6
Boys	54.2	44.7
Girls	67.2	57.1

Source: Tables 2 and 3 estimated from Census data for 1981-91

It is, perhaps, worthwhile to note that much higher proportion of children in the rural areas (8.9 percent in 1981 and 6.4 percent in 1991) was working in comparison to those in urban areas (2.7 percent in 1981 and 2.0 percent in 1991). Moreover, the gender differences in the incidence of child labour were proportionately lower in the rural than in the urban areas. At state level, the worker participation ratio among the children in rural areas was higher in the States of Andhra Pradesh, Gujarat, Karnataka, Madhya Pradesh, Maharashtra, Orissa and Rajasthan in 1991. For the urban areas, it was higher in Andhra Pradesh, Karnataka, Tamil Nadu and Uttar Pradesh.

Let us now consider the incidence of child labour broadly defined, i.e. children in the age group 5 to 14 who are participating in the labour market as also those who are neither enrolled/attending school nor are categorized as working. The proportion of such children declined from 60.4 percent (65.1 percent for rural areas and 44 percent for urban areas) in 1981 to 50.6 per cent (55.8 percent in rural areas and 34.3 per cent for the urban areas). The proportion of such girls was 67.2 percent (being 72.7 percent in rural areas and 47.4 percent in the urban areas) in 1981 and this declined to 57 percent in 1991 (being 63.4 percent in the rural areas and 37 percent in the urban areas). Though, the proportion of working girls is lower than that. of boys, the proportion of girls who are neither working nor going to schools is higher than that for the boys. This is, perhaps, because the girls are expected to perform more household chores and provide seasonal labour on the farms as well. The gender gap though has declined between 1981 and 1991; it has declined very slowly and only in the urban areas and not in the rural areas.

An analysis of the state-wise information reveals that working children as well as those who were neither going to school nor were working, accounted for nearly two-thirds of the total children (being over 75 percent for girls) in the age group 5 to 14 in the states of Bihar, Madhya Pradesh, Rajasthan and Uttar Pradesh. This proportion was over 70 percent in these states in the rural areas (being over 85 percent for girls). The percentage of NWC to total children in the age group 5 to 14 was in the range of 40-45 percent in the better off states like Gujarat, Maharashtra, Punjab and Tamil Nadu but just was 19.2 percent in Kerala. The situation in 1991 improved in all the states with the exception of Madhya Pradesh, where the pace of improvement was very slow. The proportion was in the range of 60-65 per cent (72-75 percent for girls) in Bihar, Rajasthan and Uttar Pradesh; it being 65-70 percent in the rural areas (being close to 80 percent for girls) in these states. Even in the urban areas, the combined proportion for these states was in the range of 40-45 percent, and between 45-55 percent for girls. This proportion was much lower than the national average in the State of Kerala, Maharashtra, Himachal Pradesh, Punjab and Tamil Nadu. The rural-urban difference of over 20 percent and gender differences of over 15 percent in the rural areas in 1991 were fairly significant.

Another way of looking at child labour can be in terms of the proportion of children in the total labour force. As per the 1991 Census, children in the age group 5-14 accounted for 3.6 percent of the total work force in the country with rural areas accounting for higher ratio (4.1 percent) than the urban areas (1.6 percent). Working boys in this age group accounted for 2.8 percent of the male workers (3.2 percent in the rural areas and 1.3 percent in the urban areas). The corresponding ratio for the girls was 5.7 percent (6 and 3.2 percent for the rural and urban females, respectively).

According to the National Sample Survey Organization (NSSO) rounds conducted in 1987-88 and 1993-94, the percentage of child labour in the total labour force declined from 4.1 to 3 percent during this period. The ratio of female child labour to total female labour force has been higher than that of males. Male children accounted for 3.4 percent of the total male labour force in 1987-88 and this declined to 2.4 percent in 1993-94. The corresponding ratios for females were 6 and 5 percent respectively. Similarly, the ratio of rural child workers to total workers has been higher than those in the urban areas. Nearly 4.5 percent of the total rural workers were children in 1987-88 as compared to 3.4 percent in 1993--94. The corresponding shares in the urban areas were 2.4 percent and 1.7 percent respectively. The estimates are summarized in the Table 4.

As per the 1991 Census, nearly 91 percent of the total child labour was in the rural areas. This can be partly explained by the fact that much lower proportion of the children in rural areas attended schools as compared to the urban children. The literacy rates in the rural areas were 36.1 and 44.7 percent in 1981 and 1991 respectively. Secondly, it is more difficult to enforce minimum age for working as well as the minimum years of schooling in rural areas. The seasonal nature and bunching of agricultural operations generates a fluctuating demand for labour that is seen to be best met by household hands, including the children. Most of the children are pushed into work because of this nature of rural economy. In addition there is always the consideration of augmenting family incomes.

Table 4
Percentage of Child Labour in Labour Force in India

Child Labour	*1987-88*	*1993-94*
Rural Children	4.5	3.4
Boys	3.8	2.7
Girls	6.2	5.3
Urban Children	2.4	1.7
Boys	1.9	1.4
Girls	4.5	3.4
Combined Children	4.1	3.0
Boys	3.4	2.4
Girls	6.0	5.0

Source: NSSO Rounds.

The 1991 Census also gives the distribution of child labour in different sectors of the economy. Accordingly, over 90 percent of the rural boys and girls were engaged in agriculture and related activities. While the boys were equally likely to work in own cultivation as agricultural workers, the proportion of girls as agricultural workers was much higher. The employment structure of the urban child workers has been quite different and more diversified. Only 20 percent of the urban boys and 30 percent of the urban girls were employed in agriculture. Around 35 percent of the urban boys and girls were engaged in household and non-household industries. Within this group, boys tended to work more in the non-household industries vis-a-vis the girls who worked mainly in the household industries. Much larger proportion of boys worked in trade and commerce than the girls. Nearly one fourth of the working girls and one-sixth of the working boys in the urban areas were engaged in services.

Child Labour: Some Policies

From the time of its independence, India has committed itself to be against child labour. Article 24 of the Indian constitution clearly states that "No child below the age of fourteen years shall be employed to work in any factory or mine or employed in any hazardous employment" (Constitution of India cited in Jain 1985, 218). Article 39 (e) directs State policy such "that the health and strength of workers. . . and the tender age of children are not abused and that citizens are not forced by economic necessity to enter avocations unsuited to their age or strength" (Constitution of India cited in Human Rights Watch 1996, 29). These two articles show that India has always had the goal of taking care of its children and ensuring the safety of workers. The Bonded Labour System Act of 1976 fulfills the Indian Constitution's directive of ending forced labour. The Act "frees all bonded laborers, cancels any outstanding debts against them, prohibits the creation of new bondage agreements, and orders the economic rehabilitation of freed bonded laborers by the state" (Human Rights Watch 1996, 30). In regard to child labour, the Indian government implemented the Child Labour Act in 1986. The purpose of this act is to "prohibit the employment of children who have not completed their 14th year in specified hazardous occupations and processes" (Narayan 1988, 146). ILO convention No. 138 suggests that the minimum age for employment should not be less than fifteen years, and thus the Child Labour Act of 1986 does not meet this target (Subrahmanya 1987, 105).

A recent advance in government policy occurred in August of 1994, when then- Prime Minister Narasimha Rao announced his proposal of an Elimination of Child Labour Programme. This program pledges to end child labour for two million children in hazardous industries as defined in the Child Labour Act of 1986, by the year 2000. The program revolves around an incentive for children to quit their work and enter non-formal schooling: a one hundred rupee payment as well as one meal a day for attending school (Human Rights Watch 1996, 119-120). Where the funds for this program will come from is unknown. The government needs eight and a half billion dollars for the program over five years, and yet "about 4 percent of the five-year estimated cost was allocated for child labour elimination programs in 1995-1996" (Human Rights Watch 1996, 120).

All of the policies that the Indian government has in place are in accordance with the Constitution of India, and all support the eradication of Child Labour. The problem of child labour still remains even though all of these policies are existent. Enforcement is the key aspect that is lacking in the government's efforts. No enforcement data for child labour laws are available: "A glaring sign of neglect of their duties by officials charged with enforcing child labor laws is the failure to collect, maintain, and disseminate accurate statistics regarding enforcement efforts" (Human Rights Watch 1996, 131). Although the lack of data does not mean enforcement is nonexistent, the number of child labourers and their work participation rates show that enforcement, if existent, is ineffective.

The concept of compulsory education, where all school aged children are required to attend school, combats the force of poverty that pulls children out of school. Policies relating to compulsory education not only force children to attend school, but also contribute appropriate funds to the primary education system, instead of higher education.

An example of a country where compulsory education has worked to reduce child labour is Sri Lanka. The Sri Lankan government decided to enforce compulsory education in the 1920's and 1930's (Weiner 1991, 173). With this compulsory education policy, school participation rates rose from 58 percent in 1946 to 74 percent in 1963 (Weiner 1991, 173). The literacy rate also increased from 58 percent in 1946 to 86 percent in 1984 (Weiner 1991, 172). The corresponding result has been that the employment rate of children in the ten to fourteen age group has shown a substantial decline from 13 percent in 1946 to 6.2 percent in 1963 (Weiner 1991, 174), and currently stands at 5.3% for males and 4.6% for females (International Labour Organization 1995, 113). These trends lead Weiner (1991) to the conclusion that "Sri Lanka has achieved a remarkably high enrollment rate, high retention rate, and a corresponding decline in child labour" (p.175).

The Indian state of Kerala distinguishes itself from the rest of India with its educational system. The government of Kerala allocates more funds to education than any other state, with a per capita expenditure of 11.5 rupees compared to the Indian average of 7.8 rupees (Weiner 1991, 175). It is not only the expenditure of more funds, but where the funds are used that makes the difference. Kerala spends more money on "mass education than colleges and universities" (Weiner 1991, 176). No correlation exists between expenditure on education and literacy when comparing different countries because some countries, such as India, spend more funds on higher education than primary education (Weiner 1991, 160). Kerala's emphasis on primary education has lead to a dropout rate of close to 0%, a literacy rate of 94% for males and 86% for females (The World Bank 1995, 113), and a low child work participation rate of 1.9% (in 1971) compared to the Indian average of 7.1% in 1971 (Weiner 1991, 175). Weiner (1991) points out that "The Kerala Government has made no special effort to end child labor. It is the expansion of the school system rather than the enforcement of labour legislation that has reduced the amount of child labour" (p. 177).

Article 45 of the Constitution of India states that "The State shall endeavour to provide within a period of ten years from the commencement of this Constitution for free and compulsory education for all children until they complete the age of fourteen years" (Jain 1985, 219). It is obvious that "the State" has not achieved this goal, shown by the literacy, dropout, and child work participation rates discussed previously. A National Policy on Education was adopted in 1986, and it addresses the need to "expand and improve basic education" (The World Bank 1995, 124). Recently, the central government implemented The District Primary Education Program (DPEP), in an attempt to act on the recommendations of the National Policy on Education. The program involves the subsidizing of approved investments, by the Government of India. The central government will provide a grant of 85% on expenditures by the states (The World Bank 1995, 123). Since these measures have been implemented very recently, results cannot be obtained and the effectiveness of the DPEP cannot be commented on at this time.

Concluding Remarks

Child labour is a significant problem in India. The prevalence of it is shown by the child work participation rates which are higher in Indian than in other developing countries. The major determinant of child labour is poverty. Even though children are paid less than adults, whatever income they earn is of benefit to poor families. In addition to poverty, the lack of adequate and accessible souces of credit forces poor parents to engage their children in the harsher form of child labour – bonded child labour. Some parents also feel that a formal education is not beneficial, and that children learn work skills through labour at a young age. These views are narrow and do not take the long term developmental benefits of education into account. Another determinant is access to education. In some areas, education is not affordable, or is found to be inadequate. With no other alternatives, children spend their time working.

The Constitution of India clearly states that child labour is wrong and that measures should be taken to end it. The government of India has implemented the Child Labour Act in 1986 that outlaws child labour in certain areas and sets the minimum age of employment at fourteen. This Act falls short of making all child labour illegal, and fails to meet the ILO guideline concerning the minimum age of employment set at fifteen years of age. Though policies are in place that could potentially reduce the incidence of child labour, enforcement is a problem. If child labour is to be eradicated in India, the government and those responsible for enforcement need to start doing their jobs. Policies can and will be developed concerning child labour, but without enforcement they are all useless.

The state of education in India also needs to be improved. High illiteracy and dropout rates are reflective of the inadequacy of the educational system. Poverty plays a role in the ineffectiveness of the educational system. Dropout rates are high because children are forced to work in order to support their families. The attitudes of the people also contribute to the lack of enrollment — parents feel that work develops skills that can be used to earn an income, while education does not help in this matter. Compulsory education may help in regard to these attitudes. The examples of Sri Lanka and Kerala show that compulsory education has worked in those areas. There are differences between Sri Lanka, Kerala and the rest of India. What types of social welfare structures do these places have? What are the attitudes of the people? Is there some other reason why the labour market for child labourers is poor in these areas? These are some questions that need to be answered before applying the concept of compulsory education to India? India is making progress in terms of educational policy. The DPEP has been implemented only four years ago, and so results are not apparent at this time. Hopefully the future will show that this program has made progress towards universal education, and eradicating child labour.

Child labour cannot be eliminated by focusing on one determinant, for example education, or by brute enforcement of child labour laws. The government of India must ensure that the needs of the poor are filled before attacking child labour. If poverty is addressed, the need for child labour will automatically diminish. No matter how hard India tries, child labour always will exist until the need for it is removed. The development of India as a nation is being hampered by child labour. Children are growing up illiterate because they have been working and not attending school. A cycle of poverty is formed and the need for child labour is reborn after every generation. India needs to address the situation by tackling the underlying causes of child labour through governmental policies and the enforcement of these policies. Only then will India succeed in the fight against child labour.

The in-depth study rightly reflects that children are the blooming flowers of the garden of the society. It is, therefore, our duty to protect these tender flowers from damaging effects of excess exposure, Justice Subba Rao has rightly opined that

"Social Justice must begin with children. Unless tender plant is properly nourished, it has little chance to grow into a strong and useful tree. So first priority in the scale of social justice will be given to the welfare of children." There are no two opinions that children are the future of the nation and thus they should be given adequate opportunity and facilities for developing themselves into good citizens.

References

Grootaert, C., and R. Kanbur (1995), Child labour: An Economic Perspective. International Labour Review 134:187-201.

Human Rights Watch (1996), The Small Hands of Slavery - Bonded Child Labor in India, New York.

ILO (1992), World Labour Report, Geneva.

ILO (1993), World Labour Report, Geneva.

ILO (1995), World Labour Report, Geneva.

Jain, S.N. (1985), "Legislation and Government Policy in Child Labour" in *Child Labour and Health: Problems and Prospects*, edited by U. Naidu and K. Kapadia. Bombay: Tata Institute of Social Sciences.

Mehra-Kerpelman, K. (1996), Children at Work: How Many and Where? World of Work, 15:8-9.

Nangia, P. (1987), Child Labour: Cause-Effect Syndrome. Janak Publishers, New Delhi.

Narayan, A. (1988), "Child Labour Policies and Programmes: The Indian Experience" in *Combating Child Labour*, edited by A. Bequele and J. Boyden, International Labour Organisation, Geneva.

Subrahmanya, R.K.A. (1987)," Can the Child Labour Act of 1986 Effectively Control Child Labour?" in *Young Hands at Work - Child Labour in India*, edited by M. Gupta and K. Voll, Atma Ram & Sons, Delhi.

The World Bank (1995), Economic Developments in India: Achievements and Challenges, The World Bank, Washington:

Weiner, M. (1991), The Child and the State in India, Princeton: Princeton University Press

Shandilya, Tapan Kumar (2003), Child Labour: A Global Challenge, Deep & Deep Publications Pvt. Ltd, New Delhi.

Shandilya, Tapan Kumar (2006), "Child Labour: Eradication ", Deep & Deep Publications Pvt. Ltd, New Delhi.

Raj, M.S. and Chauhan, D, "Child Labour in India: Causes, Magnitude and Way Out", Published article in ed. volume of Sen, R.K., Dasgupata Asis, Problems of Child Labour in India, Deep & Deep Publications Pvt. Ltd., New Delhi, p. 20.

Hariharan. G., "Child Labour: A case of Vellore District", Published article in ed. Volume of Sen. R.K. and Dasgupta, Asis, Problem of Child Labour in India, Deep & 'Deep Publications Pvt. Ltd., New Delhi. p.160

S. Sharma, M.V.N., Frankline, G.B. and Rao, T.H., "Problems and Prospects of Child Labour-A Case Study of Guntur District, Andhra Pradesh," article Published in ed. Volume of Sen & Dasgupta, Problem of Child Labour in India, Deep & Deep Publications Pvt. Ltd., New Delhi, p. 149.

Anker Richard (1998), article Published in Economic of Child Labour in Hazardous Industries of India, ed. By Anker Richard, Barge Sandhya, Rajagopal, S., Joseph, M.P., Published by Centre for Operations Research and Training (CORT) Baroda (Gujarat), p. 1.

Khan, M.E., Anker Richard, Barge, Sandhya (2001), "Child Labour Economics Gain or Social cost?" Article published in IDPAD International Conference on Child Labour in South Asia, Vol. II, New Delhi, p. 1.

13

Education and Child Labour in India

Kumkum Jha

Introduction

Child labour is multidimensional global menace. The developing world is suffering all the more. According to UNICEF 2009 estimates (State of World Children), more than 30 million children in India are engaged in someway or the other in various labour activities.

Nearly 40% of our population consists of children (below the age of the fourteen.) The Constitution of Indian as expounded by the Supreme Court, makes free and compulsory education upto that age a fundamental right. However, a large number of children in that age group do not have blessing but on the contrary, are condemned to backbreaking labour under harrowing conditions. Mahbul-ul Haq, in his tireless campaign for Asian development, exposed the myth of economic constrains on literacy. He pointed out that countries with far lower per capita GDP than India had achieved spectacularly higher levels of literacy. He demonstrated that it was lack of political commitment and not economic constraints that devastated the country with the course of illiteracy.

Child labour is a harsh reality. Millions of sons and daughters of India are victims. Regretfully, most of them have been placed at a situational disadvantage that is not their own creation. They are in theory, free citizens of a free country, entitled to the same inalienable human rights as others. Yet in practice, they have been victims of generations of neglect, discrimination and deprivation. Whether, their victimhood relates to birth or caste or employment or sex, they had perforce to reconcile themselves to it.

Science and technology is changing the face of the world rapidly and in coming decades it will change beyond recognition. No. country can afford to remain in isolation. Globalization is no longer a matter of choice. So long child labour persists, child education will be impossible. It is a vicious circle which if not broken, will entrap and immobilize India to the position of a mere bystander, watching the great excitement of the new transformation of the world passerby. The Agenda for governance adopted by the Indian Government in March 1998 exhorted, "We will present a national charter of children. Our aim is to ensure that no child will remain illiterate, hungry or lacks of medical care. We will take measure to eliminate child labour".

Impact of Education on Child Labour

There are three thoughts regarding education's impact on child labour. The first school of thought treats education as the fundamental human right of every child in 5-14 age groups. It holds that any child in this age group who is out of school should be treated as a working child. According to 1991 census, total child population in India was 297 million of which school going age (5-14) constitute around 203 million. But only 112 million children are lucky enough to reach formal schools. Obviously, 100 million plus are children who do not attend school. It is the responsibility of the state to create the infrastructure and environment for facilitating free, compulsory and universal access to both primary and elementary education. Thee can be no excuse for 100 million children in the 5-14 age group being outside the school system whether formal or non formal. Access to educational opportunities for all children is the barest minimum obligation of the state which can not absolve itself from the obligation on the ground of poverty and other economic compulsions or due to lack of infrastructure, logistical support and resources. It is child labour that induces poverty rather than poverty that induces child labour. A child below 15 years is not physically and emotionally matures and fit to enter in the world of work. If they are forced to do so, it would result in retardation and impoverishment of their evolution and growth.

According to second school of thought, the magnitude of the problem is so enormous that the state will hardly afford to create the environment and provide the infrastructure to send the additional 100 million plus children to school. It would require about forty thousand crores annually. This school of thought, therefore, advocates a gradual, sequential and selective approach to the entire issue of out of school children vis-à-vis working children. According to them, elimination of child labour can be achieved progressively rather than at a stroke.

The third school of though believes that both civil society and the state have failed in the following:

- Making education a fundamental human right.
- Creating the appropriate infrastructure and environment and providing incentives to ensure access to educational opportunities to all.
- Creating a positive and conducive school atmosphere that will enable universal retention and participation of children who have enrolled themselves in school.

They advocate that it should be left to the children themselves to decide whether or not they want to go to school. Their need of education should be provided by the state or the society. If, however, the children find that the educational system is dull, not motivating and irrelevant and would prefer to work, the state should create opportunities for forms of work that is in consonance with their physical and mental capacities. 2009 report of World Bank on education reveals that less than

60% children complete education upto 8th standard in India. We are far behind China, Vietnam and Sri Lanka.

Dimension of Child Labour in India

In 1981, the total workforce in the country was about 223m and the number of working children 13.6m or 6% of the total work force. In 1991; however, the total workforce in the country was 314m, of which child labour formed its share as 3.59% only.

The proportion of working children to the total labour force is also lower in India than in many other developing countries. Child labour accounts for 5.2% of the total labour force in India as against percentages of 27.3 in Turkey, 20.7 in Thailand, 19.5 in Bangladesh, 18.8 in Brazil, 16.6 in Pakistan, 12.4 in Indonesia, 11.5 in Mexico, 8.2 in Egypt, 6.6 in Argentina. This is not, however, any consolation. The fact that the proportionate share of child labour as a subset of the total child population has been declining over time is also no consolation as the absolute number continues to be very large, as in fact the highest in the world.

Prof. D.P. Choudhary of the Department of Economics, University of Wollongong, Australia has scientifically classified working children in India in three major groups. In the first, less than 6% of about 13-14m full time child workers are employed for wages in activities that are prohibited under the child labour (Prohibition and Regulation) Act. In the second category, children are employed for wages, but in activities that are not so prohibited under the Act. In the third category, over 80% of India's full time and part time child workers are trapped in a situation where the parents of working children and their families work jointly within family economic enterprises (farm, household, industries, petty trades), small and marginal cultivators, share croppers, who are engaged in farming activities in the parched conditions of different parts of India. Southern Orissa, Central India (the Chattisgarh region), the desert tracts of Rajasthan are good examples of this. A very large number of the children are reported to be neither workers, nor in schools. They are engaged in activities such as collection of firewoods in rural areas, rag-picking in urban areas and household work. They are not considered to be economic activities and none of our laws provide any social or economic protection to this group. According to Prof. Choudhary, these children who he terms "nowhere children", numbered around 74-98m in 1991, neither at school nor at work they represent a colossal waste of a sizeable percentage of potential manpower. At its most formative stage on account large scale educational deprivation when they entered in adulthood without literacy, they will be in no position to develop their innate capacities and skills. They would constitute a major liability for the nation. A large number of data suggest that child labour in India is more a rural than an urban phenomenon. Approximately 90% of working children are in the rural areas, engaged in agricultural and allied activities. Cultivation, agricultural labour, forestry fisheries, pottery and carpentry account for 84.9% of child labour. In urban areas; manufacturing, service and repairs account for 8.64% child labour. Even urban child labourers are actually rural labour forced to migrate to urban areas due to poverty and other economic compulsions. Of these, only 0.8% works in factories. The unorganized and informal sectors, both in urban and rural areas, account for almost entire child labour force.

Table 1
Distribution of Child Labour in Major States

State	*Percentage*
Andhra Pradesh	14.3
Madhya Pradesh	12.5
Maharashtra	11.4
Utter Pradesh	10.5
Karnataka	8.3
Bihar	8.1
Tamilnadu	7.1
Rajasthan	6.0
Orissa	5.1
Gujrat	4.5
West Bengal	4.4

Source: Annual Report, Government of India

The distribution of child labour in different states appears to indicate certain correlations. States with a large population living below the poverty line have a higher incidence of child labour. A higher incidence of child labour is accompanied by a high drop-out rate in the school. The incidence of child labour is partly linked to the level of socio-economic development of an area and partly to the attitude of the parents, employers and socio-cultural atmosphere. The following table shows distribution of child labour in eleven major states according to 1991 census.

Etiology of Child Labour

The incidence of child labour negatively correlates with per capita income, infrastructure development, school enrolment ratio, the position of women in society and female participation in non-agricultural work. It positively correlates with parental poverty, illiteracy, unemployment, under employment and the percentage of the labour force in agriculture.

A detailed review by Lloyd (1994) found relationship between child labour and size of the household. His study revealed following factors in the regard:

- *Level of Socio Economic Development*- The effect of household size is larger in urban or more developed areas.
- *Level of Social Expenditure by the State*- The effect of household size is less if state expenditure is high.
- *Family Culture*- The effect of house hold size is weaker where extended family systems exist.
- *Phase of Demographic Transition*- The effect of household size is larger in the later phases.

In the rural areas, the relationship between household size and child labour correlates with land holdings. There is evidence to show that children in landless and marginal farm house holds generally engage in wage labour while those in households with larger farms engage in agricultural work.

Research provides further evidences that poor households send children to work in order to augment household income and also as a safe guard against the uncertainties of income they face, such as the loss of job, the occurrence of a natural calamity (flood, cyclone, drought, and famine), failed harvest, prolonged illness, etc. Such an interruption can be really threatening for poor households whose income is low, who have no savings and are not in a position to borrow for want of collateral.

Child labour supply is determined by the characteristics of the community as a whole. The social infrastructure, casts large influence. Education is the most powerful infrastructure with regards to child labour. In an economic environment where there is shrinkage of jobs in the organized sector on account of recession, rationalization, retrenchment or closure as well as in the unorganized or informal sector, the survival depends on work, many parents are forced to conclude that taking children out of school and putting them to work will be the most sensible option for existence. Another important determinant of child labour supply relates closely to the dynamics of labour market. It has been observed that flexibility of wages is a key factor in influencing employment of children. In India under the Minimum Wages Act, 1948, children are permitted to work for no more than four and half hours a day and entitled to receive fifty percent of the wage of an adult. Since there is no way of measuring the working hours in an informal work environment in actual practice, children are made to work the whole day while wages payable continue to be half those paid to adults. All assumptions regarding the behaviour of labour markets tend to go awry in a situation, as in India, where there is no stability and durability of employment. Employment in the Indian labour market is susceptible to violent fluctuations and is characterized by rapid mobility of labour or migration. This has a considerable bearing on child labour in terms of employment status, wages, working conditions and merits fairly detailed treatment.

One in three Indians is a migrant, according to United Nations Human Development Report, 2009. Millions of our people are leaving their homes in search of jobs and greener pastures. Migration has tremendous impact on child labour.

The social cost of migration is too heavy. The earnings are never adequate due to low wages and a large sum is siphoned by the middlemen and contractors. It seriously deprives children of their access to educational opportunities. Besides, the children of migrant parents find if difficult to be taught in languages which are not familiar to them. The surroundings and situations are also hostile. Millions of innocent and guileless children of migrant parents are thus exposed to acute and heart rending deprivation and exploitations for no fault of theirs. The joy and excitement of a normal childhood are totally lost to them. Their parents migrate from Santhal Parganas, Chotanagpur and the Singhbhum regions of Jharkhand, Darbhanga, Madhubani, Sitamarhi and Jehanabad Districts of Bihar as well as many backward districts of Madhya Pradesh, Chattisgarh, Rajasthan, Uttarakhand and Himachal Pradesh to the Plains of Punjab, Haryana, Jammu and Kashmir, hydro electric projects and thermal stations of Himachal Pradesh, Delhi and the north-east and the prosperous states like Gujarat and Maharashtra. They migrate on account of poverty, landlessness and a total lack of assets.

Combating Child Labour

In the landmark judgment of the Supreme Court in Civil Writ Application No. 465 of 1986, MC Mehta Vs State of Tamil Nadu and Ors, dated 10 December 1986, the learned Judges remarked 'Child is the Father of the man'. It emphasizes how a child should be groomed and receives education and nutrition, so as to enable the petals of childhood to blossom to the flowers of youth and manhood. For the foundation of a healthy, vibrant, strong and self-reliant Republic all children must be given the opportunities to develop into healthy all rounded personalities. Child labour can best be combated through education, social awareness and activism; the removal and rehabilitation of child labourers, legislation and proper enforcement of those laws. Government should devote resources for educations. Schooling should be compulsory, of good quality and relevance. It should be little or no cost financially to poor families. In 1994 Malawi made primary education free. From one economic year to the next, enrolment increased by roughly 50% and more of the new students were female than man. The International community has the funds to provide free Primary education. It is a question of budgeting priorities. The following initiatives can be effective in combating child labour.

(i) *Improving Child Labour Legislation and Laws:* Many countries have national child labour laws that establish a minimum age for work and regulate working conditions. These laws tend to be effective in combating child labour abuses in the formal sector in urban areas. In developing countries, legal protection for child labourers does not extend beyond the formal sector to the kinds of work in which children are most involved such as agriculture and domestic service. In addition, labour laws in many countries do not cover factories employing less than ten people. The carpet industry in Pakistan, for examples, is largely a cottage industry, deliberately organized in this way to avoid labour laws. So it is important to extend protection in such a manner that laws should cover the most exploitative forms of child labour and the main places where children work.

(ii) *Enforcement of Child Labour Legislation and Laws:* Lack of enforcement of laws especially in the main areas in which children work and their exploitation is the key obstacle to combating child labour. Laws cannot be effective if they are not enforced.

(iii) *Increasing Access, Quality and Relevance of Education:* Education is the key to the ending exploitation of children. Children who attend school are less likely to be involved in hazardous or exploitative work. The main obstacle is in achieving universal primary education is the inability and or the unwillingness of governments to provide adequate and quality educational facilities for poor children in rural areas, city and towns. Evidence from around the world has shown that poor families are willing to sacrifice by sending send their children to school when it is economically and physically accessible and truly productive in terms of future employment prospects. The focus should not just be on education of children. Emphasis should also be on education programmes for adults especially women. Evidence shows that there is an inverse relationship between adult literacy rate and the incidence of child labour in the long run. Educated adults have fewer and better educated children.

(iv) *Vocational Training:* Vocational education and training for order child labourers can play an important role in combating child labour. Training provides the marketable skills for gainful employment which in turn, contributes to local and national development.

(v) *Equality for Women and Girls:* The campaign to abolish child labour cannot be separated from women's struggles for recognition, decision-making, power, autonomy, equality in gender, a fair division of paid and unpaid work and other measures to end poverty and violence. The social welfare of children is closely related to the position of women. Throughout the world, it is the women who spend the most time caring for children. Women are the hardest hit by World Bank and IMF structural adjustment programmes, their spending power is reduced, their workload is increased and they are often lent to care for families alone. They may have no choice but to let the children work for the sake of the family as a whole. As soon as a women's income improves, so too does the situation of her children.

(vi) *Women Invest in their Children:* In their food, water, housing, clothing and schooling, women need access to decent jobs and good childcare. A commitment to women's equality must be part of the commitment to end child labour.

(vii) *Replacing Child Workers with Adults:* Replacing child workers with their parents would actually increase a family's income because adults are more highly paid. The small increase in production costs which would result from replacing child workers with adults would have a small effect on sales in importing countries.

Conclusion

Child labour is a global problem and can only be fought on a global scale. Policies against child labour can only be successful if they are the result of international cooperation. Government should work together with international and supranational organisations such as UNICEF and the ILO. They should cooperate with NGOs that have experience in the field and support promising projects such as those addressing poverty relief and education. Policy also must encourage multinational cooperation to formulate codes of conduct.

The fight against child labour should not be separated from the issue of global inequality. Any action by government against child labour is futile, implausible and not reciprocal, if that action does not reflect their own responsibility in creating and sustaining child labour. Governments should accept that child labour is a complex issue and set as a priority elimination on its worst forms.

It must be emphasized that education is the most effective weapon against the curse of child labour. Free and compulsory education holds the promise of breaking the vicious cycle of illiteracy, poverty and finally, the elimination of child labour. Therefore, the policy makers and the administrators should focus on the issue of universal literacy which is the focal point of "Sarva Siksha Abhiyan" of the Government of India.

References

Boudhiba Abdelwahab (1983), Exploitation of Child Labour: Final Report of the Special Repporteur of the United Nations Sub-Commission on Prevention of Discrimination and Protection of Minorities, Geneva, UN.

Mishra, Lakshmidhar (2000), "Child Labour in India" Oxford University Press

Choudhary, D.P. (1997), Child Labour in India in the Asian Perspective, Social Change, 27(3 & 4), Sept-Dec.

Llyod, Tim (1994), Poverty, Inequality and Rural Development (St. Martin's Press, Newyork)

UNICEF (2009), State of World Children.

World Bank (2009), State of Education in Asia

UNDP (2009), Human Development Report

SECTION – III

CHILD DEVELOPMENT – SOME ISSUES

14

The In and Out of Child Abuse: Issues and Prospects

Mohammad Reza Iravani

Introduction

A study, which is conducted by a Mumbai based Womens College has shown that 68.5 percent of female criminals had been sexually abused as children. Child abuse is one of the worst, hidden and invisible crimes of the civilized society. Child abuse can be defined as "a condition having to do with those who have been deliberately injured by physical assault". This definition is limited only to physical violence, which produce a diagnostic injury. Thus, it is evident that acts of neglect and maltreatment of children, which do not produce an injury but are equally harmful, cannot be included in this definition. No definition of child abuse can be considered as valid unless it includes physical, physiological and psychological ill treatment of a child. Burgess has given a wider definition of child abuse. According to him, child abuse refers to "any child who receives non-accidental physical and psychological injury as a result of acts and omissions on the part of his parents or guardians or employers..."Verbal abuse, threats of physical violence and excessive physical punishment are also included in the definition of child abuse. So, we can say that the term abuse has different meanings and it varies according to the time and space.

We can say that child abuse is more common among child labourers, children in remand home, physically handicap children, children under mental stress and abandoned children are more vulnerable to different kinds of abuses. This child abuse can be broadly divided in to three major types– 1) physical, 2) sexual and 3) emotional. It is more unfortunate to say that it is evident that all these mentioned kinds of abuses exist among child labourers. A number of explanations have been given by social scientists to reveal the major motivational factors behind the child abuse.

Child Abuse: Psychiatric Explanation

Psychiatric explanation was propounded by many scholars. It links with child abuse factors such as mental illness and personality defects or intra-individual abnormalities. It also links abusive parents' own childhood experiences to the individuals' weak personality development and poor self-control. The thesis that personality disorder is responsible for child abuse was further advanced by reports that abusers often had a propensity for impulsive and/or anti social acts that extended beyond the preventing role. A parent, according to this explanation, may abuse his/her child due to unmet emotional needs and capabilities with own (parental) expectations, or emotional scars from their own abusive or deprived family background affecting their ability to care for their own offspring (Bhasak, 1998). This explanation initially drew makers support from many fields, including law-makers and public-interest groups because it directed most of the responsibility for abusive behavior squarely at the individual involved and absolved society from blame in contributing to the risk of child abuse through lack of education, adequate housing, family support programmes, employment opportunities and so on. However, recent researches have disproved the role of psychopathology in child abuse.

Child Abuse: Socio–Cultural Explanation

Socio-cultural explanation says those external forces or a socio-demographic variable within the society causes child abuse. This theory has three major sub fields– 1) social situational, 2) social habitability and 3) social control. The social-situational explanation proposes that abuse and violence arise out of two factors: structural stress and cultural norms. As the social structure in which a parent lives becomes more stress ridden greater becomes the possibility that family violence will surface as an attempt to gain control over irritating, tense events. Cultural sanctioning of violence as an appropriate conflict resolution technique further provides a foundation for the use of corporal punishment in child rearing. If a parent was frequently exposed to harsh physical punishment as a child, he/she may have great propensity toward viewing such behavior as normative and inhibition against physical force may be lessened.

Some western scientist have maintained that factors such as low income, unemployment, isolation, unwanted pregnancy and conflict with spouse/in-laws cause structural stresses which, combined with the cultural acceptance for violence to resolve conflict, lead to the use of force and violence against children at home. Talking of social factors, which cause stress, it has been referred to social class and family size. The major problem in this explanation is that it is unable to account for the finding that given the same set of deprivation or advance conditions, many parents do and others do not abuse their children. According to one study, parents use violence against their children because they have neither fear of being hit back, nor of being arrested thus, violence is used when (i) the cost of being violent is to less than the rewards, (ii) the absence of effective social control over family relations decreases the cost (of one member being violent towards another), and (iii) family structures reduce social control in family relations and therefore, reduce the costs and increase the rewards of being violent. Recent studies have showed that: (a) inequality in home reduces both social control and the costs of being violent, and (b) the privacy in the family serves to reduce the degree of social control exercised over family relations. In case of social habitability, the nature of child maltreatment depends upon the quality of the environment in which the person and family live, or the level of family support in the environment. Maltreatment of children increases when family support decreases

As social control point of view, some parents use violence against their children because they have no fear of being hit back. Social interactional explanation approach the etiology of child abuse in terms of the interplay between individual family and social factors in relation to both past and present events. The condition in which children have been raised may help to reveal why some adults are predisposed to abusive behavior, given certain setting conditions. Social learning theory lays emphasis on the learned nature of parenting and the fact that many parents have lack of knowledge and skill to carry out the highly complex task of child-rearing.

Types of Abuse

Neglect

Child abuse and neglect can be defined as the intentional, non accidental injury, mal-nutrient of children by parents, caretaker, employers or others including those individuals presenting Government/non-government bodies which may lead to temporary or permanent impairment of their physical, mental, psycho-social development, disability of death. Children, particularly infants, are perhaps the most vulnerable victims of crime because of their great dependence upon their parents. It is a tragic fact that children suffer to a fall greater extent as the hands of parents and their friends then they do as the hands of strangers. This type of abuse can be further classified into physical neglect, emotional neglect, moral neglect and social neglect.

Emotional Abuse: Child emotional abuse can be refereed to as a pattern of behavioural that impairs a child emotional development or sense of self worth. This may include constant criticism, threats or rejection as well as withholding love, support, or guidance. Emotional maltreatment is rarely manifested in physical signs. A few physical indicators of emotional maltreatment are speech disorders, lag in physical development and failure-to-thrive syndrome. The behavioural characteristics of emotional maltreatment are habit disorders, conduct disorders, neurotic trait, psycho-neurotic reaction behavior extremes (passive, aggressive, rigid reserved, demanding stubborn), lag in emotional and intellectual and attempted suicide. Four important causes emotional abuse are poverty, deficient parental control and non-cordial relations within family, maltreatment faced by parents in their child hood or inter generational transmission of child mal treatment, and alcoholism of parents. A significant proportion of abusing parents were themselves abused as children.

Physical Abuse: It can be defined as situation in which a child suffers, or is likely to suffer, significant harm from an injury inflicted by the child's parent or caretaker. It is more visible form of abuse among working children than children who normally resides with the parents. If a child failed in execute the order of his boss, the boss may get angry and beat, burn, fracture, abrasion etc. Boys are more beaten than girls. Also school going children well be more beaten by the other children. The studies have revealed that mothers abuse children physically more than of the fathers. Also this study further says expressive violence is one in which the use of physical is an end in itself. Instrumental or power oriented violence is one in which violence is intended not only as a meance of including the child to alter his behavior but also to establish parental authority. Child precipitated violence is one in which the victims of violence contribute to their own victimization either through action defined as deviant by the aggressor parent or through provoking their antagonism.

Causes of Physical Abuse

Many social scientists have given different causes of physical abuse. Some consider the psycho-pathology of the individual perpetrators as the primary cause factor, other view the psycho-social pathology of family interaction as the main cause and still others put major emphasis on situations of acute as tress. The situational stresses pointed out four models of dominant causes of a child's physical abuse. They are:

- Relations between couples
- Relations between parents and children
- Structural stress, and
- Child-produced stresses

Totally we can say that through the role of the personality traits of the abusers cannot be ignored but family environment and stress radian family situations are more crucial in child battering.

Sexual Abuse

It can be defined as contacts or interactions between a child and an older or more knowledgeable child or adult, when the child is being used as an object of gratification for the older child's or adult's sexual needs. Child sexual abuse can be defined as the involvement of dependent and immature children in sexual active's they do not fully comprehend, to which they are unable to give informed consent. Sexual abuse is not often identified through physical indicators alone. Frequently, a child confides in a trusted person (parents, relatives, friends, teachers, etc) that she/he has been sexually assaulted. There are some behavioral indicters too of sexual abuse. The sexually abused child may appear withdrawn or retarded, may have poor peer relationships, may be unwilling to participate in activist, may indulge in delinquent behavior, may runaway, etc.

The recent studies has shown that the lower caste girl children are more frequent victims of sexual abuse and victims age distribution is more homogenous, the assault age distribution is more heterogeneous. Also it is noted that more then 11 percent of child abuse takes place in side the family. Persons having blood relationships constitute a considerable percentage of perpetrators.

Causes of Sexual Abuse

Literature survives shows that it has four main reasons–

- Adjustment problems of the perpetrators,
- Family disorganization,
- Victims' characteristics, and
- Psychological disorders of the abusers.

The four variables related to sexual abuse are family environment, family structure, and individual predisposition's and situations factors. The analyze of family environment revealed that congestion in family was not related of sexual abuse but conflict between parents and weakening of inhabitation's leading to neglect of the children, absence of affectionate parent-child relationship within the family that fails to give support and protection to child, alcoholism of the earning male member, lack of accountability of the parents, absence of control on children, mass media, male dominated family, extra martial relationship and social isolation of the family are the major factors behind this sexual abuse. The environment in the work place also contributes to sexual molestation. Several cases of assault by employees ad mutation by co-workers of the young victims when they were all alone in the house or work place. The reserved and loneliness of young girls make them more susceptible to the overtures of the perpetrators.

Sexual abuse is the most common and invisible child abuse more among the girl child labourers. Girls are more vulnerable to the sexual abuse than boys. Usually, the victims will be 14 or above 14 years of age and they will be more from lower economic classes and are deprived of all parental care. Basically boys are the victims of employment-related abuse and girls are usually the victims of 'acquaintance related abuse'. Also we can give some other reasons that push children in to commercial sexual exploitation are economic disparities, inequitable socio-economic structure, traditional and religious practice. The circumstance surrounding child abuses are often complex. Thus, the most appropriate form of state response whether to impose criminal sanctions or whether to rely intend on some therapeutic alternative–is a difficult decision. Child victims of sexual abuse may experiences enduring feelings of guilty shame and emotional isolation. The infliction of serious bodily injury upon a child leaves psychological scares, which endure long over after physical wound is healed. The developing of healthy personalities will be seriously jeopardized for a child, who feels unsafe, unwanted and uncared for in its parent's response. This may leads to poor development in terms of initiative and low school performance. In some cases, it can be stated that the child survives rather than develops.

The study of sexual abuse of girls in India is in its infancy. The real problem is inadequacies of data relating to sexual abuse of girls because of the secrecy and stigma attached to it. Nevertheless, the notion of the 'girl child' has been reified, as if there is something essential about all female children regardless of wealth or ethnicity, something that makes them more vulnerable than boys in general. This focuses on vulnerability to sexual violation, early marriage, female feticide and infanticide unplanned teenage pregnancy and is a new manifestation of the old control over women's sexuality and fertility. All over the world, the child's susceptibility to commercial sexual expatriation lies in his or her family circumstances. Study has shown that most of the sexually exploited children are either from marginalised families in the cities and destitute families in the country or children of women already for commercial gain can no more be hidden. Recently, the increasing incidences of children suffering from sexually transmitted diseases have gradually raised awareness regarding the likelihood of sexual abuse. The literature on child prostates were sought after because they were believed to be free of STDs, including the apparently world wide belief that "penetrative sex with a virgin is a cure". Not only this also some other myths are embedded in this child trafficking since time immoral.

In India, domestic child workers and street children are further vulnerable to sexual abuses more particularly the innocent girls. Incidents where facts are fudged at Policy station are not uncommon. There is some report that victims raped by the Policy personnels. In case of India especially girl children are victims of extreme discrimination and neglect by the parents. Latest report says that India has around 4 lakh under 15 child prostitutes for child sex tourism. Thus India has got second place in the world after Thailand with 6-lakh child prostitutes. One more study says more then one million sexual exploitation children only is in Asia. In India, Bangladesh, Korea, Taiwan, child trafficking has become a kind invisible business. It has become a new feature of economic life in several countries.

In India, the demand for children comes mainly from the local population. However, India and other South Asian Countries are gradually replacing South East Asia as the venue of choice for foreigners, as there are fewer laws against child sexual abuse, and South Asian children can be bought at more affordable prices. The Convention on Rights of the Child has been rectified and supported by 178 countries including India. It may be given the NGOs, lawyers, government officials, and Policy officers, no choice except to take all possible measures in ensuring protection of the rights of children. We do not need more legislations. We already have a number of laws, which are not being implemented.

The NGOs role has almost become a pattern of speech. The chosen rhetoric is that the NGOs are the closest to the target groups, that the NGOs role is the critical and most important one. It is a way of transferring responsibility from one sector to another. The government and we, however, cannot shun the responsibility. NGOs can be partners, not substitutes in the government's efforts. There is need to raise public sensitivity and awareness about these problems that confront us in our work. The problem of child prostitution has to be worked out not merely through rehabilitation, but with greater emphasis on prevention. There are backward villages and districts that provide the base for the traffickers. That is where the real problem. NGOs working towards rural development should focus on such poor families that are willy-nilly-forced to send their children to earn. We lack the skills to search the underworld mafia that is dangerous. There are people who are making a lost of money in trafficking. We have witnessed the power of community action in Manila where the parents of the children came out on the street and demanded justice; and in Goa where protestation are going on; the beach areas of Sri Lanka, where small community groups are committed to monitor the problem in order to protect their own children. The community has to rise up and join hands, though it is not something that is going to be easy.

Recently, there has been increasing awareness in the country regarding the menacing aspects and repercussions of child prostitution. The difference between reality and application of the law shows that the issue of child prostitution is more hidden than exposed. This sorry state of affairs rather compound the problem in the country and the Human Rights Commission has decided to have this issue considered on regular basis by a core group comprising, inter alia, the National Commission for Women, the Department of Women and Child Development, selected NGOs and UNICEF. This group is, among other things, considering sufficiency of existing laws and the ways of improving upon their enforcement, necessity of making development on such issues of holding public meetings, seminars in the specific areas and so on in order to eliminate or minimize the child prostitution. There is a strong correlation between family abuse of children, especially girls, and the drive to enter the sex trade. The mother in particular plays a pivotal role in her daughter's life decisions. The record indicates that there is direct commercial sexual exploitation of children because of the family situations.

Poverty, despair and newly dislocating values support such incidence of sexual exploitation among the children. Even though poverty is often prescribed to be cause of sale of children into labour, actually no poor families sell their children. Some families sell the child due to poverty, unemployment, consumerism and other adverse situations. At time, however, a child is sold into commercial sex by parents who have themselves sexually or otherwise abused the child.

The child is prepared and made "ready" for sex and able to earn money for the family. Such parents get lumpsum money for their children and push their children into "bondage", a situation in which the child is forced to provide sex to earn money to repay the family's debt to the exploiter.

Commercial sexual exploitation of children is above board in an organised industrial sector from small business to larger factories. There are people who use technology to sell the product to increase "good business". This "industry" is on abuse of children involved in fraud enslavement, bribery and corruption at various levels. The impact of commercial sexual exploitation on child has assumed staggering positions. The child loses its childhood, its dignity, often its future. These are unquestionable causes but these are evil effects of exploitation, which are more miserable. The most obvious of these relates to the health of the child. HIV/AIDS is both reason and consequence of commercial, sexual exploitation of children.

The evidence indicates that the miscreant people who consider sex with a child as "safer" is choosing children as sex partners. Having sex with a child, it is a notion, protects and abuse from HIV/AIDS because the child is more likely to be "clean". But the fact is otherwise because of their vulnerability and weaknesses. Children in flesh-market who are often forced to take more clients than adult might accept and are generally too weak to protest or avoid the situation. Moreover, children are physically more vulnerable to infection because of their socio-economic weakness. The 'virgin' child is asked by many customers as the "safest". Presently another problem is reconstruction surgery, which promotes commercial exploitation of sex children making multiple operations. Thus, the child is more infected with HIV as is found thorough some studies. Thus, the innocent child is met with death sentence meaning thereby that his/her life, respect and options. There are, besides, various physical and psychological reasons among the children forcing then in to sex. Children trapped in the cycle of commercial sex are frequently abused, beaten, burnt, tortured and deprived of food, air etc. They are also prone to different kind diseases. Drugs are often used to keep children taken into prostitution's easily. They may also be a self-medicating menace to numb the pain of hunger or despair. At the national level, many countries laid down laws making children's abuse a crime. Recently, there has been growing awareness of commercial sexual explorations of children. Children are transferred across borders Exploiters travel to set up their network. Clients go to buy service on foreign shores for promotion of their trade, it is said that making laws and enforcing them are two different things. It is certainly difficult to make laws work well against such odds. It is more difficult when local laws make them scot-free and safeguard the culprits exploiting the children. Indian Constitution articles 24 and 39 seek to protect children of tender age from abuse, exploitation, moral and material abandonment, employment of children under 14 years in any factory of hazardous jobs. The national policies for children also seeks to prevent exploitation of children against neglected and abandoning Juvenile Justice (Care and Protection) of Children Act also contains measures such as care and protection for abandoned and delinquent children. The Indian Penal Code declared kidnapping, maiming, selling or buying, seduction and sexual exploitation of children as an offence liable for punishment.

The present day media technology although develop consumption leading to sexual trade, they can erase the menace. The advent of the Internet has opened up new channels of informations of those looking for children for sex. The dark aspect of Internet technology menace that informations can be shared really time and again on special request dealt with by promotes and supplies of children for sex. Pornographic pictures and video clips can be up loaded and down –loaded anonymously. Besides technology, the press and media also play an importent role in domain of commercial, sexual, exploitation of children, both positive and negative.

On the negative side, the media contributed to the liberation of sexuality explicit imaginary and to shift any moral values. Satellite technology, international travel and support infrastructure means, that such image are quite frequently revised in a non-supportive context. Many TV viewers are adolescent and their attitude to adolescence itself is worthless. On the negative side, many reporters investing commercial sexual exploitations leading have unwitting corrupted evidence by paying for stores, enabling to escape convection. Press and media can play both positive and negative roles in exploitations of children for sex. The press and media can help immensely to advocacy, highlighting positive moral values and human rights. They can support positive family values and apprise parents when their children are at stake. They can hold children themselves to draw moral values on there on behavior and to identify risk factors of their social situations. According to rights of the children, child labour may be viewed as denial child rights. Under this right come rehabilitation, protection of child workers and betterment of their working conditions. Hence regulation of these facets of child labour is felt essential. Right to education and access to recreation and to childhood itself is linked with the right of the child. The notion of child hood is relatively of recent significance especially in the context of children rights. The enforcement of economic, social and cultural rights is made conditioned to the availability of the resources while civil and political rights have same obligations and regressive implementation of economic, social and cultural rights. A country's richness is measured by the norms like maximum extent of utilization of valuable resources in order to tackle child labour more effectively. In this context, child labour is now considered in a humanitarian as well as human rights approach. Child labour is considered as a violation of civil and political rights or a violation of economic, social and cultural rights. Nonetheless, all these rights are interacted and immediate steps need be taken for talking all these facets or effectively breaking a point in the vicious circle.

No doubt, we cannot resolve the problem in while, but no time can be delayed for taking adequate initiation in the matter. Under the Child Rights Convention, there are various sections relating to child labour –discriminations, abuse, encroachment to privacy and recession impeachment on child's education and safely and security of the child. Child labour is attributed mainly exploration, discrimination, helpless, caste and gender operation. There are different attitudinal factors which contribute to taking children to hazardous jobs on dignified services and insecure and indeed lie calling. Even the World Bank is setting restrictions on the misuse of child labour. It is surmised that the greater productively of these children who remain in primary schools for sufficient time will enable them to earn over six times the cost of giving them the extra education. A number of NGOs are now active to control the quantum of child labour and reduce its harmful effects and repercussions. Governament has also established a few committees to deal with child rights in its various sections of the society. It has also set up the National Human Rights Commission to examine not only the human rights in general, but also children's rights in particular. The policies approach that can be considered to prevent child abuse are 1) the punitive approach, which views abuse and neglect as crimes for which parents or other adults as should be punishable and 2) an intervention approach, which views abuse as a family problem requiring learning appropriate parenting and child development skills and therapy.

References

Aptekar (2004), Child Abuse in Paraguay", *International Journal of Educational Development'*, 15(1), 47-60.

Bovden (1998), 'Risk, Financial Markets and Human Capital in a Developing Country', *Review of Economic Studies*, 64, 311-335.

Babu (1999), Child Labour versus Abuse: Some Evidence from Latin America, *Journal of Population Economics*, 10 (4), 377-386.

Basu, K., & Tzannatos, Z. (2003), The Global Child Labour Problem: What Do We Know and What Can We Do? The World Bank Economic Review, *17*(2), 147-173.

Charles Brody, Effects of Child Work Experience a Decade Later: Evidence from the National Longitudinal Survey. Sociology of Education; 196 9(1), 66-81.

Caldwell, John C. (2007), 'The Socio-Economic Explanation of Child Labour', Canberra; Australian National University, p.89.

Chelliah, and Sudarshan (1999), 'Poverty and Beyond: Human Development in India', New Delhi: Social Science Press , p.45.

Hussain, M., & Mashus, K.E. (2005), Child Labour Use and Economic Growth: An Economertic Analysis. Malden: Blackwell Publishing Ltd, p.7.

Lindert (2008), Explaining Household Vulnerability to Idiosyncratic Income Shocks, *American Economic Review,* Vol. 85(2), No. 5.

Mason, A.D. and S.R. Khandker (2005), Household Schooling Decisions in Tanzania, mimeo, Washington (D.C.), *The World Bank,* p.38.

Maggie Black (2004), Household Work as a Deterrent to Schooling: An Analysis of Adolescent Girls in Peru, *Journal of Developing Areas,* 32(3), 339-356.

Morrow, and Mueller, E. (2007), The Value and Allocation of Time in Rural Botswana, *Journal of Development Economics,* p.329-360.

Nowicki, S. and Strickland, B.R. (2003), A Locus of Control Scale for Children, *Journal of Consulting and Clinical Psychology,* Vol. 4 No. 5.

Weiner (2006), Family Size, Schooling and Child Labour in Peru- An Empirical Analysis, *Journal of Population Economics,* p.387-405.

15

Understanding Multiple Perspectives of the Child Support Grant in South Africa

M. Kasiram, R. Sathiparsad and D. Holscher

Introduction and Context

Following the change from over 350 years of colonial and apartheid rule in South Africa, the first democratically elected government that came into power in 1994 was faced with the challenge of having to address vast levels of inequality and poverty. Poverty and the distribution of wealth were so skewed in terms of race, gender and region that children who grew up in rural, black and female-headed households were disproportionately affected by severe levels of poverty (May, 1998; Cassiem *et al.* 2000; Landman *et al.* 2003; UNDP, 2004). Consequently, child mortality levels in South Africa in general and amongst this group of children in particular were unacceptably high, with, by now constitutionally enshrined children's rights and basic needs unmet for the majority of South African children (Manuel, 2007). Poverty continues to be the biggest challenge faced by the government with The Times (Brandon and Pather, 13/11/07:1) citing 24 million South Africans as living below the poverty line, half of whom are dependent on government grants.

One of the South African government's initiatives to address poverty in 1998 was the introduction of a R100 flat rate grant for children up to the age of seven years, payable to the child's care - giver and subject to a means test. In 2003 this amount was extended to R200 and the scope was broadened to include children up to the age of 14, reaching by now just under 8 million beneficiaries (Manuel, 2007). The Child Support Grant (CSG) replaced the previous State Maintenance Grant (SMG) which was considered to be biased towards White, and later Indian children and families. The CSG's expressed intention was to alleviate poverty (Lund, 2007) and to enable primary care givers to better provide for their children's needs (Makiwane and Udjo, 2006). Thus, the introduction of the CSG was celebrated as an important post apartheid milestone towards the attainment of social security and more generally, social justice in South Africa (Ewing, 2004).

However, recent studies have been prompted by public perception that the Child Support Grant is unnecessary; that it might indeed be counter-productive in that it contributes to a rise of teen pregnancy; that it is frequently abused by care givers rather than used for the benefit of children; that it stretches scarce government resources; and that the HIV/AIDS pandemic in the country necessitates better support for the care of children (Lund, 2002, 2007; Makiwane and Udjo, 2006). It is before this tension between the expressed intentions behind the grant on the one hand and critical public appraisal on the other that three educators at the University of KwaZulu-Natal and a group of final year social work students embarked on a study of public perceptions of the Child Support Grant.

Aim and Objectives

The overall aim of the study was to explore public perceptions around the CSG. Research objectives were to explore with participants:

- the extent of factual knowledge about the CSG
- perceptions of uses/abuses of the grant

- differences in perceptions of the CSG across race, class and gender lines
- their views on how child poverty may be addressed.

Research Methodology

A mixed methodologies paradigm was adopted to glean multiple perspectives of the CSG using qualitative and quantitative approaches. Exploratory and descriptive methods worked complementarily to yield rich data that was described in detail.

The qualitative component comprised:

- 25 interviews using a semi-structured interview format
- 38 participants in 4 focus group discussions

The quantitative component comprised:

- 72 questionnaires that contained mostly closed and a few open-ended questions

Details of the Sample

Two sampling strategies were adopted for both the qualitative and quantitative components, namely purposive and convenience sampling. Hence, besides participants needing to have basic knowledge about the CSG and interest in the study, no further qualifying criteria were employed to secure participation. Seventy two social work students in their first year of study completed the questionnaire in the quantitative study.

In the qualitative study, 38 social work students in their third year of study, and 15 volunteers at a Durban-based social service organisation consented to participate in focus group discussions. In total, four once-off focus group discussions were held with the students, and one with the volunteers.

Interviews were also conducted with 25 professionals and non professionals who participated in the study. There was a racial and gender mix, but not in equal proportion in accord with the sample being an available one, thereby limiting the scope for crosses sectional analysis by specific criteria. However, the interviews enabled us to engage in a deeper exploration of knowledge, perceptions and observations pertaining to the topic.

Data analysis for the qualitative section was thematic content analysis and for the quantitative part, the Microsoft excel program was used to calculate frequency and range. Ethical requirements were adhered to with participation being voluntary whilst allowing the participant the option to withdraw at any time. Further, ethical clearance was secured from the University Research Ethics Committee to conduct this study.

Results and Discussion

This section is discussed under sub-headings that relate directly to the objectives of the study.

Knowledge of the CSG

Amongst all participants, there was generally a good understanding of qualifying criteria for the CSG and its purpose to supplement family income, to improve care for children and to contribute to alleviating poverty. This was understandable since many participants were social workers or social workers in training. Predictably, qualitative analysis revealed that professionals knew more than non-professionals, although in the student sample in the quantitative component, only 43% knew the year of introduction of the grant. Also, not all participants knew that the grant was increased to R200, despite media focus, suggesting that the public may be "saturated" and inattentive and/or that it is difficult to keep pace with detail in this respect. Documents required to successfully access the grant were numerous and not all participants could identify all of them.

While some social workers had some general understanding of the CSG, others were not able to engage on the topic adequately. Several gaps in the knowledge that social workers had about the CSG were noted. These included some degree of ignorance regarding the application procedures, the amounts paid and the difficulties experienced in accessing the grant. This is a matter of concern as social workers, being at the forefront of service delivery, need to be well informed to enable them to provide support and guidance to their clients. A lack of such knowledge may point to a need for in-service training/continuing education for social workers at their organizations.

Frustrations, Uses and Misuses

An interesting frustration was that paying this grant eroded *"ubuntu"*, the culture of helping and caring without reward. This comment from social workers reflects conflicting philosophies of caring by professionals who themselves receive payment for services.

Frustrations that prevented grant access and benefits were similar across all participants, with quantitative measurements pointing to long queues (93%); corruption/bribery (73%) and communication problems (58%). Participants were quick to acknowledge that a major obstacle to access is that many children do not have birth certificates and therefore cannot apply for social grants while others are not even aware that they are entitled to assistance (UNICEF, 2006).

In a similar vein, Dlungwana (2007) reported from her study on child-headed households in Durban that those not having proper documents such as birth certificates, identity documents and death certificates ended up with their grant applications not being processed. Similar findings were reported by Mfecane *et al.* (2006) from their study on orphans and vulnerable children in the Free State. A further issue highlighted by Hall, Leatt & Rosa (2005) and Dlungwana (2007) is that rural areas are particularly affected on account of location, meagre resources and lack of infra structure.

There was general consensus that even if the grant was used for other basic necessities such as caring for other family members in the home, this should not be seen as constituting "abuse". The point made was that poverty gave people no option but to 'spread' the grant in many directions.

As regards potential benefits and uses of the grant, few believed that the grant served its intended function (21% met basic needs and 25% alleviates poverty). Focus groups and interviews qualified further benefits/uses such as providing basic necessities at home, empowering women, sending children to school and using the monies to start up small businesses.

On the other hand, several participants maintained that the CSG was used for personal gain (90.2%). Misuse of the CSG yielded some emotive responses such as: *"for boyfriends, clothing, drugs, cell phones, cosmetics and lingerie to seduce other men"*! The link with teenage pregnancy was 63% in the quantitative study. This was supported by comments in the qualitative study such as: *"people get more babies just for the grant"*. One social worker explained that a twelve year old girl openly admitted to falling pregnant in order to receive the grant as she needed money. This sentiment is clearly articulated in a recent report in the Sunday Times (Govender, 2007:7 "School pregnancy shock") with one school guidance counsellor asserting that 80% of teen pregnancies were among orphans who wished to access the CSG as income for themselves.

However some participants did not believe that the grant encouraged teenage pregnancy as they indicated that it was too little to make any difference in caring for a child. Another Sunday Times (2005) report draws attention to studies conducted by the Soul City and Love Life publications which show that the major causes of teenage pregnancies are sexual ignorance and coercive sex such as rape. This has little to do with the CSG grant. In general, the CSG was cited as encouraging dependency and laziness and that it will continue to be misused because no support exists for whistle blowing.

A further problem was explained by one participant thus: *"it encourages some people to leave their children with their parents and then neglect their responsibilities and still receive the grant."* In many instances grandparents face the responsibility of caring for their grandchildren while the mothers of the children receive the grant and live elsewhere. Similarly, research by

Hall, Leatt & Rosa (2005) revealed that the elderly and other primary care givers in the community are being abused by mothers/fathers who are not taking responsibility for their children. For the social workers in our study, it was clear that for many young women, the money was a primary focus and not the responsibility of their children.

Differing Perceptions

Differences across race, gender and profession were evident from respondents in both the qualitative and quantitative studies. The perception amongst respondents was that Non Africans: *"are ashamed to receive CSG; they can't comment realistically because they have no primary experience of it; it is a waste of taxpayers' money"*. Clearly, experience of poverty and/ or receiving the CSG was perceived to directly correlate with a better understanding of the CSG and its purpose.

Across profession and status, students were judgemental against young, female sexually active, unmarried grant recipients. Gender differences were also found in that females were perceived to be more knowledgeable and sympathetic. It was also suggested that males do not apply for the CSG because they: *"believe the grant is for girls"*, suggesting that they may be afraid of being viewed as emasculated. Such attitudes have a ripple effect in that children needing care may be severely disadvantaged.

Participant Views on Addressing Child Poverty

There was overall agreement among the participants that the CSG should be increased. The view was that despite receiving the grant, many children were still affected by poverty as the grant was inadequate to address basic needs. The majority of participants felt that the grant should be extended to children up to the age of eighteen to enable them to complete schooling. Suggestions were also made that additional pay points needed to be established especially in areas far from the city centre. This would save on transport costs for families who were already financially stretched. Consistent with findings by Mfecane *et al.* (2006), some participants in our study expressed the view that people should make efforts to be self-supporting instead of being dependent on the government to support their children. By the same token, some participants asserted that if the government invests in job creation, dependency on grants may decrease.

Conclusion and Recommendations

Our research demonstrates clearly that there are indeed multiple perspectives regarding the Child Support Grant in South Africa, with a clear finding that the majority of our sample felt that the grant is being misused more than used. Hence it does not meet a child's needs nor address poverty. Participants demonstrated a tension between recognizing the need for the CSG, yet making value judgments about recipients. Participants also appeared to lack factual knowledge of the CSG and poverty and instead used stereotypes to interpret personal observations and to make broad generalizations.

Despite the impact on the alleviation of poverty by increasing children's access to food, education and health care, not all poor children benefit from the grant as many primary care givers bear the brunt of ineffective implementation procedures and cumbersome bureaucratic requirements. A review of some of these processes may go a long way towards improving accessibility and the realisation of all people's rights to social assistance, as set out in Section 27 of the South African Constitution (Hall, Leatt & Rosa, 2005).

With regard to accessibility, the view was that the grant is more easily accessible in urban than in rural areas where people live far from pay points. Such disadvantage to children and families in rural areas needs to be addressed. As suggested by Mfecane *et al.* (2006), one way to address this would be to decentralize the social security department so that services are taken to the people, thus saving high transport costs. This may be done via the establishment of satellite offices and mobile units to service the rural areas. To avoid long queues and waiting periods, it is recommended that there should be set days for the payment of specific grants. A further suggestion is that additional administrative resources such as office space and technology be made available, and additional trained staff be employed to attend to queries and to facilitate the payment process. It may be convenient if facilities are made available at the social security application points for CSG applicants to have birth certificates and identity documents photocopied and certified. This calls for collaboration between the Department of Home Affairs and the Department of Social Development.

To address possible abuse, cash payments to care givers may be replaced by food vouchers. To prevent fraud, mechanisms must be set in place to effectively administer and monitor the payment of the CSG including the immediate dismissal of corrupt officials.

As stated previously, most participants in our study felt that the amount applicants receive is inadequate to cover even the basic needs of the child/children concerned. We agree that a review of the amount paid is necessary and annual inflation needs to be taken into account. With regard to self-help efforts, we are of the view that people, especially women, must be empowered and given education and appropriate skills to enable them to find jobs and support themselves. It is incumbent on the government to drive this process.

We support the participants' suggestion that the CSG be extended to all children up to the age of 18 years as many of these children are still at school. It is also felt that children aged 16 should be eligible for the grant if they are primary care givers of children who in many cases are their siblings. This will provide some assistance to children heading households, especially where AIDS has robbed children of their parents. Applicants should also be aware that they have a right to appeal and monitoring mechanisms need to be put in place to track application processes and outcomes. To address the issue of long waiting periods we recommend that a set period of, for example, 90 days be allowed for processing applications. This may contribute to ensuring administrative accountability.

It is recommended that to update social workers and other helping professionals, the government must conduct continuing workshops that provide information and discuss issues and needs relating to the child support grant and other grants. More awareness-raising campaigns need to be launched on local radio stations and via road-shows, especially in marginalized areas such as townships, informal settlements and rural areas. These campaigns could clarify the eligibility requirements for the CSG and the administrative requirements for application. We recommend further that issues regarding policies and practices relating to social security be included in social work curricula at Universities. This will ensure that qualifying social workers have sufficient grounding in this area to be able to assist their clients.

Finally, it must be emphasized that the Child Support Grant is one initiative by the South African government to address child poverty. As evidenced in our study, there are mixed responses regarding the effectiveness of the grant in adequately meeting the needs of children. This area begs further research along with research to explore other initiatives that may contribute to alleviating poverty in South Africa. It is hoped that that the study has relevance for other emerging democracies that struggle to bridge the divide across wealth and poverty and that this study may point to areas of redress as well as areas that warrant further investigation.

References

Brandon, M. & Pather, S. (2007), Eight Million on Child Support. The Times, 13/11/2007.

Cassiem, S., Perry, H., Sadan, M, and Streak, J. (2000), Child Poverty and the Budget, Cape Town, Idasa.

Dlungwana, N.E. (2007), The Experiences of Children Who Are Heads of Households in Hammarsdale, Unpublished Masters Dissertation, University of KwaZulu-Natal, Durban, South Africa.

Ewing, D. (2004), Constitution of South Africa, *Children First*, (8) 57-58.

Govender, P. (2007), School Pregnancy Shock, The Sunday Times, page 7.

Hall, K, Leatt, A. & Rosa, S. (2005), Does the 'Means' Justify the End? Targeting the Child Support Grant. In: Leatt A & Rosa S (eds) *Towards a Means to Live: Targeting Poverty Alleviation to Make Children's Rights Real.* Cape Town: Children's Institute.

Landman, JP, Bhorat, H., van der Berg, S. & Van Aardt, C. (2003), Breaking the Grip of Poverty and Inequality in South African 2004-2014: Current Issues and Future Policy Options. http://www.sarpn.org.za. Accessed 14 May 2007.

Lund, F. (2002), Consensus and Contestation: The Policy for Child Support in South Africa, Draft Monograph, School of Development Studies: University of Natal.

Lund, F. (2007) Lecture: The Child Support Grant. Address to Social Work Level 4 Students, March.

Manuel, T. (2007), Budget Speech 2007 by the Minister of Finance, Trevor A Manuel, MP. http://www.info.gov.za. Accessed 25/05/07.

Mfecane, S, Skinner, D, Mdwaba, T. Mandivevenyi, C. Ntjantja, N. (2006),. A Situational Analysis of OVC Services in the Kopanong Municipality, Free State. In

D. Skinner and A Davids (Eds). *A Situational Analysis of Orphans and Vulnerable Children in Four Districts of South Africa.* (pp 31-46). Cape Town: HSRC.

Makiwane, M. & Udjo, E. (2006), Child Support Grant Associated With the Increase of Teenage Fertility in South Africa: Evidence from National Service and Administrative Data, Human Resource Council, Pretoria, South Africa.

May, J. (1998), Poverty and Inequality in South Africa, Report prepared for the Office of the Executive Deputy President and the Inter-Ministerial Committee for Poverty and Inequality, Summary Report.

http://www.welfare.gov.za/Documents/1998/Pov.htm Accessed 29/05/2007.

The Sunday Times–24 April 2005, cited at http://www.sagoodnews.co.za /search/jobs/435600.htm.

UNDP (2004), South African Human Development Report 2003, Pretoria, United Nations Development Programme, Oxford University Press.

UNICEF (2006), Saving Children, Enhancing Lives: Combating HIV and AIDS in South Africa, Pretoria.

www.childrencount.ci.org.za Accessed: 27/03/2007 Children's Institute, University of Cape Town.

16

Criminal Behaviour Among the Children of Women Prisoners in Karnataka

Ravikanth B. Lamani

Sexual violence against women is a significant public health problem. This violence adversely affects both psychological and physical health. About 5, 00,000 American women-annually are forced to have sexual intercourse against their will. The short and longer term psychological impacts of sexual assaults include anxiety disorders, major depressive disorders, post-traumatic stress disorder, suicidal ideation and actions, substance abuse, and eating disorders. The physical health impact of sexual assaults includes genital and non-genital injuries, a risk of unwanted pregnancies, and a risk of acquiring a sexually transmitted infection. Longer term physical health consequences of sexual assaults include chronic pelvic pain and pelvic inflammatory diseases. Women who have sexually abused in forced sex during childhood were from the category who have less education, lower incomes, run away home during childhood, to exchange sex for drugs or money and to either smoke cigarettes, drink alcohol, etc.

The children of any country are its valuable asset. No nation on this globe can ignore the responsibility to ensure the proper growth and development of children as the future of the country lies with them. In the world, children are used by boot leggers and drug peddlers. An innocent soul is put on the most hideous type of job. Children are trained for pickpocketing, thefts. Hardly any police has been available. Non-Government organisations can definitely play an important role with the help of the police to check such evils in the society.

The fact that children are physically and mentally immature necessitates special rights for their nurture, protection and fulfilment of unique needs. The rights of the child should be a matter of great concern to one and all as the children constitute one of the most vulnerable sections of the society. A deprived child may belong to any religious, ethnic, linguistic, socio-economic category and hence universal acceptance and promotion of child rights needs greater emphasis than the rights of other deprived section of the society.

The female prisons some young children staying with mothers under the most undesirable atmosphere and under inhuman conditions. In Calcutta, Bombay and Lucknow Non-Government organisations succeeded in getting the children released from Jails and they are then rehabilitated. Even today, the helplessness and vulnerability the child is the worst sufferer inspite of all the "National Plans for the Health, Happiness and Survival of the child". Let us all, the concerned Government departments, the police and the Non-Government organisations and welfare organisations join together to protect the child and its rights.

In 1997-98, there were 2807 women prisoners in Karnataka's seven central jails and sub-jails. Even if only fifty per cent of these women have two or three small or growing children that means 3,500 children were left to look after themselves, feed themselves, find a place to live and cope with relatives, neighbour or strangers, not all of whom could be trusted. In fact, there are no available statistics on information about these children, their number, where and how they live, who looks after them, whether go to school, what happen to them when they fall sick etc. - speaks for itself. In such a situation, we do not know if child's need for the warmth, love and affection of his/her family, particularly the mother, can even be considerered as being among the priority needs in the overall scheme of things. The world over, the mother is the main care giver. Woman prisoner's children especially vulnerable when she is taken away, if women prisoner is illiterate, as is the case most times, the bewildering circumstances of her arrest make it impossible for her to make any alternate arrangements for her children's custody and care. She has no information about what is happening to her children.

The Report of the National Expert Committee on Women Prisoners, 1987, headed by Justice V.R. Krishna Iyer, represents the most comprehensive treatise on the issue. The committee realised that despite constitutional mandates and exhortations at many forums, there is a heavy short-fall in the delivery of services to women in custody. It has articulated that women hood even in criminal wrappings and behavioural aberrations deserves to be nursed with dignity and restored to a normal life, using all the material, moral and spiritual resources at society's command. It has forcefully pleaded for the necessary improvement in the services for women prisoners in terms of basic amenities or basic needs, living conditions, facilities for education, vocational training, legal aid and after care, so as to protect their human dignity and to revive among them the essence of life. Lamenting as to how, women prisons are denied of their basic human rights, the committee has evolved three basic instruments to rationalise the policies and programmes for their well being and welfare in custodial setting. The national policy for custodial justice to women urges upon the Government to restructure laws and procedures governing women prisoners in consonance with constitutional provisions, international standards and judicial pronouncements. The legislative-cum-administrative code for custodial correctional and rehabilitative justice, as worked out by the expert committee, incorporates an elaborate framework for gender justice in prisons. The rules cover all the vital aspects of institutional management of women offenders such as segregation and classification, admission, property, dependent children, general treatment and daily routine clothing and equipment, accommodation, cleanliness and sanitation, amenities, letters and interviews, vocational training and labour, medical facilities, legal aid, counseling and restorative measures, facilities for foreign nationals, education, premature release, transfer, social relations and aftercare, insane and mentally ill female prisoners, discipline, punishment, requests and complaints, and female personnel.

Taking Care

Many non-government organisations in the country has taken up the care of women prisoners' children as a necessary corollary and a meaningful added dimension to their work with women in the cells. Taking this on has meant looking for and identifying the children based on, the often, sketchy information given by the mother. Arrangements have to be made for their food, clothes and medicines, as most children are found in states of extreme neglect. Along with these basics, the care-giver at the non-government organisations centers has to deal with the ill-effects of trauma on the child manifested through distress behaviors like excessive crying, incessant rocking, shock etc. If the period of the child's separation from his/ her family is prolonged, then arrangements have to be made for child's education to be taken up and sustained. At regular intervals, the social workers obtain permission from the prison authorities and take the children to spend time with their mothers in the prison.

Legislative

Any legal back-up that can bring about certain musts to the situations faced by these children appears rather obscure. Only young children below five are allowed to stay in the prison with their mother. Here too, it has happened that very young children have been overlooked. A support system consisting of the child's relatives/community is largely presumed to be available to look after the older children. In reality, such support is hardly sustained or consistent and in several instances, it is not even safe for the child. The Juvenile Justice Act makes a generalised reference to neglected juveniles. According to the Act, any such juvenile if brought to the notice of the police, has to be produced before the juvenile welfare board and can be sent to a state observation or remand home. At present, care of the women prisoner's children is thought of if:

- The mother, at the time arrest, makes a special request. Then, the children may be put into remand homes.
- While in the cell, the mother comes into contact with social workers, the circumstances demand a great deal of NGO initiatives for any thing to happen.

Inside the prisons, the female staff, who look after the women's cell and are in constant contact with the women prisoners, are the ones who can probably elicit such information. But in reality, they play a limited role and see their main responsibility as security. Also, given the prevalent, punitive atmosphere, the insensitive, often indifferent attitudes within prisons, the possibility of such humane interactions seems rather farfetched.

Needs

A silver lining has been the positive and sometimes compassionate response that has come from some senior officials and lower level staff of the police and prison departments, where Non-Government organisations could approach them in individual cases. But all of them are part of a system where any spark of desire to help in immediately crushed by the anxiety to maintain status quo; maintaining status quo is definitely the easier option considering there are no legal bindings for them to do otherwise.

To start with, departments and the people involved - police, prisons and courts must recognize and acknowledge and existence of the issue concerning their children. Part of the procedure at the time of arrest of a woman should include making enquiries about her children and their whereabouts.

The women should have the right to have immediate contact with an appropriate organization a bonafide non-government organisations-that can assist in making a decision about the immediate care of her children. However, it is highly unlikely that under the circumstances, the woman herself will be able to insist on this or be aware of whom to contact. So, representatives of such organisations, whose presence is not intimidating to the woman or her children, unlike the police, should be part of the arrest part.

At present, the Government department for women and children plays no role in issues concerning women prisoners or their children. To start with, they can augment and help expand the existing facilities availed at Non-Government organisations centers for children, to keep the children in safe surroundings, so that apart from the basics, the children's education and overall development can be looked after till such time that they are able to go back to their families. Another aspect in whole system that can make a vital difference is the attitudes of police and prison staff i.e. constables, prison wardens and other such staff. Sensitizing them to the whole issue should be taken up as a collaborative exercise involving the departments of police, prisons and non-government organisations working with children. The media heeds to be taken up the issue effectively so that society will eventually recognise its significance.

We stress effectively to emphasise that it does not help to present the pathetic situation of the children as a tearjerking "good story" of Non-Government organisations as doing "good work". The media should be part of lobbying groups and have a specific role to present facts so as to highlight the rights that these children have been denied.

The mother may or may not be guilty, but her children should not be punished.

- In the light of the recommendations of the National Experts Committee on Women Prisoners, 1987, the All India Committee on Jail Reforms, 1980-83 and the All India Jail Manual Committee, 1957-59 through the Ministry of Home Affairs and the Ministry of Welfare

are also legitimately concerned with prison administration and social defence, Department of Women and Child Development in the Ministry of Human Resource Development is ideally suited to assume the responsibility for the planning, implementation and monitoring of the programme for the welfare of women prisoners and their children.

- Department of Women and Child Development with representative of National Commission for Women, Central Social Welfare Board, National Institute of Public Cooperation and Child Development, Bureau of Police Research and Development and National Institute of Criminology and Forensic Sciences, along with eminent experts leading prison administrators may also serve as a vehicle for on-going research, training and standard-setting in this field.
- The rules relating to the treatment of women prisoners under the State Prisons Manuals may be revised immediately on the lines indicated by the National Expert Committee on Women Prisoners in the legislative-cum-administrative code for custodial, correctional and rehabilitative justice to women and the rules for the superintendence and management of female prisoners and children with them in jails.
- With a view to building up a national consensus on various aspects of the welfare of women prisoners, the Department of Women and Child Development may convene National Conference of State Jail Ministers and Home Secretaries. The implementation of the recommendations of the National Expert Committee on Women Prisoners may be taken up as the substantive agenda item for discussion at the proposed conference. The Ministry of Home Affairs, the Ministry of Welfare and the Planning Commission may also be actively involved in this endeavor.
- The Department of Women and Child Development may formulate a comprehensive scheme for the

welfare of women prisoners and their children. Additional female staff for custodial correctional and rehabilitative purposes, up gradation of basic amenities, nurseries/creches for dependent children. Training of staff responsible for women prisoners and support to voluntary welfare organisations associated with the programmes for women prisoners and their children in jails.

References

Bachman, R, & Saltzman, L.E. (1995), Violence Against Women: Estimates from the redesigned survey. Washington D.C.: U.S. Department of Justice, Bureau of Justice Statistics.

De young, M (1982), The Sexual Victimization of Children Jefferson, NY: Mc Farland.

Finkelhor, D & Browne, A. (1985), Child Sexual Abuse. American Journal of Ortho-psychiatry.

Fletcher, B.R. Shaver, L D & Moon, D.G. (1993), Women Prisoners: A Forgotten Population. Westport, C.T.: Praeger

Gutman, L.T. St. Clairae, K.Herman - Giddens, M.E. Johnston, W.W. & Phelps, W.C (1992), Evaluation of Sexually Abused and Non-Abused Young Girls for Intra-vaginal Human papillema Virus Infection, American Journal of Diseases in Childhood.

Report of the National Expert Committee on Women Prisoners, 1987

Schiff, A.F. (1977), A Statistical Evaluation of Rape, Forensic Science.

Wyatt, G.E. (1985), The Sexual Abuse of Afro-American and White American Women in Childhood, Child Abuse Neglect.

Zierler, S., Feingold, L. Laufer, D., Velentgas, P., Gordon, I., & Mayer, K., (1991), Adults Survivors of Childhood Sexual Abuse and Subsequent Risk of HIV Infection, American Journal of Public Health.

SECTION – IV

CHILD LABOUR AND HUMAN RIGHTS

17

Child Labour Welfare Legislations in India

Asha Singh

Introduction

Children constitute principal assets of any country. Children's Development is as important as the development of material resources and the best way to develop national human resources is to take care of children. India has the largest child population in the world. There are more children under the age of fourteen in India than the entire population of the United States. The great challenge of India, as a developing country, is to provide nutrition, education and health care to these children. Children under fourteen constitute around 3.6% of the total labor force in India. Of these children, nine out of every ten work in their own rural family settings. Nearly 85% are engaged in traditional agricultural activities. Less than 9% work in manufacturing, services and repairs and about 0.8% work in factories.

All out efforts are being made by India for the development and welfare of children. While child labor is a complex problem that is basically rooted in poverty, there is unwavering commitment by the Government and the people of India to combat it. India has been playing a lead role in advocating protection of children by signing various international declarations and agreements and has all along followed a proactive policy with respect to the problem of child labor. In addition, various state governments have also stood for constitutional, statutory and developmental measures to combat child labor and have passed acts to protect children from exploitation through employment. Six ILO conventions relating to child labor have been ratified; three of these as early as the first quarter of this century.

The first Act in India relating to child labor was the Enactment of Children (Pledging of Labor) Act of February 1933. Since then there have been nine different Indian legislations relating to child labor. The strategy of progressive elimination of child labor underscores India's legislative intent, and takes cognizance of the fact that child labor is not an isolated phenomenon that can be tackled without simultaneously taking into account the socio-economic milieu that is at the root of the problem.

The Government of India is determined to eradicate child labor in the country. The world's largest child labor elimination program is being implemented at the grass roots level in India, with primary education targeted for nearly 250 million. In this a large number of non-governmental and voluntary organizations are involved. Special investigation cells have been set up in States to enforce existing laws banning employment of children in hazardous industries.

Some special measures are urgently required to protect them from various kinds of adverse effects of the work undertaken by them.

Child Labour-Exploitation in Ancient Times

The concept of child protection was not unknown to ancient India. Manusmriti reveals the fact that education was necessary for the children. The fathers and mothers were punished by the community if they did not send their girls and boys to the hermitage of a Guru or University after their attaining the age of eight years. It means that after eight years no children should be left at home. They should be sent to schools for education.

Near the middle of the 19th century, mechanized large-scale production came into existence. At that time, employers in any industry were not subject to any legal restrictions. The employers were free to bargain with labour. Therefore, labour in this country was exploited by the employers for their benefits.

Child labour is a grave problem in India. The principal reason for the prevalence of child labour is economic. Poverty compels the low income, poor households to depend primarily on children's work and wages to supplement and support the family. The absence of social safety increases the dependence on child labour. It has existed in some form from time immemorial. But it was only after the advent of factory type units in the middle of the 19th century that children began being employed in industries where they worked for long hours under appalling conditions. The question of the regulation of the conditions of work for labour was first breached in 1875 by the appointment of a committee by the Bombay Government. After much deliberation, the first Act was passed in 1881. It only provided for the regulation of the working hours of children below twelve years of age. Children below seven years were not allowed to work. Between seven to twelve years of age, they could work for nine hours. This Act however applied only to units having 100 or more workers and using mechanized power.

Taking note of the situation, various legal measures were taken in the western countries as well as in India to protect the interests of the working child. Impressed by the developments in the West, Bombay Factory Labour Commission, 1885 stated: "On the average, only 15 holidays are given in Indian factories, while in England, besides 10 holidays there are 52 Sundays and 52 half Saturdays, making a total of 88 days altogether." It was also pointed out by this Commission that in the ginning and pressing works of Khandesh, in which majority of workers were women or children, the usual working hours were from 4 or 5 AM to 8 or 9 PM, but when working at high pressure they work sometimes day and night for eight days consecutively, until their hands are tired out and they lose their health.

In the beginning, any Act introduced by the British Government to restrict the employment of children in Indian Factories was criticized by the Indian Press. Even the leading nationalist and social reform newspapers, such as Indu Prakash (22 March 1880, 21 March 1881 and 4 August 1884), the Gujarati (28 March 1880 and 27 March 1881), the Indian Spectator (20 March 1881), the Native Opinion (27 March and 19 June 1881) and Dhyan Prakash (30 June 1881) protested against the legal measures affecting the industrial employment of children in India. According to these critics, children working in the mills enjoyed better health than those who attended the school. They also felt that if the boys were thrown out of employment they would be forced to beg, borrow or steal. The strongest objection to the factory legislation was based on the belief that it would retard the growth of the rising cotton textile industry by raising the costs of production and thus reducing competitive capacity vis-a-vis the mills of Lancashire.

In 1891, another Act was passed which applied to units having 50 or more workers. The minimum age for children was fixed at nine, and hours of work were seven for children between nine and fourteen years of age. However, the smaller units, where the worst abuse existed were not covered by the Act. Regulations however were not always enforced and evasion was frequent. In 1889, in a report on the working of the Factory Act, it was stated that in the Jabalpur Mill children worked from sunrise to sunset with a rest period of one hour. In the coalmines in Bengal, children were employed extensively underground. During the 1905 industrial boom with the introduction of the electric light, it was found that children often had to work 14 to 16 hours. The physique of the factory children was poor in comparison to other children. They had no opportunity of education, no training in skills and hence no chances of upward mobility. People gradually become conscious about the need to have some form of legislation, which could lead to the abolition of this evil practice.

Government has always put efforts to understand the problem of child labour. Various Committees have been set-up from time to time to look into the extent, distribution, working conditions and the related problems of the working children.

A brief resume of some of the reports of these committees is being discussed.

Report of the Royal Commission on Labour in India, 1930

The objective of the Royal Commission, also known as Whitley Commission, was to collect as much information on labour as possible in very short span of time. This information was derived from the published reports of the labour office and other printed matter in the possession of the labour office from unpublished data and the personal knowledge of the staff of the labour office.

In the comprehensive Report of the Commission, it was observed, inter alia, that the most noteworthy effect of the 1922 Act was that the employment of children in the mills, cotton spinning and weaving industry had reduced. In its occasional references about the working conditions of children, the Report mentions, "children usually work five hours a day without any interval. . . . In the smaller factories, hours of work are often long and machinery unfenced. Sanitation too, is often defective." It was also reported that Section 26 of the Indian Mines Act, 1923 under which no child could be employed in a mine, caused some hardship. It was observed that poverty, undoubtedly, induced some parents to sweat their children.

In the opinion of the Bombay Textile Labour Union on the employment of children as mentioned by the Royal Commission's Report (Vol. I, pp. 342-43), "the provisions of the Factories Act require amendment. The maximum age limit for the employment of children should be raised from twelve to fourteen years. This change may have an effect in reducing, to some extent, the ranks of unemployed persons in the industry. The employment of children in factories before eight in the morning and after five in the evening should be prohibited." This Union was also opposed to the double shift system in the factories, which, it was felt, affects the health.

The Employment of Children Act, 1938

1. The Act prohibits the employment of children below the age of 15 in any occupation connected with the transport

of goods or mail by railways, connected with a port authority within the limits of any port, or connected with any work on railway premises/Section 3(3)/a child who has completed his fourteen years will be allowed in the schedule is carried on/Section 3(3).

The Schedule

- Bidi-making,
- Carpet weaving,
- Cement manufacture,
- Cloth printing and dyeing and weaving,
- Manufacture of matches, explosives and fireworks,
- Mica cutting and splitting,
- Shellac manufacture and soap manufacture, 8. Tanning, and
- Wood cleaning.

2. The (State) government after a notification in the gazette and a notice period of three months may add any description of process to the Schedule.
3. The Act clearly states in Section 3(3) that family units and training schools of Government will not come under this provision.
4. Section 3-B states that before any work set out in the schedule is carried out in any workshop, the inspector must receive a notice from the 'occupiers' giving full details about the name and situation of the workshop, name of actual manager, and the nature of the processes to be carried on in the workshop.
5. Certificate of age of the child workers are required from a prescribed medical authority.
6. All employers employing children must maintain registers (Section 3-D), showing the name and date of birth of every child under 17 years of age so employed or permitted to work, the work and rest periods, the nature of work, etc.

7. Notices clearly stating abstracts of sub-sections 1 and 2 of Section 3 and Section 4 are to be prominently displayed at all railway stations and ports.
8. Violation of this Act can mean imprisonment from 3 months to one year and a fine from Rs. 500 to Rs. 2000. For someone who has been convicted earlier, the period of imprisonment can go up from 6 months to two years.

Report of the National Commission on Labour, 1969

The Commission was appointed in 1966 by the Ministry of Labour, Employment and Rehabilitation under the Chairmanship of Dr. P.B. Gajendragadkar to review the conditions of labour and suggest measures for their improvement. The Commission noticed that 8 percent of the workers were below 15 years of age, with most of them employed in agriculture and the allied activities. However, in the organized industries, the employment of children was declining. The employment of child workers below the prescribed age was also reported to be continuing in far off places and in rural areas where the enforcement of statutory provisions was more difficult. The Commission found that in certain industries such as glass, bidi, carpet manufacturing, etc., the conditions under which children worked were deplorable. It realized that the employment of children was more than an economic problem than anything else. The Commission felt that the early employment resulted in the denial of education to children; therefore, it suggested that the employment hours of children should be fixed in such a way so as to enable them to attend school. Where the number of children is adequate, the employers with the assistance of the State Governments should make arrangements to combine work with education.

Report of the Harbans Singh Committee, 1977

This Commission was to investigate the problems of child labour in various factories and industries in Ramanathapuram district of Tamil Nadu. The report was submitted in 1977, but was not made public. This report says that 40-45% of the labourers employed in the match industry are children. Girls outnumber boys; the ratio is three to one (3:1). Children work more than the stipulated hours of work, i.e., four-and-half hours per day. Leaving their homes as early as 3 a.m., children spend nearly sixteen hours away from home. "The provisions of both the Factories Act and Employment of Children Act are being violated with impunity." For violation of these Acts, if at all, some factory owners are punished but the punishment is very nominal.

The Committee feels that the "Child labour is one of the most crucial factors for the development of the match and fireworks industries in Ramanathapuram area . . . a community of interests has developed between the employers and employees as a result of which employment of children continues without protest. The government agencies have also been responsible for this" (para 10:4).

Accepting that banning child labour would not remove all the children from the labour force, the report suggests that the working hours should be reduced, wages should be increased and instead of the prevailing piece-rate system, the wages should be linked to the cost of living index. It is also recommended that the non-formal education should be given to children in the factories. School attendance should be made compulsory and it should be a precedent condition for employment in factories. However, the various recommendations suggest the radical measures to end the scourge of child labour.

Report of the Committee on Child Labour, 1979

The Committee was appointed in 1979 by the Ministry of Labour under the chairmanship of M.S. Gurupadswamy to look into details of the causes leading to and the problems arising out of the employment of children in India. The Committee investigated: (i) the dimensions of child labour and the occupations in which children were employed, and (ii) the existing laws, their adequacy and implementation. After making a statistical survey, the Committee documents the nature of exploitation of child labour in rural and urban economic activities. It highlights the condition of child labour in bidi manufacturing and glass bangle industry, handloom and carpet weaving industry, the precious stone polishing industry and in the domestic work, hotels, machine tools and repair shops. The Committee visited the match and fireworks industries of Sivakasi to make a through enquiry of the working conditions of children in this noxious occupation.

The Report highlights that it is not uncommon to find children working at the age of seven or eight in most of these industries. At meager wages, they work for prolonged hours and develop many physical problems. The extent of their exploitation can be guessed from the findings, such as, the young diamond-cutters develop eye defects very soon, but as the early signs of eye fatigue are detected, they are retrenched by the employers quite ruthlessly.

The Committee summarizes the situation of children in India as one of 'continuing drift'. "Though there is little evidence of children at work in the organized sector. . . the overall position is as had been observed by the Whitely Commission nearly fifty years ago. Bulk of the children continues to be employed in the rural environment. While most of them work without wages, there is an increasing number amongst them employed for wages and also of many working on jobs, which are hazardous. They handle dangerous chemicals and are also employed on machines with sharp edges and blades. Definite efforts are called for to prohibit their working in such occupations." The Committee emphasized that unless a systematic evaluation is made from time to time in respect of jobs in which children are employed and certain purposeful policy decisions are taken to meet the deficiencies, the existing situation is not likely to undergo any dimensional, qualitative or quantitative change.

The Committee has examined in details the laws dealing with children. It has found that the existing legal framework for employment of children in India is rather dispersed and patchy. It, therefore, concludes that there is a need for single model legislation on child labour in India, such that there are no anomalies on the issues like minimum wages, working hours, medical examination, penalties of offences, etc. It has suggested fixing the minimum age for entry in the workforce at fifteen years. To overcome the administrative inadequacies for the implementation of the laws, it suggested the need to involve social workers, voluntary organizations and trade unions as well as parents to assist the enforcement of legislative measures.

Report on Child Labour in Indian Industries, 1981

This Report is the result of a rapid survey conducted by the Labour Bureau in certain organized and unorganized sectors of Indian industries. The Report presents an account of the various aspects of child labour, e.g.; employment, wages and earnings, working conditions, welfare facilities, etc. In the organized sector, the following manufacturing products were covered: tea factories, cashew processing and making, wood and wood products, cotton textile and hosiery industries, match and fireworks, stone crushing and plantations. In the unorganized sector, survey was conducted in hand loom, bidi, glass bangles, carpet weaving, coir, fishing, and shops and commercial establishments.

It was found that in most factories the hours of work, as prescribed under the Act, were not being strictly adhered to. The Report, therefore, emphasizes the need to strengthen the enforcement machinery to make the employers fully conscious of their obligations towards child employees.

During the survey, it was found that children of very tender age were found working in certain industries, such as match box, hand loom, bidi, fishing, hotels and restaurants, repair shops, etc. The wages paid to the children varied from state to state and from industry to industry-from less than one rupee in plantations, and match and fireworks units to a maximum of five rupees in cashew processing, gur making and textile manufacturing. In most of the cases, the payment was on piece-rate basis.

The Report states that the majority of working children come from poor families to supplement their family income.

They are compelled to discontinue their studies, as there is no provision of night schools for those who want to continue studies. The Report emphasizes on bringing about a change in the social attitude towards child labour, besides tightening the laws and activating the enforcement machinery.

Legislative Framework for Child Labour

Apart from setting up various Committees to look into the conditions of working children and suggesting measures to improve their lot, government has passed various Acts to minimize the exploitation of this most vulnerable group of the society. The legislative measures, which have been taken from time to time, have been discussed below in chronological order. The need for such protective measures was felt when the industrial revolution started.

Legislations before Independence

- In 1850, an Act was passed regarding Apprentice Contractors, according to which any child would be bound as an apprentice for learning trade, craft or for employment upto a maximum of seven years.
- The Indian Factories Act, 1881, prohibits (a) the employment of children below 7 years in any factory, (b) the employment in two factories on the same day, (c) working period exceeding 9 hours a day. The Act also stated that at least four holidays should be provided in a month. This Act covered only those factories, which employed 100 or more persons
- In 1891, the Factories Act was revised. The new Act raised the minimum age for work to 9 years and reduced the working period to 7 hours in a day with the prohibition of work at night between 8 p.m. and 5 a.m.
- In 1901, the Mines Act was passed, which prohibited the employment of children below 12 years in mines, as it was dangerous to their health and safety.
- The Factories Act of 1911 prohibited the work by children in factories (a) between 7 p.m. and 5.30 a.m., and (b) in

certain dangerous processes. According to this Act, the certificate of age and medical fitness for the employment of children was also required.

- In 1922, the Factories Amendment Act was passed, which (a) raised the minimum age to 15 years in general, (b) fixed the working hours to a maximum of 6 hours and an interval of half an hour in between, (c) prohibited employment of children below 18 in certain processes. The scope of this Act was extended to establishments employing 20 or more persons with mechanical power.
- The Indian Mines Act, 1923 raised the minimum age from 12 to 13 years in mines.
- The Indian Ports (Amendment) Act, 1931, laid 12 years as the minimum age for handling goods in ports.
- The Children (Pledging of Labour) Act, 1933 stressed a penalty for parents and guardians who pledged the labour of the child. This Act was aimed at the most direct and blatant exploitation of children by adults.
- The Factories Act of 1934 made elaborate arrangements regarding the employment of children. The employment of children was prohibited under 12 years of age and restricted to only 5 hours for children between 12 to 15 years.
- The Indian Mines (Amendment) Act, 1935, inter alia, prohibited the employment of children in mines below 15 years of age.
- The Employment of Children Act, 1938, prohibited their employment in occupations connected with the transport of goods, passengers or mails on railways. It raised the minimum age for handling goods in docks from 12 to 14 years.

Legislations after Independence

At the time of independence, constitutional provisions were made to protect the rights of the child in India. Article 24 of the constitution provides, "No child below the age of 14 years shall be employed to work in any factory or mines or engaged in any other hazardous employment." Article 39 protects the children against arising due to their forced entry into vocations unsuited to their age and strength. Article 45 directs the State to provide free and compulsory education to all children until they complete the age of 14 years. Apart from that, various Acts have laid down provisions to provide legal protection to working children. These Acts, enacted chronologically, are as follows:

The Factories Act, 1948 prohibits the employment of children below 14 years to 18 years of age to obtain a certificate of fitness from a certifying surgeon and periodical examination. The Act prohibits employing children between 14 to 17 years at night (between 10 p.m. to 6 a.m.) between 14 and 15 years for not more than 4-$4^1/_2$ hours in any day, only one shift and in one factory. The Act prohibits employing children in certain processes within factories. They shall not be allowed to work on machines, which are considered dangerous. They shall not clean, lubricate or adjust any part of prime mover or of any transmission machinery while it is in motion or if they stand the risk of injury. They shall not be employed to press cotton if a cotton opener is at work in that area. The (State) Government may make rules prescribing the maximum weights, which may be lifted, carried or moved by children employed in factories. Every factory is supposed to maintain registers giving all details of child workers and weekly holidays and paid leave are also specified. The Factories Act does not apply to such factories where there are less than 10 workers with power and less than 20 workers without the aid of power.

The Minimum Wages Act, 1948 defines a child as a person below 15 years. It provides for minimum wages for children and apprentices. It also has provisions regarding hours of work (4-$4^1/_2$ hours in the case of a child) and physical fitness.

The Mines Act, 1952 also defines a child as a person below 15 years. The Act not only prohibits the employment of children in mines, but also prohibits the presence of children in any part of the mine, which is below ground or above ground where any mining operation is being carried on. A young person (between 16 to 18 years) is allowed to work in any part below ground if he has a medical certificate from a certifying surgeon about his fitness. Even then such person cannot work at night (between 6.00 p.m. to 6.00 a.m.). Punishment for violation is imprisonment upto three months or a fine upto Rs. 1,000 or both.

The Plantation Labour Act, 1951 prohibits employment of children below 12 years of age. It also regulates hours of work with no work at night. No child can be allowed to work for more than 40 hours a week and only between 6 a.m. and 7 p.m. It prescribes a few welfare measures for the children as well as education facilities for children of the plantation workers. The Act has the same provisions for offences and penalties as the Factories Act.

The Merchant Shipping Act, 1958 bars employment in any capacity of a person below 15 years in a ship except a training ship, home-trade ship or a ship of less than two hundred ton gross, or a ship where other family members work. No person below age 18 can be a trimmer or stoker in any ship and all persons below the age 18 years require a medical certificate. Such medical certificates are required at intervals of one year. The Act imposes a modest penalty of fine upto Rs. 50 for violation of the provisions.

The Shops and Establishment Act defines a child as a person below 12 years (in some states the minimum age is 14 years) and prohibits their employment in shops, commercial establishments, restaurants, hotels, etc. The hours of work are 7 per day in Andhra Pradesh, Bihar, Tamilnadu, Tripura, Pondicherry and West Bengal, 6 per day in Gujarat, Maharashtra, Jammu and Kashmir, Uttar Pradesh and Delhi, 5 per day in Himachal Pradesh, Madhya Pradesh, Karnataka, Orissa and Punjab, 3 per day in Rajasthan. Night work for children and young persons is also prohibited under State laws relating to shops and commercial establishments. It varies from 6 a.m. to 7 a.m. in the morning upto 7 p.m. to 9 p.m. at night. The various state governments have passed the Shops and Establishment Acts which are applicable within their states. The Act has often been amended to suit the given situation.

The Motor Transport Workers Act, 1961 defines a child as a person below 15 years and their employment is prohibited. A person between 15 and 18 years can be employed after obtaining a certificate of fitness and can work only 6 hours a day with a half hour rest period and not between 10 p.m. and 6 a.m.

Atomic Energy Act, 1962 has the minimum age as 18 years. The Beedi and Cigar Workers Act, 1966 prohibits employment of children below 14 years. No young person (between 14 and 18 years) shall be required or allowed to work except between 6 a.m. and 7 p.m. But this Act does not apply to private dwelling houses where a large percentage of Beedi and Cigar manufacture takes place on a sub-contracting system. The Factories Act will however apply if the number of workers employed exceeds the minimum laid down in the Act.

Radiation Protection Rules, 1971

A person shall not be qualified for being engaged as an apprentice to undergo apprenticeship training in any designated trade, unless he is above 14 years of age. The total number of hours for an apprentice shall be 42 hours to 48 hours per week, including the time spent on related instructions. No apprentice other than a short-term apprentice shall be engaged in such training between 10 p.m. and 6 a.m. The Act applies to such areas or industries as may be specified by the Central Government.

As can be seen from the above list of various Acts, the consciousness of the evils of child labour has been manifested in these legislative processes. However, it would be unrealistic to state that child labour can be completely and immediately abolished because it would result in untold misery to the affected families. Even the ILO has realized this and in its recent publications advocates regularizing child labour with improved working conditions as an interim measure before abolishing it. This does not mean that one overlooks the evils and the harm this does to the overall development of a child. The ultimate aim has to be the complete abolition of child labour as soon as possible. With this end in view, the new Bill on Child Labour called the "Child Labour (Prohibition and Regulation) Bill, 1986" was introduced and passed in Parliament during its winter session in 1986. The aim of the Act is "To prohibit the engagement of children in certain employments and to regulate the conditions of work of children in certain other employments." It will also obtain uniformity in the definition of "child" in the related laws. In the earlier Acts a child could be any person below the age of 12 to 16 years. From henceforth, "child means a person who has not completed his fourteenth year of age.

Child Labour (Prohibition and Regulation) Bill, 1986

The Act states right in the beginning that its aim is to 'prohibit the engagement of children in certain employments and to regulate the conditions of work of children in certain other employments'. According to this Act, the Employment of Children Act, 1938 is repealed. All rules made in this Act will be in addition to the provisions of the Factories Act, 1948, the Plantations Labour Act, 1951 and the Mines Act, 1952.

- According to this Act "child" means a person who has not completed his fourteenth year of age.
- Again, family units and training centers are not included in the purview of the Act.
- The Act provides for the setting up of "Child Labour Technical Advisory Committee" for the purpose of addition of occupations and processes to the Schedule. A notice of at least three months will be given by the Central Government before adding any occupation or process to the Schedule.
- The Act clearly lays down that no child will be allowed to work for more than six hours per day with a rest period of one hour after three hours of work. Once a week he will be given a holiday.
- No child will be allowed to work between 7 p.m. and 8 a.m. and no overtime will be permitted.
- The Act clearly states that the Government can make rules for the health and safety of children who are

permitted to work in any establishment. These rules can provide for matters such as cleanliness, ventilation, dust and fumes, lighting, drinking water and sanitary facilities, etc. but there is no mention of nutrition of medical facilities.

- The penalty for violation of the Act will range from three months to one year of imprisonment with a fine of Rs. 10,000 to Rs. 20,000.
- If a person is found guilty he will be liable for punishment under any of the previous Acts.
- Any person, police officer or an inspector can file a complaint of an offence under this Act in any Court of Competent Jurisdiction.
- Part B of the Schedule has added one more process into the existing list and that is "building and construction industry." All other provisions are similar to the ones already existing in the Act of 1938.

Comments on Child Labour Act, 1986

1. Both, the Acts of 1938, cover only the children in the organized sector and not the 90% in the unorganized urban and rural sectors and family units. How do occupations and processes, which are hazardous in the organized sector, become safe when performed in family or unorganized units? How can children be allowed to work anywhere in these occupations and processes? All Government training schools are exempt and hence can continue to train children at the young age of 7 and 8 and also use them for the production of items, which are sold commercially through Government emporia.
2. In the Schedule, many occupations which are really hazardous are not included, such as the glass and bangle factories, the slate industry, etc. However, the Technical Advisory Committee has been empowered to add other occupations and processes to the existing schedule.
3. The government in the Act of 1986 gives itself the time of 10 years in which, it claims, will abolish the serious

problem of child labour. The Government has had enough power to deal firmly with employers violating the provisions of the Children's Act of 1938, Factories Act of 1948, Minimum Wages Act, etc. for the past decades and yet this abhorrent exploitation continues. How does the government now feel that they can do away with this problem in 10 years time? The enforcement of the new legislation has again been left in the hands of Inspectors who have proved rather ineffective through all these years.

4. The great merit of the Act of 1986 is that it brings about uniformity in the definition of a child, minimum age for employment and conditions of work by repealing the Employment of Children's Act of 1938 and making necessary amendments in the other Acts.
5. The new Act does not specify how the welfare, health and safety of working children are to be protected. The Government has taken upon itself the task of providing all welfare measures leaving the employers rather free of this responsibility. From where will the Government get the massive funds, which are required for providing these facilities?
6. Increasing the penalty is not enough because the real deterrent for employing children would only be the closure of the erring units. As pointed out by Neerja Chowdhury in her article in The Statesman on 16th December, 1986, the Government should give economic incentives to those industrial units which switch to new methods of production, using new machinery and new technology so that children need not be employed and the work could easily be done by adults which, in the long-run would help to minimize adult unemployment. The Government could levy heavy tax on these industries, which continue to employ children.
7. The new Act empowers anybody to file a complaint against an offender in any court of competent authority. However, in the end the age of the working child will have to be proved for which dependence on a recognized medical

practitioner will be necessary. It has already been seen how unreliable some of these age certificates tend to be.

Role of International Labour Organization

The ILO has played an important role in the gradual elimination of child labour, since its inception in 1919. The programmes of ILO focus their attention on the five main issues: prohibiting child labour; protecting children at work; attacking the basic causes of child labour; helping children to adopt to future work life; and protecting children of working mothers. Highest priority was given to the abolition of child labour in the activities of ILO. A series of conventions and recommendations have been formulated to regulate and limit and gradually abolish child labour. The very first International Labour Conference adopted a convention which fixed the minimum age at 14 years for the industrial employment of children. The subsequent sessions of ILO adopted various conventions and recommendations concerning the minimum age of entry into economic activities. Till now, Conventions and 16 recommendations have been adopted by the ILO in the interest of working children all over the world. The conventions are as follows:

- Minimum Age (Industry) Convention (No.5), 1919.
- Night Work of Young Persons (Industry) Convention (No.6), 1919.
- Minimum Age (Sea) Convention (No.7), 1920.
- Minimum Age (Agriculture) Convention (No. 10), 1921.
- Minimum Age (Trimmers and Stockers) Convention (No. 15), 1921.
- Medical Examination of Young Persons (Sea) Convention (No.16), 1921.
- Minimum Age (Non-Industrial Employment) Convention (No. 33), 1932.
- Minimum Age (Sea) Convention (Revised) (No. 58), 1936.

- Minimum Age (Industry) Convention (Revised) (No. 59), 1937.
- Minimum Age (Non-Industrial Employment) Convention (Revised) (No. 60), 1937.
- Medical Examination (Sea-farer) Convention (No. 73), 1946.
- Medical Examination of Young Persons (Industry) (No. 77), 1946.
- Medical Examination of Young Persons (Non-Industrial Occupations) Convention (No. 78), 1946.
- Night Work of Young Persons (Non-Industrial Occupation) Convention (No. 79), 1946.
- Night Work of Young Persons (Industry) Convention (Revised) (No. 90), 1948.
- Medical Examination of Young Persons (Underground Work) Convention (No. 124), 1965.
- Minimum Age (Underground Work) Convention (No. 123), 1973.
- Minimum Age Convention (No. 138), 1973.18

The Convention No. 138 replaced all the previous relevant conventions. Its purpose was to establish minimum standards valid for all sectors of economic activity with a view to achieve total abolition of child labour.

To make this convention apply its principles easily, Recommendation No. 146 was adopted, which advocates, inter alia, a firm national commitment to full employment; the progressive extension of socio-economic measures to alleviate poverty and ensure high living standards to keep children away from economic activity; the development and progressive extension of social security and family welfare measures aimed at ensuring child maintenance including children's allowances; the development and progressive extension to adequate facilities for education and appropriate vocational training for children and young persons; the development and progressive extension of appropriate facilities for the protection and welfare of children and young persons, and for the promotion of their development; adoption of special measures for migrant children and young persons who do not live with their families; introduction of compulsory full time attendance at school till the age of admission to employment.

Due to poverty and unorganized nature of the Indian economy, the child labour laws have not been able to reach the standards set forth by the International Labour Organization. This is the reason why India has been able to ratify and implement only 6 conventions out of 18 adopted by ILO. These are:

- Minimum Age (Industry) Convention, 1919.
- Night Work of Young Persons (Industry) Convention, 1921.
- Minimum Age (Trimmers and Stockers) Convention, 1921.
- Medical Examination of Young Persons (Sea) Convention, 1921.
- Night Work of Young Persons (Industry) Convention (Revised), 1948.
- Minimum Age (Underground Work) Convention, 1973.

This minimum age convention of 1973 prescribed that the normal entry in the labour force should not be below 14 years of age in any of the occupations except the hazardous jobs, where it should be raised to 18 years.

Conclusion

The phenomenon of child labour is thus so complex and deep rooted in the socio economic fabric of the society that it may not be wise to rely on one single approach to dealing with it. There are many causes of this complex problem so a comprehensive integrated approach is required. There is no touch and vanish type solution of the problem. We will have to design our action plan keeping in view short-term and long-term perspective. We should first take measures for immediate improvement in conditions of work because in near future in the existing socio-economic climate, chances of complete eradication of child labour problem seems remote possibility.

Therefore, there is urgent need for attitudinal change, social awareness and aggressive campaign against the sources of child labour. It becomes our national obligation to ensure physical and mental development of these young ones. With measures for regulating and humanizing child labour along with attack on poverty, we hope that there would be gradual elimination of this problem. The eradication of the problem is a long process which requires intensive effort on many fronts and also creation of general social awareness and needs cooperation from different sections of society.

References

Gangrade, K.D. (1982), "Child and the Law", National Seminar on Child and Law, NIPCED, New Delhi.

Report of the Bombay Factory Labour Commission of 1885, p. 8.

Bipin Chandra (1969), "The Rise and Growth of Economic Nationalism in India", People's Publishing House, New Delhi, p. 336.

Central Act 9 of 1850.

Central Act 15 of 1881.

Central Act 11 of 1891.

Central Act 8 of 1901.

Central Act 12 of 1911.

Central Act 2 of 1922 Amending Act 12 of 1911.

Central Act 4 of 1923.

Central Act 11 of 1931.

Central Act 2 of 1933.

Central Act 25 of 1934.

Elias Mendelievich (ed.) (1979), Children at Work, ILO, Geneva, p.

Economic and Social Commission for Asia and Pacific (1980), No.1, September, p. 18.

"Child Labour in India", The Indian Journal of Public Administration, XXV (3), July-September, 1979, p. 936.

Elias Mendelievich; .op. cit., p. 156.

Constitution of India, Act 15 (3) Articles 23-24.

Dr. S.N. Dhyani, Jurisprudence: A Study of Indian Legal Theory, 1980, p. 70.

Indian Express 26th Aug. 1982.

Indian Factories Act, 1948, Section 24.

Journal of Labour Legislations (vol. XVIII, No. 3-6.)

Journal of Labour Legislations, Aug. 1987, National Labour Institute, Noida

Mohd. Mustafa and Onkar Sharma, Child Labour in India; A Bitter Truth, Deep and Deep Publications, New Delhi, p. 110.

Plantation of Labour Act, 1951, Section 24.

Prasad, Umesh, "Socio-Economic Problems of Child Labour: A Case Study", The Hindustan Review, Vol.-9, No.-7, Jan-April, 2002.

Section 3 (3)

Section 40 (i)

Section 70 (2)

Shandilya, T.K. and S.A. Khan (ed),(2003), Child Labour, A Global Challenge, Deep and Deep Publications Pvt. Ltd., New Delhi.

Shandilya, Tapan Kumar (1977), Child Labour in India, Dr. Ambedkar Journal of Social Sciences, MHOW (M.P.).

The Mines Act, 1952, Section 2 (i)

Vide Notification No GSR 847 (E) dated August 10 1988, Published in Gazette of India Extraordinary Pvt. II, Section 3 (i), dated 10.8.1988.

Working Children in India, Child Labour Cell, National Labour Institute, NOIDA, 1993, pp. 2-4.

18

Does Child Labour Displace Children Rights?—Issues and Prospectives

Nanjunda D.C.

Introduction

The decade since the adoption of the Convention on the Rights of the Child was marked by some significant advances on behalf of children. Many countries used the convention as the basis on which to revise domestic legislation and improve protections for children, or have appointed special ombudsmen persons or envoys for children. As the Committee on the Rights of the Child evaluated country reports under the convention, it developed new standards of protection and pressed governments for specific reforms.

United Nations Report (1996) on the impact of armed conflict on children raised international concern about the plight of children in war, prompting varied initiatives to end the use of child soldiers and other wartime abuses. The number of children killed every year by antipersonnel landmines dropped in the wake of massive efforts to end the use of the weapon and the adoption of the1997 Mine Ban Treaty. The adoption of the statute for the International Criminal Court held out the hope of ending the impunity of those responsible for the recruitment of children under the age of fifteen in armed conflicts, as well as those who commit other war crimes, crimes against humanity, and genocide.

However, despite these advances, the promises of the Convention on the Rights of the Child were broken for countless children around the world. The armed conflicts that raged in all quarters of the world produced appalling abuses of children's rights. Hundreds of thousands of children were pressed into service as soldiers. Millions became refugees, displaced from their homes, often separated from their families, their future and safety uncertain.

Children living outside war zones were also subjected to routine violence. Street children on every continent endured harassment and physical abuse by Policy. Even schools, intended to promote the healthy development of children, were the site of abuse. In some countries, the use of corporal punishment by teachers resulted in injury and even death. In others, gay and lesbian students endured harassment and violence by their peers while school authorities failed to intervene.

Millions of children had no access to education, worked long hours under hazardous conditions, or languished in orphanages or detention centers where they endured inhumane conditions and daily assaults on their dignity, in violation of the rights guaranteed to them under the convention. The issues selected for attention below represent those which were the focus of Human Rights Watch investigation and advocacy over the past half-decade. The tenth anniversary of the Convention on the Rights of the Child marked an important milestone. The rights of children were recognized as never before. But it also posed a challenge for governments and civil society to take stronger action to implement its provisions, strengthen protections and fulfill the promises made to the children of the world.

The Use of Children as Soldiers

In dozens of countries around the world, children were direct participants in war. Denied a childhood and often subjected to horrific violence, some 300,000 children served as soldiers in current armed conflicts. These young combatants participated in all aspects of contemporary warfare. They wielded AK-47s and M-16s on the front lines of combat, served as human mine detectors, participated in suicide missions, carried supplies and acted as spies, messengers or lookouts.

Physically vulnerable and easily intimidated, children typically made obedient soldiers. Many were abducted or recruited by force and often compelled to follow orders under threat of death. Others joined armed groups out of desperation. As society broke down during conflict, leaving children with no access to school, driving them from their homes, or separating them from family members, many children perceived armed groups as their best chance for survival. Others sought escape from poverty or joined military forces to avenge family members who had been killed.

Child soldiers were used in more than thirty countries around the world. Human Rights Watch investigated the use of child soldiers in some of these conflicts, including in Angola, Colombia, the Democratic Republic of Congo, Lebanon, Liberia, Sierra Leone, Sri Lanka, Sudan and Uganda. In Sierra Leone, thousands of children abducted by rebel forces witnessed and participated in horrible atrocities against civilians including beheadings, amputations, rape and burning people alive. Children forced to take part in atrocities were often given drugs to overcome their fear or reluctance to do so. In Colombia, tens of thousands of children were used as soldiers by all sides to the country's ongoing bloody conflict. In Southern Lebanon, when boys fled to desert or avoid conscription by the South Lebanon Army, an Israeli auxiliary militia, their entire families were subject to expulsion from the occupied zone.

Girls were also used as soldiers in many parts of the world. In addition to combat duties, Human Rights Watch found that girls were subject to sexual abuse and taken as "wives" by armed groups in Angola, Sierra Leone, and Uganda. Girls who were impregnated by rebel commanders were sometimes forced to strap their babies on their backs shortly after giving birth and take up arms against opposing forces.

Some governments took positive steps. Colombia significantly reduced the number of under-eighteens in its national security forces after pledging to uphold a minimum recruitment age of eighteen. The Sierra Leonean government excluded under-eighteens from its newly-formed military, based on pledges made to Olara Otunnu, the special representative for the secretary-general on armed conflict and children. The U.K. Government made a military aid agreement to the Sierra Leonean Government contingent on non recruitment of children and the demobilization and rehabilitation of former child soldiers, although it continued to use sixteen-and seventeen-year-olds in its own military force. Other states, including the Czech Republic, Germany, Norway, Portugal, and South Africa, passed legislation or introduced measures to exclude under-eighteens from their military forces.

Under the Convention on the Rights of the Child, the general definition of a child is any person under the age of eighteen. However, Article 38, governing children and armed conflict, uses fifteen as the minimum age for recruitment and participation in hostilities. This low standard of protection remained a glaring and troubling anomaly among the convention's other strong provisions.

Several years after the convention's adoption, a U.N. working group was created to draft an optional protocol to the convention that would raise the minimum age for recruitment and participation in hostilities to eighteen. However, as the tenth anniversary of the convention's adoption arrived, agreement on the optional protocol still had not been reached, largely because of opposition by governments who continued to recruit minors, notably the United States.

Despite these obstacles, efforts to stop the use of child soldiers continued to grow. In 1998, the recruitment of children under the age of fifteen and their use in hostilities was identified as a war crime in the statute of the International Criminal Court. Once established, the court will have jurisdiction to prosecute those responsible for the use of child soldiers. The use of children as soldiers was also recognized as a child labour issue. A labour treaty banning the worst forms of child labour adopted in June 1999, prohibited the forced recruitment of children for use in armed conflicts.

In 1998, the Coalition to Stop the Use of Child Soldiers formed in order to campaign for a strong optional protocol to the Convention on the Rights of the Child which would prohibit any recruitment of children under the age of eighteen or their use in armed conflict. Established by six international NGOs, the coalition worked with national campaigns in more than thirty countries around the world, mobilizing political will and public pressure to end the use of children as soldiers. In addition to media campaigns, the publication of new research and advocacy within regional and international fora, its activities included a series of high profile regional conferences focused on the use of children as soldiers in Africa, Latin America, and Europe. Despite this growing momentum, efforts to stop the use of child soldier did not reach fruition. Recruitment of child soldiers continued around the world, those responsible for their recruitment escaped justice and key governments continued to resist efforts to establish and enforce the prohibitions necessary to end the use of children as soldiers.

The International Criminal Court

On July 17, 1998, in Rome, delegates representing 160 countries voted by an overwhelming majority to establish a permanent International Criminal Court (ICC) to try persons charged with committing war crimes, crimes against humanity, and genocide. Upon its establishment, the court will provide a powerful deterrent to the conscription, enlistment, or use in hostilities of children under the age of fifteen years conduct defined as a war crime in the ICC statute. The statute also included other important measures to protect children in armed conflict: it recognized intentional attacks on educational institutions as a war crime, provided special arrangements for children as victims and witnesses, and exempted children below the age of eighteen from prosecution by the court.

Delegates reconvened at the United Nations headquarters for three weeks in July and August of 1999 to draft the rules of procedure and evidence for the court and the elements of the crimes covered by the statute. Two proposals introduced by the United States and by Costa Rica, Switzerland, and Hungary would have restricted the scope of the statute's provisions on the war crime of conscripting, enlisting or using children in hostilities. The U.S. proposal would have required the prosecutor to prove that the accused knew the child in question was below the age of fifteen. The proposal by Costa Rica, Switzerland, and Hungary would have required a showing that the accused knew of or was "willfully blind" to the child's minority. In addition, both proposals would have required proof that the accused caused the child's conscription, enlistment or use in hostilities.

Human Rights Watch said that the court should have jurisdiction over cases in which the accused recklessly failed to take steps to ascertain the child's age. Such a position, we argued, would be consistent with Protocol I. Additional to the Geneva Conventions, which requires states to "take all feasible measures" to ensure that children under the age of fifteen do not take an active part in hostilities. Human Rights Watch also pointed out that encouragement, acceptance or authorization of a child's enlistment or participation in hostilities should be sufficient conduct for the court to exercise jurisdiction.

A subsequent discussion paper, produced by the coordinator of the delegates' working group on the element of crimes, reflected these recommendations. It required prosecutors to show that the accused "knew or should have known" that the child in question was under the age of fifteen years phrasing that recognizes an obligation to attempt to determine the child's age. The discussion paper did not reflect a consensus among delegates, and was introduced to provide a basis for further discussion. It nevertheless reflected awareness that the court must have adequate discretion to interpret the statute's language for the benefit of children in armed conflict.

Refugee Children

Refugee children were among the most vulnerable children in the world. Not only had they suffered from war or other forms of persecution in their countries of origin, but many refugee children continued to suffer human rights abuses in countries of asylum. Children made up more than half of all refugees around the world, yet their rights and special protection needs as children were frequently neglected.

The human rights abuses that drove children into flight were only the first chapter of hardship for many refugee children. Even after travelling across an international border to seek refuge, they remained vulnerable to hazardous labour exploitation, physical abuse, denial of education, sexual violence and exploitation, cross-border attacks, militarization of refugee camps and recruitment as child soldiers.

Article 22 of the Convention on the Rights of the Child grants special protection to refugee children. Children who are not being cared for by their parents, known as "separated children" are entitled to special protections under Articles 20 and 22. Refugee children fleeing war are also entitled to special protection under Article 38 of the convention, as children affected by armed conflict. Refugee children, like all children, are entitled to all other rights granted under the convention including the rights to life, physical integrity, adequate food and medical care, education and to be free from discrimination, exploitation and abuse.

Separated and unaccompanied children were particularly vulnerable. In the United States, Human Rights Watch found that unaccompanied children were held by the U.S. Immigration and Naturalization Service in detention facilities where some were confined for lengthy periods of time before being released to family members or appropriate guardians. Rarely understanding what was happening to them, children were often denied information about their detention and their right to be represented by an attorney in immigration proceedings in a language they understood. In some cases they were housed with juvenile offenders and subjected to a rigid and punitive environment.

In 1999, Human Rights Watch conducted an in-depth investigation into the protection of Sierra Leonean refugee children in Guinea, where children made up 65 percent of the 300,000 Sierra Leonean refugees there. Most of the children interviewed by Human Rights Watch had been in refugee camps in Guinea just over a year, with little hope of returning home in the near future. Internally displaced children within Sierra Leone were thought to suffer many of the same problems on an even larger scale.

The plight of separated children and girls in the Guinean refugee camps was found to be particularly severe and warranted special attention. Separated children were taken in by families along the way while fleeing, or in the camps. These families acted as care givers or foster families. However, some children in such care were neglected, physically or sexually abused, denied food, denied education or exploited for their labour. Social workers charged with protection of separated children in the refugee camps in Guinea had not even identified most children of concern, much less monitored their care and protection.

Human Rights Watch found that Sierra Leonean refugee girls as young as twelve felt they had no choice but to work as child prostitutes in order to support themselves and in some cases, their families. These girls had little or no access to education or health care and little hope for their future. Better identification and monitoring systems were clearly needed to ensure effective interventions.

Refugee children who lived in camps close to the porous Sierra Leone-Guinea border were vulnerable to cross border armed raids which resulted in murder, mutilation and abduction of dozens of refugees over the past year. According to international law and standards, as well as United Nations High Commissioner for Refugees (UNHCR) policies, the refugees should not have been in camps located dangerously close to the border in the first place.

Refugee children were also at risk of being recruited and used as child soldiers. In Guinea, Sierra Leonean refugee children as young as seven risked being abducted by raiding rebel forces or being used by the government civil defense forces, known as Kamajors.

Despite the fact that these children suffered enormously and remained extremely vulnerable, their plight was largely ignored by the international community. UNHCR faced substantial political, financial, and logistical challenges in protecting the human rights of refugee children in Guinea. The focus of international attention on refugee crises in Europe as well as "donor fatigue" with respect to Asian refugees, served to limit resources available for Guinea. One manifestation of this was a grossly insufficient number of staff present inside or near camps. UNHCR also faced severe logistical constraints in the Gueckedou area of Guinea, which housed more than sixty camps. One was the poor state of the unpaved roads, which were often impassable during Guinea's June to November rainy season. However, the failure to adequately protect the rights of refugee children was only partially attributable to a lack of resources.

Although UNHCR had used the Convention on the Rights of the Child as the basis for extensive policies and guidelines designed to protect the rights of refugee children in many cases, these policies were not implemented. For Sierra Leonean children in Guinea, the international community failed to identify vulnerable children; to monitor for abuse and labour exploitation; to protect girls from sexual abuse and exploitation; to move the refugees to safe locations away from the border; to preserve the humanitarian character of the refugee camps and to prevent refugee children from serving as child soldiers.

Policy Abuse and Arbitrary Detention of Street Children

Attention to street children focused largely on their pressing economic and social plight poverty, lack of shelter, denial of education, AIDS, prostitution and substance abuse. With the exception of mass killings of street children in Brazil and Colombia, little attention was paid to the Policy violence and abuse inflicted on these children, or their treatment within the justice system through which they regularly passed. Civil and political rights violations against street children were largely overlooked, symptomatic of the larger failure to take seriously the full scope of children's rights enshrined in the Convention on the Rights of the Child.

Viewed as "anti-social" or criminal elements, or a scourge on a city's tourist-filled streets and business districts, many Policy and ordinary citizens simply wished street children would disappear, by whatever means. Street children throughout the world were subjected to routine harassment and physical abuse by Policy, government and private security forces, out to wipe the streets clean of a perceived social blight. Street children faced extortion, theft, severe beatings, mutilation, sexual abuse and even death.

They were often arrested and jailed because of their homelessness (on vague grounds such as vagrancy or loitering) or their involvements in small businesses deemed to be illegal, such as unlicensed hawking, or were accused of petty theft, drug-related crimes, or prostitution. Some were arrested as scapegoats, or in order to finger or catch others. Many Policy believed street children had information about crimes committed on their beat, or attributed crimes in the area to them directly, imputing criminal associations and activities to the children generally.

They were held for excessive periods of time in Police lockups, for days and even weeks, usually mixed with adults. In jails, they were sometimes further beaten by Police, or forced to pay bribes in order to be released. Girls were sometimes coerced into providing sexual services to Police in exchange for release, or were raped. From jails, street children were transferred eventually to long-term penal institutions, sometimes euphemistically called "homes" or "schools" where they languished out of sight for years.

Few advocates spoke up for these children, let alone lawyers or prosecutors, and street children rarely had family members or other concerned adults able to intervene on their behalf. Often, family members were not informed of their children's arrest and detention in the first place. Contrary to popular belief, many street children actually had family members and homes to which they returned periodically and were not orphans.

Over the years, Human Rights Watch had attempted to highlight the serious nature of the human rights abuses committed against street children by law enforcement personnel in Brazil, Bulgaria, Colombia, Guatemala, India, Kenya, and Sudan, and on the gross lack of Police accountability for abusive actions. Widespread impunity and the slowness of law enforcement bodies to investigate and prosecute cases of abuses against street children allowed violence against street children to continue unchecked.

Even in Guatemala where the NGO Casa Alianza had been singularly active in seeking Police accountability for the rape, torture, and killing of street children, only a handful of prosecutions resulted out of hundreds of criminal complaints filed. Frustrated with the failure of the national judicial system to address these cases, Casa Alianza and the Center for Justice and International Law brought a landmark case involving the Policy killings of five street youth in 1990 to the Inter-American Commission on Human Rights and subsequently to the Inter-American Court of Human Rights, where the case was pending at the time of this writing. Still, violence against street children in Guatemala continued and the government was as slow as ever in responding to the abuse.

The case of Guatemala demonstrated that even where there were strong advocates willing and able to assist street children in seeking justice, without the commitment of governments, the judiciary and most importantly law enforcement itself, the abuses would continue.

Children in Conflict with the Law

In the ten years following the adoption and near-universal ratification of the Convention on the Rights of the Child, a growing number of countries modified their juvenile justice laws to guarantee children the rights set forth in the convention and in other international instruments. This trend was most evident in Latin America, where many countries enacted reforms to bring their legislation into compliance with the convention. Brazil, one of the first to reform its national laws comprehensively in response to the Convention on the Rights of the Child, adopted its Children's and Adolescent's Statute in 1990. Ecuador and Peru passed Juveniles Acts in 1992,

Mexico adopted its Law on the Treatment of Juvenile Offenders in 1991, El Salvador enacted a new juvenile justice law in 1995, and Nicaragua adopted a Children's Legal Code in 1998 after a two-year delay Grounded in the principle that all children possessed rights which must be respected by the state, these reform efforts represented a significant departure from earlier legislation directed exclusively at "minors" in "irregular situations" and in need of protection.

In other countries, reforms were under consideration but had not yet been enacted into law. Efforts to reform Guatemala's juvenile justice system stalled in early 1998, when the government delayed for the second time the implementation of a new Minors' Code that would represent a vast improvement over current legislation. Among other protections, the code would guarantee the right to a lawyer at government expense to children accused of crimes, would forbid placing children in protective custody in juvenile detention centers and would end the practice of imprisoning children for "status offenses" such as running away or being homeless. A similar proposal was pending in Venezuela.

Nevertheless, a large number of countries in the region and elsewhere in the world had not taken action to bring their legislation into compliance with the convention. In America, Argentina and Paraguay, among others, retained outdated juvenile laws that did not adequately protect children's rights; in Colombia, the 1989 Juveniles Act was little more than a repackaging of earlier legislation.

Where legislative reforms had taken place, the practices in many countries fell far short of their new legal standards. In Mexico, as the U.N. Committee on the Rights of the Child observed in 1994, a large number of children complained of ill-treatment at the hands of Policy and military personnel. In Nicaragua, although the law provided that children should be housed separately from adults, children continued to be commingled with adults because of the lack of appropriate juvenile facilities. In the Dominican Republic, the government's near-complete failure to enforce the country's 1994 minor's code led to the confinement of hundreds of adolescents in adult prisons, where youth were not afforded sufficient protection, education or rehabilitation.

Trial and Sentencing Practices

Far too often, children around the world were brought to trial and sentenced in ways that violated their rights. Human Rights Watch documented systemic failures to guarantee children legal representation and otherwise provide them with fair hearings in Brazil, Bulgaria, Guatemala, India, Jamaica, Kenya, Pakistan and Russia. Of particular concern were sentences that violated the International principle that deprivation of liberty should be a measure of last resort and for the shortest appropriate period of time and prohibiting measures that constituted torture or cruel, inhuman or degrading treatment.

In many cases, children were detained arbitrarily or indefinitely on the basis of vague legal provisions. In Kenya, Human Rights Watch's investigation found that street children were committed for years to juvenile correctional institutions after they were found to be "in need of protection or discipline" in summary proceedings without legal representation. Similarly, in Paraguay and other countries in the Americas that had not brought their laws into conformity with the Convention on the Rights of the Child, children were detained on the ill-defined basis that they were in a "state of danger."

In other instances, state authorities simply flouted laws intended to protect the due process rights of juveniles. Our 1996 investigation of Bulgaria found that children were often detained in Policy lockups far longer than the legally permissible periods without being formally charged and without any judicial review. In India, we found that Policy regularly detained street children without giving them any grounds for arrest and failed to bring them before magistrates in the time period required under India's Juvenile Justice Act. In a 1999 investigation of Policy practices in Russia, adolescents in various cities told Human Rights Watch that Policy routinely violated Russian law and international standards by interrogating them sometimes under torture in the absence of attorneys.

In Jamaica, Trinidad and Tobago and elsewhere in the English-speaking Caribbean, juvenile court judges were authorized to impose sentences of flogging for certain crimes. In addition, children in detention in these countries were subjected to corporal punishment as a method of discipline. Similarly, Pakistan's Hudood Ordinances permitted judges to include whipping, usually between fifteen and thirty lashes, as part of children's sentences; in practice, however, that portion of the sentence appeared to be routinely overturned on appeal. In Kenya too, corporal punishment by cane or rod is authorized by law in sentencing children and as a disciplinary measure in correctional institutions for children. The imposition of corporal punishment is prohibited by international standards. Moreover, the U.N. bodies charged with monitoring states parties' compliance with the International Covenant on Civil and Political Rights, the Convention against Torture and Other Cruel, Inhuman or Degrading Treatment or Punishment, and the Convention on the Rights of the Child have all indicated that corporal punishment is incompatible with those human rights treaties.

Conditions of Confinement

Throughout the world, children were subjected to appalling conditions of confinement that violated international standards. Often held with adults and subjected to beatings at the hands of guards and other detainees, children in confinement were frequently denied adequate food, medical and mental health care, education and access to basic sanitary facilities. All of these children would eventually return to society, meaning that the failure to prepare them for their return was shortsighted as well as cruel, carrying enormous social costs.

The practice of holding children in adult facilities, common in many parts of the world, exposed children to abusive conditions including physical and sexual abuse far worse than those they would have experienced in juvenile facilities. In Cambodia, for example, children were housed indiscriminately with adult detainees and reportedly sexually abused and subjected to other forms of physical and psychological violence at the hands of adults. In Guatemala, Human Rights Watch interviewed children commingled with adults who reported beatings and rapes by adults and being forced to give up their clothing to adults, or to pay money to adults in order to get a place to sleep.

The United States continued to incarcerate large numbers of children in response to a perceived upsurge in violent juvenile crime. In fact, the number of juvenile offenders consistently fell from 1994 to 1997; according to U.S. Federal Bureau of Investigation data, juvenile arrests declined each year with an overall decrease of nearly 4 percent for the period. Juvenile arrests for violent crimes were down by 6 percent during the same time period.

Many youth in the United States were charged in the adult criminal system under state laws that made it easier for children to be tried as adults. Between 1992 and 1998, at least forty U.S. states adopted such legislation. A similar measure was pending at the federal level in 1999. Forty-two U.S. states detained youth in adult jails while they awaited trial. As a result, whether or not they would ultimately be found innocent, many children faced the prospect of spending six months to one year or more of their formative adolescent years behind bars pending trial.

In State of Maryland (U.S.), Human Rights Watch found that youth held in adult jails were subjected to the risk of violence at the hands of other juveniles and, in some facilities, from adult detainees. These risks were particularly high in the Baltimore City Detention Center, where some 150 adolescents faced daily risks to their personal safety, at times from fights condoned or even organized by corrections officers. Disciplinary measures there often appeared to be arbitrary and excessive with many youth and sometimes the entire juvenile section, receiving the maximum sanction of ninety days confinement to their cells. With few exceptions, the Maryland jails visited by Human Rights Watch suffered from serious deficiencies in the amount of education provided a dearth of age-appropriate recreational activities and an apparent lack of specialized training programs for staff in adolescent development and behavior management. In addition, children in all facilities reported that they did not receive enough to eat.

Commendably, some countries took positive steps to acknowledge and correct abusive conditions of confinement. The South Asian government initiated a program in November 1997 to keep children out of the country's prisons, although delays in implementing the program threatened its effectiveness. Another deficiency in the program was that children between the ages of fifteen and eighteen who were accused of the most serious crimes would remain in adult prisons. In Bangladesh, the government accepted the need for improvements in conditions of confinement for children in conflict with the law, in particular noting in its 1997 supplementary report to the Committee on the Rights of the Child that "Too many minors are held in jails and Policy stations alongside adult offenders." In Jamaica, following the July 1999 release of the findings of a Human Rights Watch investigation of the practice of detaining children in filthy and overcrowded Policy lockups, the government announced that it would move all detained children to juvenile facilities.

The Death Penalty and Juvenile Offenders

The Convention on the Rights of the Child unequivocally prohibits the use of the death penalty on juvenile offenders, those who were under the age of eighteen at the time of their crimes. Nevertheless, countries like Iran, Pakistan, Saudi Arabia, the United States and Yemen are known to have executed juvenile offenders in the 1990s.

The ten executions of juvenile offenders in the United States during this period represented more than half the known worldwide total, making it the worldwide leader in executing juvenile offenders. Five executions took place in the U.S. State of Texas; the States of Georgia, Louisiana, Missouri, Oklahoma and Virginia each executed one juvenile offender in the same period. Sean Sellers, executed in Oklahoma in February 1999, was the first sixteen-year-old offender to be put to death in the United States in forty years. Seventy juvenile offenders were on death row in the United States as of July 1, 1999.

In positive developments, the highest court of the U.S. State of Florida ruled that the imposition of the death penalty on sixteen-year-old offenders was cruel and unusual punishment in violation of the state constitution and effective October 1, 1999, the State of Montana abolished the death penalty for those under eighteen at the time of their crimes. As a result, nineteen of the forty U.S. states that permit capital punishment now prohibit the execution of offenders who were sixteen years old and younger at the time of their crimes; fifteen of the remaining twenty-one states restrict that punishment to adult offenders.

As these conditions came to light, the international community responded. In the past decade, the European Union provided more than (U.S.) $75 million to improve the plight of abandoned Romanian children. Funds were directed not only towards emergency food, clothing and medical care but also toward creating and implementing policies to prevent child abandonment. In 1999, the United States Agency for International Development developed a program to channel (U.S.) $6 million to Russian organizations working to keep families together and further develop foster care and alternatives to institutional care for orphans and abandoned children. In China, staffing and medical care in orphanages improved and the government worked to encourage adoption of abandoned children. Despite these encouraging developments, orphans and abandoned children continued to be institutionalized at alarming rates and too often failed to receive adequate care and protection.

Finally, while numerous international standards exist which protected the rights of children confined in penal or correctional institutions and settings, no comparable international standards exist to protect the rights of abandoned or orphaned children. Human Rights Watch advocated the use of alternatives to institutionalization of children wherever possible, including support for families or extended families and foster care with placement in small residential care facilities as a measure of last resort.

Violence against Children in School

For many children around the world, violence was a regular part of the school experience. In some countries, school officials routinely used corporal punishment to maintain classroom discipline and to punish children for poor academic performance. In other countries, authorities failed to intervene to protect minority children from harassment and attacks by other students. The failure of school officials to protect children from violence in school denied them their right to be free from all forms of physical or mental violence and the full enjoyment of their right to education.

School Corporal Punishment

School corporal punishment remained widespread and an accepted part of the class room experience for millions of children around the world, where the human rights violations inherent in its use went unrecognized. In many countries, the use of corporal punishment by teachers against children was explicitly authorized by law, making it a legalized form of violence against children.

The U.N. Committee on the Rights of the Child, the U.N. Committee against Torture, the U.N. Human Rights Committee, and the European Court and Commission of Human Rights took a strong stand against corporal punishment in schools on the grounds that it may rise to the level of torture or cruel, inhuman or degrading treatment or punishment. The Committee on the Rights of the Child was particularly outspoken, stating that the use of corporal punishment against children was incompatible with the Convention on the Rights of the Child and it frequently proposed the revision of existing legislation and the development of education campaigns to prevent the physical punishment of children. The use of corporal punishment violated the right of children to be free from violence, debased their dignity and physical integrity, interfered with the development of their physical and mental health and infringed on their basic right to education. Human Rights Watch worked to highlight these abuses, undertaking a fact-finding mission to Kenya and issuing its findings in August 1999. Kenya's School Discipline Regulations authorized the use of corporal punishment in schools but failed effectively to regulate its use. Nominal restraints were routinely ignored by teachers and the regulations rarely enforced. Teachers caned children for "offenses" such as tardiness, talking in class, wearing torn or dirty uniforms, being unable to answer a question or failing to achieve target marks set on exams. These measures often resulted in bruising, swelling and small cuts; at times, however, children suffered more serious injuries such as sprained or broken fingers or wrists, knocked-out teeth, internal injuries and even death.

Unsurprisingly, school corporal punishment did little to further its supposed educative purpose and had far-reaching and harmful consequences for children. Aside from the common physical injuries and the extreme cases of death which resulted, the practice produced psychological scars that stayed with children for the rest of their lives. Research in Kenya found that the use of corporal punishment instilled a fear of the classroom for some children that impaired learning and at times led children to drop out of school altogether. Other research showed that corporal punishment could be a significant factor in the development of violent attitudes and actions in childhood and later life.

Violence Based on Sexual Orientation

In United States and other countries around the world, gay, lesbian, bisexual and trans-gendered students too often experienced school as a place that accepted intolerance, ostracization and violence against those perceived to be different. For the most part, school officials refused to intervene to protect these students, allowing what began as harassment to escalate to physical violence. Studies by the U.S. Department of Health and Human Services, the States of Massachusetts and Vermont, and the Seattle, Washington school district found that students who were subjected to harassment and violence at the hands of their peers frequently suffered from depression, low self-esteem and an inability to focus on schoolwork; most alarmingly, the studies concluded that gay, lesbian, bisexual and transgendered students were two to three times more likely to attempt suicide than their heterosexual counterparts.

Conclusion

Various policies and programs are investigated. There is no one perfect policy or program that solves the issue of child labour completely by itself, useful to reflect on the pros and cons of various approaches to eliminate child labour and to protect children. It seems any zero-tolerance approach is counter-productive since such policies fail to address the root of causes of child labour from various dimensions. Poverty itself is not the only problem; neither is poor education quality. Legislative bans, international boycotts of products, enforcement of compulsory education, etc. can harm working children and their families. The problem is that all those partially effective policy interventions have been implemented in isolation from each other. It is not until recently that even reforming basic education started to take some position as an effective strategy to eliminate/reduce child labour. Child labour is not a sectoral problem. What is important and what has been learned from experience in order to combat child labour, is to fight against the problem with a multi-faceted and multi- dimensional policy approach that balances economic, legislative, educational and social interventions. In addition, involving all the stakeholders, such as teachers, parents, children and employers in the discussion of child labour is also important. There are multiple reasons to eliminate child labour and multiple reasons to justify existing child labour among various stakeholders, which implies that positive effects for one group may be negative effects for another. National governments in most countries in the world have not been enthusiastically involved in the issue of child labour and have failed to be a leading agency to combat child labour. Many interventions to combat/reduce child labour have been implemented by international organizations and domestic and international NGO's. Although the CRC has been ratified nearly universally; for example, this impressive world-wide human rights movement does not correspond to actions in law, policy, and practices in most nations. It is political will, not poverty that constraints universalization of compulsory education and elimination of child labour. Without governments' serious commitment and involvement, it may be difficult to achieve universal compulsory education and to combat the root of child labour.

References

Alderman, H,J. Behrman, V. Lavy and R. Menon (1997), "Child Nutrition, Child Health and School Enrollment", Police Research Department, Washington DC: World Bank.

Bekombo, M. (1981), "The Child in Africa: Socialization, Education and Work." Ch. 4 in G. Rodgers and G. Standing (eds.) *Child Work, Poverty and Underdevelopment*, ILO: Geneva.

Becker, G. S. (1979), An Equilibrium Theory of the Distribution of Household Income and Intergenerational Mobility. *Journal of Political Economy, 87*, 1153-1189.

Becker, G. S. (1997, May 12), Is There Any Way to Stop Child Labour Abuses? *Business Week (Industrial/Technology Edition)* 22.

Hadded and Aldemore, (1999), Intra Household Resource Allocation in Developing Countries: Models Methods and Policy *Paper Presented in conference organised by John Hopkins University-USA*, March11-14.

Dhagamwar, 1999, Child Rights, Family Needs and State Interests: Contradictory or Complementary *Lecture delivered at the workshop on; Needs Vs Rights: Social Policy from a Child Centered Perspective:.* IDS and JNU, New Delhi, July 28-30.

Steven (2004), Compulsory Schooling Laws and the Cure for Child Labour. *Bulletin of Economic Research, 56*(3), 227-239.

Patil, B. R (1986), The Urban Industrial Working Child in India, *Paper presented in seminar conducted in Singapore*, Feb 21-23.

Ravallion and Wodon, (1999), Does Child Labour Displace Schooling? Evidences on Behavioral Responses to an Enrollment Subsidy. *Paper presented at the Annual Conference of the Royal Economics Society*, University of Nottingham, UK June 12-16, 1999.

Singh, Abha (1998), *United Nations and the Rights of the Child: A Study of Child Labour in India*. New Delhi: J.N University.

19

Child Labour and Indian Law

Savita Bajaj and S.K. Khandelia

Today there are no two opinions that the children are the hope of parents and future of the nation and thus be given adequate opportunities and facilities for developing themselves. The growth of the child into a mature and happy person with fully developed personality largely depends upon the support and attention he receives from the society. If a child does not get proper education, diet and other facilities, has very development into a self sustaining human being is dwarfed. The child because of his physical and mental imn :turity needs special safeguards; it becomes, therefore, the duty of the state to protect children's right by legislative and other means. The needs and requirements of the child, the primordial ground norm of this universe, the most innocent and helpless human being incapable of enforcing his legal rights, but to speak of demanding new rights obligate the state to secure him distributive justice. As distinguished from adults, children are peculiarly susceptible to certain harms. They cannot raise their voice against those who injure them or deprive them of their rights. The peculiar position of the child arising from his physical and mental disability and position of dependence recognizes the need for the special provisions in many matters and the law should take care of all these in the interest and general welfare of child. The protective arm of the law has; therefore, to be long and strong enough if distributive justice to the adults of tomorrow is to be secured.

Child labour is not a new phenomenon to our age. What is new, however, is its perception as a social problem the world over. There has been a distinct of the legitimizing groups of society vis-a-vis child labour because of some new developments.

A generally valid definition of child labour is presently not available either in the national or international context. Any definition turns upon the precise meaning we attach to two components of the term "child labour," i.e., "child" in terms of his chronological age, and "labour" in terms of its nature, quantum and income generation capacity. Child labour, however, can broadly be defined as that segment of the child population, which participates in work either, paid or unpaid.

The definition of child labour varies from one act to another depending upon the seriousness of the problems of children working in a particular employment. The precise age of what constitute child labour has not been laid down anywhere because of variations in the age of child as given under different legislative enactments. Section 82 of the Indian Penal Code, 1860 reads: "Nothing is an offence which is done by a child under 7 years of age. Section 83 of the Indian Penal Code provides, "Nothing is an offence which is done by child above 7 years and under 12 years who has not attained sufficient maturity of understanding to judge the nature and consequence of his conduct on the occasion. Section 105 of Indian Evidence Act, 1872, lays down, "When a person is accused of any offence, the burden of proving the existence of circumstances bringing the case within any of the general of special exception including that of childhood of the Indian Penal Code of any concerning law is upon him. Under the Indian Majority Act, 1874, the age of majority has been fixed at 18 years. Under the Vaccination Act, 1880, children have been defined as persons, "who have not attained the age of 14 years in case of boys and 18 years in case of girls." Under the Reformatory School Act, 1887, "youth offender" means any boy who has been convicted of any offence punishable with imprisonment for life or death and who at the time of such conviction, was under the age of 15 years. The Child Marriage Restraint Act, 1929 (Sharda Act) defines child as a "male below twenty-one years and a female below eighteen years of age." According to Employment of Children Act, 1938, "No child who has not completed his fifteen years shall be employed or permitted to work in any occupation. No child who has completed his fifteen years but has not completed his seventeenth year shall be employed or permitted to work in any occupation unless the period of work of such child for any day are so fixed as to allow an interval of rest for at least twelve consecutive hours which shall include at least seven consecutive hours between 10 P.M. and 7 A.M. as may be prescribed. No child who has not completed his fourteenth year shall be employed or permitted to work in any workshop within any of the processes set forth in the schedule is carried on. Under the Motor Vehicles Act, 1939, child has been defined as a person under the age of 18 years. According to the U.P. Children Act, 1951, "child" means a person under the age of 16 years. As per the Plantation of Labour Act, 1951, "child", means a person who has not completed his fifteenth year." Section 24 of the Act lays down: "No child who has not completed his twelfth year shall be required or allowed to work in any plantation. Under the Suppression of Immoral Traffic in Women and Girls Act, 1956, "girl" means a female who has not completed the age of 21 years. According to the Orphanages and Charitable Horns (Supervision and Control) Act, 1960, "child" means a boy or girl who has not completed the age of eighteen years. As per the provisions of the Children Act, 1960, "child" means a boy who has attained the age of 18 years. In the Merchant Shipping Act, 1958, employment of children below fifteen years as seamen has ordinarily been prohibited. Persons below eighteen years cannot be employed as trimmer and stokers. According to the Motor Transport Worker's Act, 1961, "child" means a person who has not completed his fifteen years. Section 21 of the Act provides: "No child shall be required or allowed to work in any capacity in any motor transport undertaking." Section 22 lays down: "No adolescent shall be required or allowed to work as a motor transport worker in any motor transport undertaking unless (a) a certificate of fitness granted with reference to him is in the custody of the employer, and (b) such adolescent carries with him while he is at work, a token giving a reference to such certificate." "Adolescent," according to Section 2(a) of the Act, "means a person who has completed his fifteenth year but has not completed his eighteenth year.' Under the Radiation Protection Rules, 1971, framed under the Atomic Energy Act, 1962, "A child has been defined as a person below eighteen years of age." According to Section 2(2) of the U.P. Dookan Aur Vanijya Adhishthan Adhiniyam, 1962, "Child" means a person who has not completed his fourteenth year. Section 1 of the Act clearly says: "No child shall be required or allowed to work in any shop of commercial establishment except as an apprentice in such employment as may be notified by the state government in the gazette." In Shops and Commercial Establishment Acts passed by other states and union territories, child has been defined as a person between 12 and 14 years. Due to this variation in age of child in different laws, the child labour will have to be defined in the context of a vocation in which a child is employed. According to Section 2(b) of the Bidi and Cigar Workers (Conditions of Employment) Act, 1966, "child" means a person who has not completed fourteenth year of age. Section 24 of the Act provides, "No child shall be allowed to work in any industrial premises."

The word 'child labour' has been differently defined in various studies. According to the committee on child labour," "Child labour, however, can broadly be defined as that segment of child population in work either paid or unpaid." In their study of working children in Bombay; Singh and others have held a view: "child labour means a working child who is between 6 and 15 years of age, is not attending school during the day, is working under an employer or is learning some trade as an apprentice. In the study titled as working children in urban Delhi conducted by the Indian Council of Child Welfare, "Every child below 14 years, who contributed to the family income or was gainfully employed including those marginally working, was treated as a worker." V.V. Giri has expressed the view: the term "child labour is commonly interpreted in two different ways: first, as an economic practice and second, as a social evil. In the first context, it signifies employment of children in gainful occupations with a view to adding to the total income of the family. It is in the second sense that the term child labour is now more generally used. In assessing the nature and extent of social evil, it is necessary to take into account the character of the jobs on which children are engaged, the danger to which they are exposed and the opportunities of development of which they have been denied. Homer Folks, Chairman of the United Nation Child Labour Committee, has defined child labour as or any work by children that interfere with their full physical development, their opportunities for a desirable level of education of their needed recreation. Kulshreshtha is of the view that, child labour in a restricted sense means the employment of child in gainful occupations, which are dangerous to their health and deny them the opportunities of development. The term child labour not only applies to the children working in the industries but also to the children in all forms of non-industrial occupations which are injurious to their physical, mental, moral and social development." According to Alakh Narayan Sharma, "Child labour means the employment of children in gainful occupations (in industrial as well as non-industrial occupations) which are injurious to their physical, mental, moral and social development. Thus, the term includes wage-labour as well as self-employed children working independently as well as in family enterprises. Child labour therefore, can be defined here as any work undertaken by children below 14 years in such works which are injurious to their health, and harmful to their proper development.

The problem of child labour in India is also of immense magnitude when one considers the number of children involved. According to the 1971 census, there were 10.74 million children working, representing 4.66 percent of total population and 5.95 per cent of the total labour force. According to the 1981 census, workers in the age group below

14 years of age (excluding Assam) were 13.59 million. On the basis of the National Sample Survey (32nd Round), the number of child workers as on 1st march, 1983 was 17.36 million. The working children mainly belong to the age group 5-14 years. Nearly 93 per cent of the total child labour force works in the rural areas and the rest in urban areas. A majority of these children work in agriculture and the unorganized sector like small commercial establishments and shops or quasi-family undertakings. 79 per cent are employed as cultivators or agricultural labourers, 8 per cent in livestock, forestry, plantations, etc., 6 per cent in household and other services, the rest in trade, commerce and transport. Various surveys conducted to do light job, such as helping in the field, in factories for packing, pasting of labels, etc., and in match factories, tea factories, tea estates, beedi manufacturing, printing, publishing, etc. Unorganized sector employs a large number of children as domestic servants, works in hotels, restaurants, canteens, wayside shops, newspaper selling, coolies, shoes-sine boys, vendor, etc. Though Indian law does not prohibit the employment of children in cottage industries, family house-holds, restaurants, or in agriculture yet it is quite evident that the working conditions of the children in these small organizations is far inferior to those of large factories.

According to the report prepared by the Indian Social Institute, 80 per cent of all child labourers belong to the scheduled castes and tribes that have been exploited and marginalized in India for centuries. A major consequence of this is the deprival of the possibility of education and the consequent upward modality. Thus child labour has become a mode of perpetuating an unjust social system and of ensuring the continued availability of subservient, unskilled, illiterate labourers who do not have the bargaining power to question the system that marginalizes them and deprives them of their right to be human."

In the long list of dubious distinctions, India famous for child labour comes on the top. The wholesale and unchecked exploitation of children of less than 14 years is a punishable crime under the Indian law. But a selfish and immoral political leadership, corrupt bureaucracy, rampant poverty, growing unemployment and a society bereft of values have all conspired to turn India into the "largest concentration of child labour in the world". In India every third child is working child and every fourth child in the age group 5-15 is employed. An estimate by the International Labour Organization puts the number of child workers in India at 44 million. But an unofficial survey estimates the number of working children at around 100 million while 21 per cent of the child workers are urban based, the rest are rural- based. There is hardly any product in India that has no child labour behind it. Lock, Carpet, Bangle, Brick, Matchbox, Cracker, Woodcarving or any other product has the invisible stamp of the tail put in by children caught in the web of poverty and an exploitative social system. Indeed, child labour in India comes cheap and easy.

The Constitution of India carries important expression of the government policies against the abuse of child labour. Fundamentally, the Constitution provides that 'no child below the age of fourteen (as against the U.N. Declaration of fifteen) years shall be employed to work in any factory or mines or engaged in any hazardous employment. It further proclaims that the state shall, in particular direct its policy towards securing that the health and strength of the tender age of children are not forced by economic necessity to enter avocations unsuited to their age or strength. It further enjoins that childhood and youth are to be protected against exploitation, also against endeavours to provide free and compulsory education for all children until they complete the age of fourteen years.

Besides the above mentioned provisions, there are also certain other provisions contained in part IV, dealing with the Directive Principles of State Policy, which although do not lay emphasis on the child welfare directly, yet the children are bound to be the beneficiaries if these provisions are implemented. The Directive Principles of State Policy embodied in the Constitution of India provides policy of protection of children with a self imposing direction towards securing the health and strength of workers, particularly to see that the same in the children of tender age is neither abused, nor they are forced by economic necessity to enter into avocations unsuited to their age or strength, and are only protected against exploitation but also from moral or material abandonment under the policy Article-45 casts a duty on the state to provide free and compulsory education for all children until they complete the age of 14 years. The pious promises of the lawmakers, the profile on eradication of child labour is not too assuring. The only solution there is to minimize the child labour exploitation.

The government agency is principally responsible for abolition of child labour exploitation. Welfare Department should set up a separate monitoring unit to maintain a continuing review of the adequacy of existing legislation. Articles 24, 38, 41, 42, 43, 46, 47, and 39 all contain such provisions, which provide strategy for indirectly promoting the welfare of the children. Article 15 (3) confers right on the states to make special provisions for women and children to protect them. Similarly, Article 23 confers a fundamental right against certain forms of exploitation. The provisions of the Indian Penal Code provide punishment for such exploitation like forced and this Article gives a constitutional sanction to punishment.

Article 24 of the Indian Constitution states "no child below the age of 14 years shall be employed to work in any factory or mine or engaged in any other hazardous employment." Article 38 (l) provides that state shall strive to promote the welfare of the people by securing and protecting as effectively as it may secure a social order in which justice, social, economic and political shall inform all institutions of national life. Naturally, an effective implementation of this principle resulting in promoting the welfare of the people through social, economic and political justice is expected to promote proportionately the child welfare.

Article 39 (e) lays down that "the health, strength of workers, men and women and the tender age of children are not abused and that citizens are not forced by economic necessity to enter a vocation unsuited to their age or strength."

Article 39 (f) states that childhood and youth are protected against exploitation and against moral and material abandonment.

Similarly, according to the provisions of Article 41, it is required that the state shall within the limits of its economic capacity and development, make effective provision for securing inter-alia, the right to education and to public assistance in case of unemployment and other cases of undeserved want. Implementation of such provisions is expected to promote the welfare of the children proportionately.

According to the provisions of Article 42 of the Constitution, the state is required to secure just and human conditions of work besides some maternity benefit. This provision envisages a healthy psychological environment to the child particularly during the significant period when the child requires a normal bringing-up.

Article 43 of the Constitution lays emphasis that the state shall endeavour to secure by suitable legislation to all workers–agricultural, industrial or otherwise; not only but also living wage with specified conditions of work ensuring a decent standard of life and full enjoyment of leisure and social and cultural opportunities. This provision also includes child labourers in its widest interpretation. Article 46 of the Constitution, similarly lays down that the state shall promote with special care the educational and economic interests of the Scheduled Castes and Scheduled Tribes and other weaker sections of the society. The children belonging to such category are the worst affected and need to be constitutionally protected. Similarly Article 47 of the Constitution lays emphasis that it shall be the primary duty of the state to raise the standard of living of its people, which includes children.

On the basis of the foregoing discussions of the Constitution provisions, the assessment of progress made against child labour exploitation or the welfare measures provided to them appears to be disappointing. However, basing on the ILO Conventions and Recommendations and the Declaration of the Rights of the Child adopted by the

General Assembly of the United Nations, more than 250 Central and States Laws were enacted pertaining to children. A broad classification in which these enactments fall is– marriage, legitimacy, guardianship, maintenance, adoption, criminal law, reformatory services, probation, prohibition of smoking, suppression of immoral traffic, child welfare, prevention of vagrancy and beggary, transfer of property, education of children, child health and child labour and many other miscellaneous matters.

In regard to child employment several laws were passed with an objective of improving working conditions of such children and in protecting them against abuse, exploitation and health hazardous. One such law, the Employment of Children Act was passed in 1938 and was amended as many as five times during the years 1939, 1948, 1949, 1951and 1978 only to ameliorate better working conditions to such children. Several other Acts such as the Factories Act, 1951; Motor Transport Workers Act, 1962; etc. regulate the conditions of work that affect children. Many such as laws are honored more in the breach than in observance. It would also be desirable to discuss the recommendations of the National Committee on Child Labour set up by Government of India in 1972, which were entrusted the task of examining laws, their adequacy and the corrective actions required to improve the implementation of such laws. Considering these, it can be stated that the economic problems involved in the employment of children are very much significant. The poverty resulting with inadequate family income and the desire to supplement the family needs compel the children to work. Indeed the parents of many of low-income group cannot afford to educate their children even if education is free or compulsory. For them an uneducated child is an asset because an educated becomes a double liability of:

- Loss of earning if the child did not work: and
- Additional expenditure on child's education

Secondly; in the legislative field, the socio-legal problems vested in the employment of children frustrate the objectives of child labour exploitation because of the following:

- Children who are orphans, restitutes, neglected and abandoned are required to work for subsistence;
- Children who are otherwise required to work for a living are circumvented to work; and
- Children belonging to the migrant families are compelled to work as child labour.

As a matter of fact, our constitutional framework and national policy for child welfare take into account the various phases of child development. But a large number of legally uncovered gaps due to administrative hindrances frustrate the objective of child welfare. In order to avoid the same a comprehensive secular law on child, placing the 'child' in the Concurrent List, by amending the Constitution, would help in proper implementation of welfare programmes for the children and the comfortable co-operation between Centre and States would render quick administrative actions.

Denial of opportunity of the children due to economic difficulties would necessarily hinder the social progress of the child forced to fate employment. Therefore, it is necessary that the hours of work of child labour be fixed in such a manner as to enable him to attend the schooling and if the number of child labourers are more than an organised non-formal education system if imparted at the child's working place, possibly it would help educating him.

The penal provision in various labour legislations is inadequate in respect of violation of working hours and there by the employer remains undeterred. It is, therefore, desirable to prescribe certain deterrent punishment (serve penalty and cancellation of license) so that the commission of similar offence is not repeated and such punishment may also set an example to other employers not top violate the legal prescriptions.

In spite of all the constitutional and conventional protection accorded to the child workers in our country; the fact remains that children of tender age are forced to take up economic pursuits to augment the income of their family in most of the cases in the lower income bracket.

At the time of making the Constitution, it was envisaged that within 10 years, all the States would make primary education compulsory. But unfortunately till 1983, the states like Bihar, Manipur, Meghalaya, Nagaland, Orissa, Sikkim, Tripura, Arunachal Pradesh and Mizoram had no Act or rule in favour of compulsory primary education. In Orissa, the State is empowered to declare any area for introduction of compulsory education under section 4 (i) of Orissa Basic Education Act of 1951, but no such declaration has been made so far regarding any area. In the states of Andhra Pradesh, Gujarat, Haryana, Himachal Pradesh, Karnataka, Maharashtra, Punjab, Rajasthan, Tamilnadu, Uttar Pradesh and West Bengal penal action for not sending the children to school is also provided in the act, but till 1983, there was not a single case of prosecution in whole of India for not sending the children to school and never any penal action was enforced. The guardians of the law are very superficial regarding the rights of the children. It seems that only the vocal groups get advantage and children will have to be vocal.

The Child Labour (Prohibition and Regulation) Act, 1986

The Act states right in the beginning that its aim is to 'prohibit the engagement of children in certain employment and to regulate the conditions of work of children in certain other employments.

According to this Act, the Employment of Children Act, 1938 is repealed. All rules made in this Act will be in addition to the provisions of the Factories Act, 1948, the Plantations Labour Act, 1951 and the Mines Act, 1952.

- According to this Act "child" means a persons who has not completed his fourteenth year of age.
- Again, family units and training centres are not included in the purview of the Act.
- The Act provides for the setting up of "Child Labour Technical Advisory Committee" for the purpose of addition of occupations and processes to the schedule. A notice of at least three months will be given by the Central Government before adding any occupation or process to the schedule.

- The Act clearly lays down that no child will be allowed to work for more than six hours per day with a rest period of one hour after three hours of work. Once a week he will be given a holiday.
- No child will be allowed to work between 7 p.m. and 8 a.m. and no overtime will be permitted.
- The Act clearly states that the Government can make rules for the health and safety of children who are permitted to work in any establishment. These rules can provide for matters such as cleanliness, ventilation, dust and fumes, lighting, drinking water and sanitary facilities, etc. But there is no mention of nutrition or medical facilities.
- The penalty for violation of the Act will range from three months to one year of imprisonment with a fine of Rs. 10,000 to Rs. 20,000.
- If a person is found guilty, he will be liable for punishment under the clauses given in section 14 (1 and 2) and not under any of the previous Acts.
- Any person, police officer or an inspector can file a complaint of an offence under this Act in any Court of Competent Jurisdiction.
- Part B of the Schedule has added one more process into the existing list and that is "building and construction industry." All other provisions are similar to the ones already existing in the Act of 1938.

Comments on Child Labour Act, 1986

- Both, the Acts of 1938 and 1986, cover only the children in the organised sector and not the 90% in the unorganised urban and rural sectors and family units. How do occupations and processes which are hazardous in the organised sector become safe when performed in family or unorganized units? How can children be allowed to work any where in these occupations and processes? All Government training schools are exempt and hence can continue to train children at the young age of 7 and 8 and also use them for the production of items which are sold commercially through Government emporia.

- In the Schedule, many occupations which are really hazardous are not included, such as the glass and bangle factories, the slate industry, etc. However, the Technical Advisory Committee has been empowered to add other occupation and processes to the existing schedule.
- The Government in the Act of 1986 gives itself the time of 10 years in which, it claims; it will abolish the serious problem of child labour. The Government has had enough power to deal firmly with employers violating the provisions of the Children Act of 1938, Factories Act of 1948, Minimum Wages Act, etc. for the past forty years, and yet this abhorrent exploitation continues. How does the Government now feel that they can do away with this problem in 10 years time? The enforcement of the new legislation has again been left in the hands of Inspectors who have proved rather ineffective through all these years.
- The great merit of the Act of 1986 is that it brings about uniformity in the definition of a child, minimum age for employment and conditions of work, by repealing the Employment of Children Act of 1938 and making necessary amendments in the other Acts.
- The new Act does not specify how the welfare, health and safety of working children is to be protected. The Government has taken upon itself the task of providing all welfare measures leaving the employers rather free of this responsibility. Where will the Government get the massive funds which are required for providing these facilities?
- Increasing the penalty is not enough because the real deterrent for employing children would only be the closure of the erring units. As pointed out by Neerja Chowdhury in her article in *The Statesmen* on 16th December, 1986, the Government should give economic incentives to those industrial units which switch to new methods of

production, using new machinery and new technology so that children need not be employed and the work could easily be done by adults which, in the long-run, would help to minimize adult unemployment. The Government could levy a heavy tax on those industries which continue to employ children.

- The new Act empowers anybody to file a complaint against an offender in any court of employment competent authority. However, in the end, the age of the working child will have to be proved for which dependence on a recognized medical practitioner will be necessary. It has already been seen how unreliable some of these age certificates tend to be.

The implementation of child labour laws in our country is very ineffective. The main reasons for this are the lack of adequate enforcement machinery, lack of political will, deliberate attempt of employers to flour the legal provisions and the lack of consciousness within the minds of the parents themselves who will obtain false age and medical certificates to enable their children to work. The number of labour inspectors is pitifully low. They can barely visit all the factories in their jurisdiction. In any case, small unregistered units and the cottage industries do not come in their purview. The inspectors can easily be bribed by the bigger factory owners who keep false certificates and make false entries in their registers (if registers exist at all). When the inspectors come, the children are hidden away or put into innocuous jobs. Few years ago, when a five member parliamentary team headed by the then Union Labour Minister, Mr. P.A. Sangma, visited Firozabad, they discovered 50 children who were locked into dark, dingy rooms to keep them hidden from the visiting team. The other units had given the children a 'holiday' because the inspection had been previously announced. After the visit, Mr. Sangma issued a time-bound ultimatum to the employers to end child labour within two months or face punitive action. Almost 4,000 children have subsequently been released from this work and four units have already been closed down.

By far the largest numbers of working children are in the agriculture sector where laws about minimum wages, hours of work, minimum age, etc. just do not apply. It would be impossible to enforce these laws because many more inspectors would be required who would have to travel vast distances to locate areas where the laws are being violated. The problem of enforcement exists in all the wage earning activities in the rural areas. Similarly, children working in family undertakings and in the urban informal sector are excluded entirely from the coverage of the relevant legislation.

Effectiveness of Child Labour Act, 1986 in Controlling Child Labour

According to Section 3 of the new Act, there is prohibition on employment of children who are below 14 years of age in any of the occupations specified in the Part A or in any workshop wherein any of the processes set forth in Part B of the Schedule (Act, 1986). The list of occupations and processes listed in the Employment of Children Act, 1938. In other words, child labour has not been abolished in any new occupation or process in which it was not already abolished. There has been no improvement in that regard.

Power is however given to the Central Government to make additions to the schedule after giving due notice. Similar powers have been given to the Government under other laws, such as Minimum Wages Act, Contract Labour Act, Payment of Wages Act, Payment of Bonus Act, Payment of Gratuity Act, Maternity Benefit Act, etc., for extending the application of those Acts. Considering the manner in which the powers vested in the Governments under these laws have been utilised one cannot be sanguine that the powers conferred on the Government to extend the scope of the Act with respect to prohibition of child labour will be employed any better in the near future.

The Act makes a provision for constituting a committee to advise the Central Government for the purpose of making additions to the schedule. This provision is also analogous to those obtaining in other Acts like the Contract Labour Act,

Equal Remuneration Act, etc. It cannot be said that these advisory bodies have been quite effective in securing better implementation of the respective Acts. There is no reason to think that the Committee set-up under this Act will be more effective unless it is invested with more powers.

In Part III of the Act certain provisions have been made to regulate the conditions of work of children employed in occupations and processes other than those specified in the Schedule. In other words, there is no prohibition on the employment of children, whatever their age is, except in the scheduled occupation processes.

Thus, according to the schemes contained in the labour legislation of some of our neighbouring countries, no child is allowed to work below a particular age that is 12 or 15 and employment of children above the minimum age upto higher age is regulated. In India, on the other hand, employment of children is totally prohibited in certain occupation processes while it is sought to be regulated in other employments without any age limit. It is a moot question whether India could also not have a provision analogous to those obtaining in the neighbouring countries.

The provisions in the Act regarding regulation of the employment of children are not complete. It is left to the appropriate Governments to prescribe the conditions except as follows:

No child shall be required to work for more than three hours at a stretch and for more than six hours in all including the time spent in waiting for work and periods of rest. No child shall be permitted or required to work between 7 p.m. and 8 a.m., no child shall be required to work overtime. Every child shall have one whole day as a holiday in each week. The Act provides for the appointment of inspectors for the purpose of securing compliance with the provisions of the Act. There is similar provision in many other Acts. While more and more provisions are being made for appointment of inspectors in various laws, necessary measures have not been taken to ensure that those provisions are operated upon effectively. Firstly, while more and more work load is being added to the inspectors, there has been no corresponding augmentation in their strength. Secondly, they lack the required training or motivation and thirdly, they do not have the required facilities. Few Governments have been able to make adequate provision of funds for their pay and allowances, especially travelling allowance, so that inspectors could not restrict themselves to move out for inspection for dearth of funds. Jan Breman in his article entitled "I am the Government Labour Officer" (*Economic and Political Weekly*, June 15, 1985) has described at length how the Government Inspectors have acquired a negative image among workers and how ineffective they are.

The provisions for inspection in the various laws call for rationalization and simplification. Unless the much needed reform is carried out in the organisation and methods of inspection, the legislative provision for inspection is not likely to achieve the object of enforcing the laws effectively. The Act has enhanced the penalties for contravention of the provisions of the Act. Under the Employment of Children Act, 1938 whoever employed a child where it was prohibited and punishable with simple imprisonment which could be extended to one month or with fine which could go up to five hundred rupees or with both. The new Act provides for a similar offence a punishment of imprisonment for not less than 3 months which may extend up to one year or with fine which shall not be less than Rs. 10,000 and may extend to Rs. 20,000.

Similarly, the penalties for other offences have also been enhanced. Effectiveness of these provisions depends on the effectiveness of the enforcement machinery and the labour judiciary. It is well known that the problem of child labour is a socio--economic problem and not a matter that can be settled by mere legislation, better enhancement of the laws or by imposition of heavy penalties. The National Commission on Labour had therefore recommended as follows:

"Para 27-39: The employment of children is indeed more of an economic problem than anything else. Nevertheless, we consider denial of opportunity to children for their proper physical development and education to be an issue of a serious nature. Keeping in view the larger interests of the society, while the economic difficulties are real, a way has to be found to give the child the necessary education in his more receptive years. We feel this can be ensured by fixing the employment hours of children so as to enable them to attend to schooling. When the number of children is adequate, the employers, with the assistance of State Government should make arrangements to combine work with education." The Committee on Child Labour has also made a similar recommendation: (Para 4-3 of the report).

Planning Commission also emphasises on improvement in the working conditions of child labour so as to make them better and more acceptable socially, improved legislation coupled with better enforcement of the laws and making efforts to bring non-formal education to child workers.

One distinct improvement the Act makes over the existing law is to enhance the penalties for violation of the law and to make provision for appointment of inspectors. If the conditions of labour can be improved by deterrents, these provisions should be more than adequate but considering that employment of child labour is more of a socio-economic problem than a legal problem and considering also that much of the child labour is outside the reach of the law, in the rural and the unorganised sector, one cannot be hopeful that these provisions will go far in regulating child labour. What child labour needs now more than anything else is a programme under which their health is protected, they receive the nutrition they require and they are given some education while they have necessarily to continue to work. No provision has been made in this regard in the Act.

Having regard to all these facts we come to the conclusion that the Child Labour (Abolition and Regulation) Act is somewhat misdirected and falls much short of the high expectations. One cannot be sanguine that its impact would' very effective so far as the child labour problem in our country in the present scenario is concerned.

It is very unfortunate that though the Indian Children and also the child labour are protected legally, in fact, there is no mechanism operating properly in the state level or in national level to look after the welfare of the children. We, the Indians, are very much vociferous of our different types of moral values but at no time, majority of us considered that protection of children is moral duty and obligation of our social and communal life. There are several legislative measures to protect the children of the country, but any number of legislative measures will be useless if the adult members of the society and the guardians of the children are not conscious of their duty and obligation to the children.

As the ILO Report on the protection of children and young workers has so rightly emphasised, the problem of prohibition of child labour is inextricably mixed up with the problem of the maintenance of the child and provision of a living wage for all employed persons adequate to maintain the family at an adequate standard. Mere passing of some legislations or giving slogans in the government-controlled media will not solve the problem, unless some sincere efforts are made by public and private organizations to scientifically examine the cause effect relationships behind child labour prevailing in different regions of our country in prescribed remedial measures.

Thus; even after independence, numerous welfare legislations have been enacted by the both centre and state governments, in the light of the philosophy contained in our National Charter. More than 250 legislations have been enacted with zeal to promote the welfare of child workers and improve their working conditions in various establishments. It is quite evident from the survey of various Articles of Constitution. Our founding fathers had in their mind an intensive care to safeguard the child workers from exploitation and improve their working conditions in various occupations. The subjects of child welfare, child care and development have been enlisted in concurrent list of our Constitution. Our National Charter imposes a duty on centre as well as state government to create a healthy environment for their all-round development. The dignity of individual, the basis of democratic setup of our society has been assured by our National Charter by declaring the fundamental rights of individual on the one hand and by forbidding the traffic in human beings, begar and exploitation of youth and childhood on the other hand.

After independence, our legislature has enacted the Minimum Wages Act, 1948; Factories Act, 1948; The Plantation Labour Act, 1951; The Mines Act, 1952; The Merchant Shipping Act, 1958; The Motor Transport Workers' Act, 1961; The Apprentice Act, 1961; The Atomic Energy Act, 1962; The Beedi and Cigar (Conditions of Employment) Act, 1966; The Shop and Establishments Act in various states and Child Labour (Prohibition and Regulation) Act, 1986 to meet the requirements of child labour from time to time.

Besides these legislative enactments, the government has also adopted a National Policy on Child Labour in 1974. The Policy resolution has evolved guidelines in the field of education, health, nutrition, integrated child development, etc. Both the Governments, i.e. Centre Government and State Governments are expected to carry out the guidelines of national policy to ensure the improvement of the working conditions of the child workers.

It is also revealed that the child labour welfare legislation in India has been influenced to a great extent by the conventions and recommendations adopted by International Labour Organisations from time to time. Besides Constitutional provisions, there are at present thirteen major enactments which provide legal protection to our children in various occupations. For making them more effective and progressive, numerous amendments have also been made in most of these legislations. Moreover, the Child Labour Deterrence Bill, 1992 which was introduced in the United States Senate recently open a new era in the field of child labour welfare. It defines a child as one who is below the age of 15 years. It is important for India because the Constitution makes it a fundamental duty of the government to ensure free and compulsory primary education to all children till the age of 14 years. The Bill prohibits the import of product in which the child labour is involved. India is a signatory to a whole gamut of international conventions prohibiting the use of the children in industries at the cost of their education and health.

National Policy on Child Labour

To curb the evil of child labour, the Government of India announced the National Policy on Child Labour in August, 1987. The action plan under the national child labour policy comprises:

- A legislative action plan,
- Focusing of general development programmes for benefiting
- Children wherever possible, and
- Project-based action plan in areas of high concentration of
- Child labour engaged in wage/quasi-wage employment.

The establishment of special schools to provide basic needs like non-formal education, vocational training, supplementary nutrition, etc. to the children withdrawn from employment has been undertaken under the NCLP. Besides the NCLP, the Child Labour Action and Support Programme (CLASP) with the aid of Government of Germany and an Action Programme under the International Programme for Elimination of Child Labour (IPEC) with the assistance from ILO since 1991 is going on. The long-term objective of IPEC is to contribute to effective abolition of child labour. Recently, the Government of India has entered into a memorandum of understanding with ILO for continuing IPEC beyond 31 December, 1996. The allocation of funds since 1992, for IPEC programme in India stands at US 4.15 million supporting 110 projects in 15 states benefiting 81,000 children.

Besides launching these projects, some more concrete steps have to be taken. The Child Labour Act, 1986 should be made applicable to the child workers in the agricultural sector and in the domestic works. Some kind of wage policy or structure must be adopted to protect the labour of the child worker immediately. India is a signatory country to the 'UN Convention of the Rights of the Child 1989' and having ratified it in 1992, is bound by the provisions of the convention. Apart from this, a number of myths surrounding child labour should be tackled to sensitize the society and the policy-makers to grapple with the situation of the child labour more effectively.

Conclusion

Hence, child labour is a heinous socio-economic problem. Countries all over the world have denounced child labour regarding it as a social evil that destroys the potentiality of the future generation in any society. Most of the developed and some of the developing countries have passed prohibitory legislations to curb the practice of child labour. However, international commitment and pressure are important but the effort of NGO's, media and government should not be ignored.

References

Constitution of India, Act 15 (3) Articles 23-24.

Dr. S.N. Dhyani (1982), Jurisprudence: A Study of Indian Legal Theory, 1980, Indian Express 26 August.

Indian Factories Act, 1948, Section 24.

Journal of Labour Legislations (Vol. XVIII, No. 3-6.).

Journal of Labour Legislations, August 1987, National Labour Institute, Noida.

Mohd. Mustafa and Onkar Sharma, Child Labour in India; A Bitter Truth, Deep and Deep Publications, New Delhi, p. 110.

Plantation of Labour Act, 1951, Section 24.

Prasad, Umesh, "Socio-Economic Problems of Child Labour: A Case Study", *The Hindustan Review, Vol.-9, No.-7, Jan-April, 2002.*

Section 3 (3).

Section 40 (i).

Section 70 (2).

Shandilya, T.K. and Khan, Shakeel Ahmad; Child labour: A Global Challenge, Deep & Deep Publication, New Delhi.

Shandilya, Tapan Kumar (1977), Child Labour in India, Dr. Ambedkar Journal of Social Sciences, MOHW (M.P.).

Shandilya,T.K (2002), "Child Labour at Work: A Case Study", *The Hindustan Review,* Vol.-9, No.-7, Jan-April.

The Mines Act, 1952, Section 2 (i).

Vide Notification No GSR 847 (E) dated Aug. 10 1988, Published in Gazette of India Extraordinary Pvt. II, Section 3 (i), dated 10-8-88.

Working Children in India, Child Labour Cell, National Labour Institute, NOIDA, 1993, pp. 2-4.

20

Child Labour and Human Rights

Bipin Kumar

Introduction

The framework of human rights can be usefully applied to address a number of deprivations that children face in society. The importance of human rights relates to the significance of the freedoms that form the subject matter of rights – freedom from hunger and freedom from escapable morbidity or premature mortality. The discipline of human rights has much to offer in systematizing the perfect and imperfect obligations that society has towards children. Human rights generate reasons for action for agents who can help in safeguarding and promoting the interests of children.

The United Nations Convention on the Rights of the Children defines the civil, political, economic, social and cultural rights of children. Child rights are fundamental freedoms and the inherent rights of all human being below the age of 18 years. India endorsed it on 11th December, 1992. The Ministry of Women and Child Development, Government of India is given the nodal responsibility for coordination and monitoring the implementation of the Convention. Though many countries have passed the Child Rights Acts; constraints of logistics and infrastructure, geo-political climate including conflicts and wars, bureaucratic bottlenecks, leading to less-efficient implementation of the same leaves much room for improvement to combat the violation of child's rights around the world.

Despite of constitutional guarantees of educational opportunity and civil rights, millions of children face widespread deprivation, discrimination and violation of their fundamental rights. A large part of this stems from being seen through the adults point of view; who make decisions for children in all spheres of their lives, and who prefer to address their welfare rather than their rights. The government's approach too remains largely welfare oriented.

Since India has the largest child population in the world; child rights need more than peripheral attention. Any understanding of human rights of children cannot be confined to specific groups of children; as they are generally being categorized-'poor children', 'working children' 'street children' and 'marginalized children'. Violations of children's rights are not limited to the poor, downtrodden and they happen in middle class and elite homes too and need to be addressed comprehensively.

Child protection is a hugely complex subject and needs strategically strengthening of existing policies to protect the child from child labour, trafficking and all kinds of exploitation cultural, commercial, religious, sexual, physical and psychological. While systematic data and information on child protection issues are still not available, evidence suggests that children in need of special protection belong to communities suffering disadvantage and social exclusion such as minority groups, scheduled castes and scheduled tribes, and the economically poor class. The lack of available services and relevant information, lack of coordination between various concerned authorities as well as the gaps persisting in law enforcement and in rehabilitation process constitute major causes of concern.

In a national scenario where there are over 17 million child labourers-being the highest in the world, where about 60 million children under the age of six live below the poverty line and where one in every six child under the age of five suffers from malnutrition, there is understandably a necessity for collective efforts, advocating children's issues, rights and national interests. Indian law has banned child labour in industries, hotels, restaurants and as domestic servants, there continues to be high demand for children as hired helpers in small scale cottage industries, offices and in homes to look after infants/babies, work in the kitchen and manage the routine household chores due to blooming economy and increasing number of the nuclear families, thereby enhancing the demand for lowly paid child labourers. Sorry plight of these underprivileged children hired by much educated, highly placed dignitaries to look after their young ones is once very aptly highlighted by Ms. Chetna Kohli, Education Specialist, UNICEF when she narrated the frequent incidence of these so called employed children being left alone in the high class society, a regular scene in party circuit.

Human rights based approach to programme planning and management meaning adhering to the principles laid down in the Convention on the Rights of the Child emphasizing upon universality, non-discrimination, the best interests of the child, the right to survival and development, the indivisibility and interdependence of human rights, accountability and respect for the concerns of the child should ensure the effectiveness of the Charter of Child Rights. Child trafficking, sexual exploitation are the problems that the society is increasingly being confronted with. The Eleventh Plan proposes to ensure that this vulnerable group is protected from further abuse. Children affected by HIV/AIDs, children in conflict with law, children in depressed circumstances and children with disabilities are going to be addressed and treated as critical target groups.

Through an Act of Parliament, the Government of NCT, Delhi has set up Delhi Commission for Protection of Children Rights (DCPCR). The Commission is meant to protect and fulfill the various rights the children enumerated under UN's Convention on Rights of Child (UNCRC) for their survival, protection, development and participation. The creation of Delhi Commission for Protection of Child Rights by the Delhi Government is a historic and pioneering initiative. The children, who are reported to be extremely deprived, marginalized and poor, suffer multiple forms of abuse and exploitation. A large number of children are legally defined as "Children a Need of Care and Protection" under Juvenile Justice Act 2000. The Commission is committed to convert these children into "Supreme Assets", which they are actually meant to be.

The problem of child labour is a global phenomenon. Even today it is not confined to the Third World Countries. It is more or less prevalent everywhere in the world, the difference, if any, is only of degree or kind. It is saddening to note that India is the largest employer of child labour in the world and has earned a dubious distinction of exploiting this human resource. We have not yet been able to grapple with this shameful menance. The prevalence of child labour in any form is a curse and at the same time it is a socio-economic evil. It is a problem as serious as one can think. It may destroy the whole country and civilization. It may block the future development of the world as a whole. The practice of child labour is as old as the history of mankind itself. Even in ancient times in pre-industrial agricultural society it existed. But the evil effects of child labour were brought into prominence only after the industrial revolution in England. It became rampant due to vast demand for manpower and capitalistic mode of production.

According to estimation, 25 per cent of the world's population will be children and 40 per cent of the entire global labour force will be below the age of 15 years by 2015. ILO in a study has concluded that in Asian countries 70 to 80 per cent of children is either working or simply wasting their lives away. Employment of children has continued therefore, it has become a serious problem.

Problems of Child Labour

Child labour is a social evil. Child slavery is a national curse. It is a grave problem in India. The phenomenon is multi-dimensional and multi-layered. It is a by-product of socio-economic structure of the society. It is not confined to the third world countries only but it has been more or less a global problem. The difference, if any, is only of degree.

The issue of child labour is concerned with human rights issue and at the same time, it is highly emotive one, these emotions tend to be coupled with very strong views both on what the child labour problem is and on what ought to be done for its elimination. The concept and practice of child labour being economically unsound, psychologically wrong and socially disastrous has posed a big threat to peace and overall world development. Therefore, the gravity of the situation and pervasive nature of the problem has attracted the urgent attention of social and political organizations, social scientists, activist groups and governments of the world including India.

The term 'child labour' is generally used to refer to 'any work by children that interferes with them in their fully physical development, the opportunities for a desirable minimum of education and their needed recreation."

Children aged between four to fourteen years doing work on family farms or in occupations with or without payment or in factories, farms outside home for wages constitute child labour. Of late, child labour has become a widespread phenomenon. It is not only confined to work on family farms or in traditional family jobs and occupations but it has also extended to other fields. Children work in agricultural and allied activities, unorganized small scale sectors and even in organized industries. The phenomenon of child labour is a symptom of disease and is consequence of exploitative system, operating at the national and international levels, lopsided development, uneven resource ownership, correlating large-scale unemployment and abject poverty among the nations.

The practice of child labour in India or in any other country of the world is an age-old phenomenon. In pre-industrial agricultural society of India, children worked as helpers and learners in hereditarily determined family occupations under the benign supervision of adult family members. The work place was an extension of the home and work was characterized by personal informal relationships. The task and technology involved were simple and non-hazardous. Radical changes, however, occurred on social economic front with the advent of industrialization and urbanization under the impact of the newly generated centrifugal and centripetal forces; there was unbroken stream of the rural people migrating to urban centres in search of livelihood. As a result, the children were in a situation where they had to earn for themselves as well as for the families. Family based economy was destroyed and work now exposed the child to unhealthy environment. The child's ability to grow and to develop into a mentally and physically sound adult was severely restricted.

The existence and perpetuation of child labour is a blot on the conscience of modern day civilized society. The child is born free and equal but often finds an uncertain future and becomes prey to exploitative set-up of the society. Children are put to work at so tender an age, which requires care, affection and education to equip them and provide better opportunities to grow and become able citizens. Unfortunately, they are denied these opportunities and are untimely subjected to enter into the workforce. In India, we have observed with an ever rising child labour growth curve. Their number is swelling unabatedly and the problem has acquired dangerous dimensions.

Children are the future of society and are destined to play important role in shaping the destiny of the nation. But unfortunately, they are suffering a lot subjected to toilsome work without having opportunities to grow. The remark sums up the sad plight of child labour : "It is really sad to note that children in most of the developing countries are living miserable, cheerless lives, toiling endlessly to ward off starvation, totally deprived of all comforts and opportunities for self-growth and development."

The phenomenon of child labour robs the child of his youthful life, restricts the prospects of education, which can enable him to reach a higher level at later stage of life and ultimately, it harms the progress and prosperity of the nation. It has been correctly stated: "Starve a child of food, of affection, of freedom, of education and you produce an adult who is stunted as an individual and holds back progress towards development rather than accelerate it. This is exactly happening in our country when put to work at a tender age, it reduces physical growth of children, lowers their efficiency, scale of intellectual growth and ultimately, their ability and thereby nation's growth in future. Thus, child labour is economically unsound, psychologically disastrous and physically as well as morally dangerous and harmful. It is inefficient utilization of labour power at a lowest productivity level, which precludes full development of children's potentialities and ultimately harms economic development.

Poverty is undeniably a major factor leading to child labour because children from poverty-stricken families are compelled to join labour force but equally important is the exploitative nature of the system. Due to poverty 'parental authority' is misused. In this context Marx said: "It was not the misuse of parental authority that created the capitalistic exploitation of children's labour, but on the contrary, it was the capitalist mode of exploitation which by sweeping away the economic basis of parental authority made its exercise degenerate into a mischievous misuse of power". There are many who view problem in this way and link it with exploitative capitalist mode of production and working of capitalist system. It has been opined: "Child labour more truly mirrors the character of the society and policy, including the nature of transition, than any other set of indicators. Thus, the exploitative capitalist order perpetuates the problem.

The roots of the problem lie in the exploitative systems prevailing not only at the national level but also at the international level. At the national level, the lopsided development process in the background of socio-economic structure results in marginalization of the poor, who are left with no option but use child labour as a survival strategy. At the international level, the need for foreign exchange, on the one hand, and stiff competition for markets in the developed world, on the other, it encourages the producers of export industries in the third world to use cheap and vulnerable child labour. Also, powerful multinational corporations use child labour directly or indirectly, to minimize cost of production and to maximize profits.

Experiences of European countries analyzed by Klaus Voll, Ester Kostal et. al. show that child labour has been an integral part of the early stages of the development of the capitalist mode of production and for a considerable extent its incidence depends on socio-cultural and religion-based values of the society. Indira Hirway regards the phenomena of child labour as both a consequence as well as cause. The vicious circle is further strengthened through the limited access of the poor to nutrition, health, education and skill. The poor access reduces the productivity as well as wages of adults, which again forces them to use their children's work for survival. The child labour system is thus used as a tool by the vested interests to strengthen their own position and further to maintain and sustain the poverty of the poor. Thus, the child labour problem has a complex dynamics having its dimension within the precinct of national boundary extending upto international level. The exploitative system both within and outside sustains and supports child labour exploitation.

Rodgers and Standing employ useful categories to classify child labour. These are; (a) domestic work; (b) non-domestic and non-monetary work; (c) bonded labour, and (d) wage labour. The first category included household work like those of maidservants, domestic servants, etc. Children are employed in the time consuming activities such as child care, cooking, cleaning, washing, etc. The examples of second category are commonly found in the form of grazing of cow, goat, pigs, etc. where child of five to six and especially female child have to bear the burden. These children may be engaged in family activity or may be a type of self-employment. In spite of ban on bonded labour in the country-side, examples are not uncommon where parents pledge their children to employ both in rural agricultural and urban unorganized sector against loans taken. The children so pledged have to work for a pittance. Children are also employed as wage labour, though their wages are often very low. Thus, they perform as unpaid worker in home or on their own fields as helpers and as paid labour on other's fields or in factories.

The concentration of child labour is to be seen in agriculture as cultivators and agricultural labourers. Children work as helpers in different agricultural operations such as sowing, weeding, harvesting and threshing. They are also engaged in road construction, digging of well and house building. A large number of them are employed in plantations. We see their concentration in agriculture and unorganized sector due to lack of enforcement of child protection laws and partly due to the legal restrictions put on employing them in organized sector. Children are found commonly in wayside restaurants, small hotels and dhabas, tea stall and sweets shop. They are engaged in casual work where there is no provision of holidays, social security. Other permissible allowances are also completely absent and they have to work in hazardous, adverse working conditions affecting their health and efficiency. As they start work at a very young age; they are deprived of education, training (vocational or otherwise) which ultimately limits their earnings and restricts upward mobility.

Besides, child labour creates many social and psychological problems. Due to their misuse for illegal, immoral works, viz. smuggling, prostitution, etc., their personality development is impaired. They grow as stunted ill-mannered citizens. This psychological deprivation (due to lack of care-free life and freedoms) harms millions of children and so not only individual or family suffers, but society loses which leads to so many adverse impacts and social problems.

Magnitude of Child Labour

Child labour is one of the major problems of the developing countries of the world. Today, it has drawn attention of the international organisations, national governments, NGOs, social organisations, administrators, reformers and thinkers. World Trade Organisation (WTO) is not in favour of products manufactured by the child labour and these products are not permitted in the international market. Nearly 200 million children all over the world are estimated to be child labourers.

In 1991, there were about 11.28 million children engaged in various activities in India and they constituted about 8 per cent of work force. The child labour is a multi-dimensional problem. Poverty, caste, tradition, size of the family, labour scarcity, wage rate, illiteracy, ignorance, schooling facilities, etc., are the major factors for the occurrence of child labour. Poverty and child labour go together and tend to reinforce on each other in poor families. Some studies show that in poor families children release women from household affairs to work outside for wages. This results into higher Child Work Participation (CWP) in household work. Child labour has been both economic and social problem in our country since a long-time. Legislative measures taken by government have proved to be ineffective in grappling with the problem of child labour. In fact, it is a paradox of the development process that despite the alarming growth of unemployment, the third world countries have failed to come to grip with the problem of unemployment while there exists high incidence of child labour. Exploitative forms of child labour have crossed the level of reasonableness in society and have become a matter of disgrace particularly in third world countries like India. There are various negative elements of child labour such as unemployment among adults, acute poverty, weak labour force, low wages due to weak bargaining power of adults, etc. which point towards the necessity of implementing various policies to curb child labour. Winner has argued that the situation in India is very grim and despite having progressive labour laws, the solution of the problem is not in the making. He also explained that poverty is less relevant as an explanation. Thus, an integrated approach is required to solve this problem.

According to an estimate, there were 52 millions child labours in the world. The South and East Asian countries accounted for 55.77% followed by the remaining Asian countries 17.50%, Africa 19% and South America 6.1%. According to the study conducted by the ILO, child labour forms 11 to 20% of the work forces in the third world countries. A large number of them are found in hazardous industries such as mining and fire works manufacturing.

According to ILO, at least 120 million of the world's children between 5-14 years did full time pay worker in 1995. When child labour includes part time workers, it numbers more than double.

A brief comparison of child labour in India with that in the World, Asia and China has been given below. The incidence of child labour is estimated by the participation rates for children between 10-14 years over a period ranging from 1950 to 2010 in Table-1.

Table 1
Participation Rates of Children (10-14 Years)

Region	*1950*	*1960*	*1970*	*1980*	*1990*	*2000*	*2010*
World	27.57	24.81	22.30	19.91	14.65	11.32	08.44
Asia	30.06	32.26	28.35	23.42	16.19	10.18	05.60
China	47.85	43.17	39.03	30.48	15.24	07.86	0.00
India	35.43	30.07	25.46	21.45	16.68	12.07	7.46

Source: Economically Active Population: Estimates and Projections 1950-2010, Geneva; ILO (1999).

Up to 1990, the participation rate of children was higher in Asia compared to the aggregate world figure; thereafter, the Asian rate has fallen below the World rate. The Chinese rate was higher than the Asian rate up to 1990. Thereafter, China has experienced a sharp fall in the rate and China is expected to be free from child labour by 2010. However, the participation rate for children was much lower in India than in China in 1950. The occurrence rate of child labour in China continued to be higher than that of India up to 1980. Thereafter, the fall in child participation rate has been much slower in India compared to China. The Indian rate exceeded the Chinese rate by 1990. By 2010, it is expected that the participation rate of children would be around 7.46 in India.

Coming to the national level, the Labour Commission Report 2001 of the Government of India has adopted an approach which earlier was limited to various NGO's and to the most foreign observers. With a redefinition of child labour, the number of working children is set at more than 100 million, 10 times more than the official figures which are available from Census and NSS reports.

The child population of India below the age of fifteen years as per 1991 census was 297 million (about 35 per cent) of a total population of 846 million. The number of children in the school going age of 5 to 14 years was estimated to be around 210 million, which comes to 68.4 per cent of the total child population. The concern of children and the elimination of child labour continue to be an area of great challenge and article of faith for successive governments. According to the census 2001 figures, there are 1.25 crores working children in the age group of 5-14 as compared to the total child population of 25.2 crores. Out of this, 1.07 crores working children are in the age group of 10-14. Existing laws prohibit the employment of children below 14 years of age in factories, mines and hazardous employment and regular working conditions of children in other non-hazardous areas of employment. In Table-2, the incidence of child labour in different states of India has been shown.

State-wise allocation of working children in the principal and subsidiary occupations, as shown in the Table-2 reveals that Andhra Pradesh comes first among the states in employing children in the age group of 5-9 years and 10-14 years in rural areas followed by Rajasthan and Karnataka. One important fact to be noted here is that Kerala is having 0% working children in the age group of 0-9 years in rural areas and 10-14 years in urban areas.

A recent state-wise figures reveals that Andhra Pradesh topped the list with over 19 lakh child labourers followed by Madhya Pradesh, Maharashtra, Uttar Pradesh, Karnataka and Bihar each accounting for over two lakhs. It is also evident that the employment of children, which is a centuries old phenomenon in India, has given rise to a number of social, physiological, economical and legal problems.

Comparing India with other countries, it has been observed that in India, the extent of child labour is not as large as in Turkey, Thailand, Bangladesh, Brazil, Pakistan, Indonesia, Mexico and Egypt. It is estimated around 5.2 per cent of the total labour force in India as against 27.3 per cent in Turkey, 20.7 per cent in Thailand, 19.5 per cent in Pakistan, 12.4 per cent in Indonesia, 11.5 per cent in Mexico and 8.2 per cent in Egypt. In a report entitled "Child Labour, Targeting the Intolerable", the ILO doubles its previous estimates of child labour saying 250 million children between ages of 5 and 14 years work in developing countries, with some 120 million working as full time and 130 million as part time workers. The report further highlighted that in the total child labour force, the share of Asia was 61 per cent, Africa, 32 per cent and Latin America 7 per cent. The ILO in an experimental survey has also found that in Ghana, India and Indonesia, the average percentage of economically active children aged between 5 and 14 years is 25 per cent. In Senegal, it is as high as 40 per cent. These estimates are based on a sample survey of 4000 households and 200 businesses in each country.

Table 2
Incidence of Child Labour Across Indian States

State	*NSS (1999-2000:Principal and Subsidiary occupations)*			*Census 1991*
	5-9 Years (Rural)	*10-14 Years (Rural)*	*10-14 Years (Urban)*	*5-14 Years (Rural & Urban)*
Andhra Pradesh	2.7	25.1	0.7	12.5
Assam	0.4	4.6	0.8	5.7
Bihar	0.2	5.0	0.3	4.3
Gujarat	0.7	11.6	0.4	7.1
Hariyana	0.1	2.6	0.2	3.0
Himachal Pradesh	0.6	8.1	0.2	4.8
Karnataka	1.1	15.2	0.6	11.1
Kerala	0	0.7	0	0.6
Madhya Pradesh	0.3	10.6	0.3	9.9
Maharashtra	0.8	8.5	0.2	8.1
Orissa	0.4	9.0	0.2	8.5
Punjab	0.5	5.5	0.4	3.6
Rajasthan	2.5	16.7	0.5	7.8
Tamil Nadu	0.4	8.6	0.5	5.9
Uttar Pradesh	0.2	6.4	0.6	4.2
West Bengal	0.4	8.8	0.6	4.8
India	0.7	9.3	0.4	6.4

Source: National Sample Survey Report No.458 (Employment and Unemployment Situation in India-1999-2000) and Population Census as reported in Thorat and Sadana (2001) EPW-Dec 28, 2002 p.5192.

Another significant feature of child labour is that in developing countries, 56 per cent of the children in the age of 10-14 years are boys. However, if it was possible in nature, the number doing unregistered works like domestic help or working at home to enable other family members to take in paid employment, the figures so arrived may show more female child laboures than male.

Table 3
Male, Female and Total Workers in the Age Group 0-14
(Constant Rate Projection)

India			
Year	Male	Female	Total
1991	83420	42765	126185
1996	86266	44161	130427
2001	86353	44119	130462

Source: Analysis of Workforce in India, p.94.

According to Table 3, the projected number of child worker has shown an increasing trend in case of both the male and female child. This trend may be attributed to the rising population because it is a function of growth rate of population.

Child labour is predominantly present in carpet, glass, matches, fire works, beedi, locks, gems, pottery and garment industries. To mention few prominent ones, the carpet industry in Mirzapur–Bhadohi belt produces 90% of carpets produced in India. As per estimates, over 1,00,000 children are employed in this industry.

India is the world's biggest maker of hand knotted carpets. Over 8.0 per cent of its production is sent abroad and the industry's most lucrative part is the exports sector. The European community is the country's biggest market and Germany is the largest international market. It is estimated that there are 80,000 child carpet makers in Kashmir and 90 per cent of them are bonded. Child labourers are exploited by the double burden of child labour and life bondage.

Shivakasi is considered as one of the biggest single construction of child labour in the world. Thousand of children in the age group of 7-12 years play with fire for nearly 8 hours day and night throughout their lives for just 7 to 8 rupees a day. Today, there are over six thousand match units in the region with a turnover of 1.1 million a year. Out of 45 thousand children, half the number employed literally plays with fire every minute of their lives. They belong to the age group of 13 to 15 years, mostly girls earning a meagre sum of Rs.2 to 8 a day as wage.

Although it is said in general terms that physical labour has a tremendous impact on the growth of the child, the socio-psychological studies reveals the real magnitude of the problem. Labour has its impact on the physical development, general health condition and morality of a child. A package of self-sustaining rehabilitation measures in necessary and efforts need to be made to intensify employment and income generating programmes both for rural and urban areas.

Child labour precludes the full unfolding of a child's potentialities. The term 'Child labour' is at times used as a synonym for employed child or working child. Conventionally, a working child is defined as a child in the age of 5 to 14 who is doing labour, either paid or unpaid. The child population can be grouped into three categories: school going children, child labour and no where children (non-labour, non-school goers). Working children suffer significant growth deficits compared to children in school. Many factors influence supply of child labour. Because child labour is cheap, the employer prefers child employment to adult employment. Vishwapriya lyengar writes about the health hazards to children in the match industry of Shivkasi. Besides these health hazards, child labour also leads to low economic growth and continuation of vicious circle of poverty. A recent state-wise figures reveals that Andhra Pradesh topped the list with over 19 lakh child labourers followed by Madhya Pradesh, Maharashtra, Uttar Pradesh, Karnataka and Bihar each accounting for over two lakh.

Child labour is widely prevalent in the state of Bihar. Table-4 provides data on the incidence of child labour in the states of Bihar, Kerala and Punjab. The performance of Bihar can neither be considered favourable in this regard nor is there any indication that the incidence of child labour is reducing in Bihar as the census data for the period from 1971 to 2001 shows.

Table 4
Child Labour as Per Census, 1971-2001

States	*1971*	*1981*	*1991*	*2001*
Bihar	1059359	1101764	942245	1117500
Kerala	111801	92854	34800	26156
Punjab	232774	216939	142868	177268
All India	10753985	13640870	11285349	12666377

Source: National Institute of Public Cooperation and Child Development (NIPCCD), Statistics on Women in India, 2007.

Initiatives of Child Labour

The essence of any legislation is to protect and safeguard the interests of the people from the onslaught of exploitation of any form. Starting from the premise that children are the most valuable asset of any nation and the child labour is injurious to the physical, mental, moral and social development of children. Hence, some special measures are urgently required to protect them from various kinds of adverse effects of the work undertaken by them.

International Initiatives

Coming to the global scenario, almost one third of the world population comprises children. They are one of the important components of the social structure and the potential careers of culture. Social justice, therefore, demands justice to children. The need for providing protection and safeguards to children have first been stated in the Geneva Declaration of the Rights of the Child, 1924 and was recognized in the Universal Declaration of Human Rights, 1948 and in the status of specialized agencies of the UNO.

The Geneva Declaration, 1924

The Geneva Declaration, 1924 on the rights of the child was the first international instrument adopted by the League of Nations in which safeguards against child labour were considered. This declaration stated, "Mankind owes to the child the best that it has to give".

Universal Declaration of Human Rights 1948

Article 25 of this declaration 1948 provides that "motherhood and childhood are entitled to special care and assistance. All children whether born in or out of wedlock, shall enjoy the same social protection.

Article 26 assures rights to free and compulsory elementary education to children.

The Supplementary Convention on the Abolition of Slavery, 1956

The slave, trade and institutions and practices similar to slavery of 1956 restrict the exploitation of children employed where the child is supplied to a third person for such purpose. According to the convention, "any institution or practice where by a child or young person under the age of 18 years, is delivered by either or both of his natural parents or by his guardian to another person (whether for reward or not), with a view to the exploitation of the child or young person for his labour".

Declaration of the Rights of Child, 1959

A concrete step has been taken through the declaration of the rights of the child in 1959 which aims that the child may have a happy childhood and enjoy for his own good and good for the society, the rights set forth in the declaration. The preamble of the declaration expresses concern of the international community for child welfare. The child due to his physical and mental immaturity needs special safeguards and care. It also call upon parents, upon men and women as individuals and upon National Governments to recognize children rights and strive for their observance by legislative and other measures. These rights which the general assembly of the United Nations calls upon to be recognized and implemented by the National Governments are contained in the following ten principles of the declaration:

- The child shall enjoy and be entitled to the rights set forth in these principles without any distinction or discrimination.

- It also ensures special protection and facilities for proper and integrated development of human personality.
- The child shall be entitled from his birth to a name and nationality.
- Special care and protection shall be provided to the child and his mother so that the child can grow and develop in health.
- For this purpose, he shall have right to adequate nutrition, housing, recreation and medical services.
- A child handicapped in any manner deserves special treatment, education and care suitable to his condition.
- For proper development of his personality, a child shall be ensured of love, atmosphere of affection and material security.
- The child shall also be entitled to free and compulsory education to promote his general culture and enable his to develop his abilities on a basis of equal opportunity.
- The child shall in all circumstances be among the first to receive protection and relief.
- He shall be protected from all forms of cruelty, reflect and exploitation, he shall not be subjected to traffic in any form and shall not be admitted to employment before an appropriate age, he shall not be engaged any employment which would prejudice his health or education or interfere with his health physical, mental or moral development. This child shall also be protected from practices which may faster racial, religious, and any other form of discrimination.

International Year of the Child, 1979

Having considered the report of the Secretary General on measure and modalities to ensure the adequate preparation, support and financing of an International Year of Child, Economic and Social Council Decision 178 (LXI) and the additional report of the secretary general prepared in the light of the discussions in the economic and social council:

- To provide a framework for advocacy on behalf of the special needs of children on the part of decision makers and the public;
- To promote recognition of the fact that programmes for children should be an integral part of economic and social development plans with a view to achieve in both the long term and short term, sustained activities for the benefit of children at the national and international levels;
- Urges the government to expand their efforts at the national and community levels to provide lashing improvements in the well-being of their children with special attention to those in the most vulnerable and particularly disadvantaged groups;
- Calls upon the appropriate Organs and Organizations of the United Nations systems to contribute to the preparation and implementation of the objectives of the International Year of the Child.
- Designates the United Nations Children's Fund as lead agency of the United Nations system responsible for coordinating the activities of the International year of the child and the Executive Director of the fund to be responsible for its coordination.
- Invites the non-governmental organizations and the public to participate actively in the International year of the child and to coordinate their programmes for the year as fully as possible, especially at the national level.
- Appeals the Governments to make contributions or pledges for the international year of the child through the United Nations Children's Fund to ensure the adequate financing or activates for the preparation and carrying out of the year.
- Expresses the hope that government organizations and the public will respond generously with contributions

to attain the objectives of the International year of the child and, through United Nations Children's Fund and other channels of external aid to increase substantially the resources available for services benefiting children;

- Requests the executive director of the United Nations Children's Fund to report to the general assembly at its thirty second session, through the economic and social council at its sixty third session on progress in preparing for the International Year of the Child, including its financing and the level of contributions pledged.

Certain number of protective measures is adopted in this declaration such as;

- The child labour below 15 years of age should be prohibited.
- Child workers should be protected from any sort of exploitation.
- There should be prohibition of hazardous and dangerous work for persons below 18 years of age.
- Medical examination of child workers.
- Vocational guidance and training to the children to make them fit, in selecting employment.

International Convention on Rights of Child, 1979

A great headway had been made in the year 1989, which marked 30th Anniversary of the 1959 Declaration of the Rights of the Child and 10th Anniversary of the International Year of the child, the General Assembly adopted an international convention on the rights of child on 20th November which was termed by the General Assembly President Joseph. N. Garba, as a binding piece of international legislation. Prior to being placed before the assembly, the draft of the convention was approved by the economic and social council and the commission on human rights during their sessions in 1989. The preamble to the convention states that a child needs special safeguards and care including appropriate legal protection before as well as after birth.

It is a comprehensive human rights convention consisting of 54 Articles drafted in full partnership between developed and developing nations. The remarkable feature of the conventions is the flexibility of its provision. In article of the convention, a child has been defined as a person below 18 years of age, but provided exceptions for countries where the age of majority is set lower. The convention recognizes the basic rights of children for survival, development, protection and participation. It provides the following provisions relating to child labour.

Article 32 of the convention recognizes the right of the child to be protected from economic exploitation and from any work that is likely to be hazardous or interfere with the child's education or harmful to the child's health – physical, mental, spiritual, moral or social development.

Part 2 of the Article stipulates that the countries "shall take legislative, administrative, social and educational measures to ensure the implementation of the present Article. It specifies the following measure:

- Provide for a minimum age or minimum ages for admission to employment.
- Provide for appropriate regulation of the hours and conditions for employment.
- Provide for appropriate penalties or other sanctions to ensure the effective enforcement of the present Article.
- The Article, in effect call for the elimination of the child labour.

Some of the main points of the convention are:

- The convention defines a child as "every human being below the age of 18 years".
- Every child has the right to life, to a name, to acquire a nationality and "as far as possible, the right to know and be cared for by his or her parents".

- Children shall have the right to freedom of expression, thought, conscience and religion, association and peaceful assembly, education, rest and leisure, social security, the highest attainable standard of living adequate for his or her physical, mental, spiritual, moral and social development.
- Children shall not be separated from their parents against their will. States parties will respect the responsibilities, rights, and duties of parents, deal with family reunification in a positive humane and expeditions manner and combat the illicit transfer and non-return of children abroad.
- Children shall be protected from economic exploitation and from hazardous work, drug use and trafficking, sexual exploitation and sexual abuse and all other forms of exploitation prejudicial to any aspects of the child labour.
- A minority of indigenous child shall not be denied the right to his or her own culture, religion or language.
- A mentally or physically disabled child should enjoy a full and decent life.
- A child who is capable of expressing his or her views should have the right to express those views freely in all matters affecting the child, including any judicial and administrative proceedings.
- No child shall be subjected to torture or other cruel, inhuman or degrading treatment or punishment. Capital punishment or life imprisonment shall not be enforced for offences committed by persons less than 18 years.
- States parties will establish a minimum age below which children shall be presumed not to have the capacity to infringe the penal law.
- States parties shall take all feasible measures so that children less than 15 years do not take direct part in

hostilities and shall refrain from recruiting them into their armed forces.

- The best interest of the child shall be the paramount consideration for adoption.
- A committee on the rights of the child, made up of 10 experts, is to be established to monitor compliance with convention provisions. It is interesting to note that the convention has been ratified by more than two third of the total members of the U.N.O. within a period of about half of the decade. The ratification requires a country to bring all its laws into line with the conventions.

International Labour Organisation (ILO)

Among other international measures, the role of ILO is remarkable. It owes its creation to the treaty of versatile at the end of World War I. The primary purpose of treaty was to maintain peace, but it was felt, that peace could be established only if it is based on social justice. Hence, on 28th June 1919, the "High Contracting Parties" agreed to establish a permanent organization to improve conditions of labour. Thus, ILO was established to serve the above purpose.

ILO Standards

Among other things; the abolition, promotion and well being of child labour are the main objectives of ILO. For which the International Labour Organization was created, and for the promotion and well being of children. A major part of that work has been the adoption of International labour conference, of a series of conventions, recommendations and resolutions dealing with the employment of children. As regards child labour, the international labour organization has adopted 18 conventions concerning their minimum age for admission to employment, medical examination and night work.

The Two Plans of ILO Policy

For the ILO, the abolition of child labour and more generally the protection of working children and young persons against work of a character or under conditions unsuitable to their age have been constant concerns since its foundation. The major part of the ILO's work regarding child labour has been the adoption by the international labour conference of a series of conventions and recommendations dealing with the employment or work of children and young persons. A further policy statement was issued by the conference in 1979, the International year of the child in the form of a resolution which called on the member states to rectify and implement International Labour standards and to take measures to ensure the proper protection of children with regard to work. Recognizing that abolition of child labour in practice will take time; the resolution stresses the need during the transitional period until its elimination for measures to regulate and humanize it. In the long run, it acquires a general improvement of living standards, a reinforcement of the educational infrastructure and perhaps, most basically, a greater consciousness of the need for change. The ILO has concerned itself with the question of child labour throughout its existence. One of the principal ways in which the ILO has tried to combat child labour is through the adoption and application of International labour standards. At its first session in 1919, the International Labour Conference adopted the first 10 conventions on minimum age for employment, and it has adopted a number of other conventions regulating the conditions of work of children and young persons when they do work.

Role of UNICEF

The UNICEF acknowledges the need to seriously address labour as a key component of the organizations policy to advocate for implementation of the convention on the rights of the child and the achievements of goals for improving the development and well being of children. Since its inception, it is trying to improve the conditions of children worldwide. It has evolved certain approaches or policies to improve the condition of working children in the world as a whole, especially in developing countries where the incidence of child labour is high.

First of all, to describe briefly about child labour, UNICEF tried to expose some well defined ways of child exploitation like.

- Starting of work at an early age,
- Prolonged hours of work within or outside the family, which denies them from attending the school.
- Excessive physical, social and psychological strenuous works for the child, like work in mines, sweat shops, and tire works thus causing damage to the health and safety of life.
- Children bearing heavy family responsibilities as taking care of their younger brothers and sisters, while parents away for work.
- Bonded labour.
- Sexual exploitation of the children.
- Negligence in their social and psychological development.

Role of UNICEF in India

The UNICEF–India is developing a strong back against child labour. In collaboration with government, NGOS, trade unions, legal exports, International agencies and private industry, UNICEF–India works to eliminate child labour and for diverting the children released from labour into the educational system as per the convention on the rights of child. It has varied objectives to protect the working children from exploitation, some of them can be stated as follows;

- To promote primary compulsory education as the fundamental strategy, elimination and prevention of child labour by enrolling and retaining children in schools.
- To advocate for revision and enforcement of legislation to prohibit child labour, especially in hazardous occupations and industries.
- To assist the central and state government to develop and implement programmes and action plans for the

release and rehabilitation of children from child labour in various industries and occupations.

- To promote convergence of all sectoral and development programmes on 'at risk' families for prevention of child labour.
- To strengthen monitoring systems on child labour.
- To strengthen alliances between NGOs, media, industry and the legal sector for social mobilization in support of elimination of child labour.

As the UNICEF aims at eliminating child labour in hazardous industries, elimination of bonded child labour, some policies and strategies are needed to fulfill this aim. The strategy of UNICEF requires the government to adopt and pursue fireman policies to eliminate child labour and to promote compulsory primary education, as a necessary supportive measure for modification and enforcement. Apart from this, it also requires the industry itself to respond and cooperate by replacing child with adult labour. It also seeks to be the helping hand of NGOs, private industry, external agencies, trade unions, media and advocates, etc. in taking innovative steps to remove child labour from their work place.

UNICEF–India also adopted some policies to strengthen its aim. They can be pointed as below,

- All forms of child labour should be eliminated to comply with agreed child labour.
- As seen in other countries, the enactment and enforcement of legislation to make primary education compulsory as a pre-requisite for the elimination of child labour.
- While poverty alleviation is clearly relevant, it is neither necessary nor desirable to await economic development as a means to eliminate child labour.
- Existing legislation on child labour is must.
- In addition, UNICEF will also seek to strengthen non-governmental alliances which are better in attracting public attention and social mobilization to eliminate child labour.

- UNICEF will focus on programmes to rehabilitate children released from labour into the educational system and to improve the livelihood of their families through anti-poverty programmes.

The UNICEF has recently made its position n child labour public and will continue to provide reliable information to the media. Affords will also be made to persuade national and state confederation of industry and chambers of commerce to adopt principles related to the abolition of child labour. UNICEF has already attached a clause requiring suppliers to certify that the products are not manufactured using child labour. When bidding for contracts, the same step has been considered by other international agencies and major industrial houses.

For achieving of success in this regard, proper monitoring on the implementation of policies, more research on the subject to know more about the problem is required. And these can be possible only in collaboration with ILO, National Labour Institute (NLI) and International Confederation of Free Trade Unions. The monitoring is presently the responsibility of the UNICEF Labour Cell. UNICEF will continue to provide support to the cell for monitoring and research activities and will explore ways of strengthening the monitoring function at national, state and district levels.

The UNESCO

The United Nations Educational, Scientific and Cultural Organisation (UNESCO) is another UN's specialized agency. UNESCO has special responsibility for every thing, involving prevention of the various forms of discrimination and promotion of the educational and cultural rights. It has also been making efforts to combat with the problem of child labour. Set up in 1946, UNESCO aims at promoting cooperation among nations through education, science and culture and thereby contributes to peace and security and enhances universal respect for justice, fundamental freedom and human rights, including rights of the child. It has tried to attack the problem of child labour through the spread of education.

World Summit for Children, 1990

Another important international step was the convention of world summit for children on 29th and 30th September, 1990. The main aim of the summit was to bring an end to the long running tragedy of the vulnerable children. Around 159 governments participated in the summit. It required all the participated countries to be guided by the principle of "first call for children" which requires that high priority should be given to the essential needs of all children. The largest global summit meeting is based on eloquent promises with ambitions. As a result of this, 90 per cent of the developing world's children are proceeding towards the goals which were set in the 1990 summit, as per the report of the UNICEF in 1995.

National Initiatives

Constitutional Provisions on Child Labour

The observations of the Whitleey Commission and Labour Investigation Committee of 1946, as well as the various statements of social-reformers on the evils of child labour, which deprives the children of opportunities of education and good health had vastly and deeply influenced the constitution, whose main aim was to provide socio-economic justice to children, the poor and the backward. Thus, the main aim of our constitution is to protect the child from various kinds of abuses and to create an environment for their fuller development.

In Fundamental rights, Articles 23 and 24 i.e. "right against exploitation" lay down that:

Article 23(i) Traffic in human beings and beggars and other similar forms of forced labour are prohibited and any contravention of the provision shall be an offence punishable in accordance with law. Thus, if a loan is extended on the condition that debtor himself or one of his family members including children will work for him till the repayment of loan with interest, such an agreement will amount to contravention of Article 23, which prohibits "Beggar". Nothing in this article shall prevent the state from imposing compulsory service for public purpose and in imposing such service; the state shall not make any discrimination on grounds of religion, caste, race, or class or any of them. Again, if a custom makes it obligatory for every householder of a village to offer one day's free labour to the headman or mukhiya of the village, it will fall with in the ambit of prohibited particles, being in contravention of Articles 23.

Articles 24: This article prohibits employment of children in factories etc. No child below the age of 14 shall be employed to work in any factory or mine or engaged in any other hazardous employment. This is a constitutional prohibition which, even if not followed by appropriate legislation, must operate vigour and construction work being plainly and undoubtedly a hazardous employment. It is clear that by reason of this constitutional prohibition, no child below the age of 14 years can be allowed to be engaged in construction work. Whenever the central Government undertake a construction project which is likely to last for some time. the central Government should provide that children of construction workers, who are living at or near project site, should be given facilities for schooling and this may be done either by the central government itself, or by the contractor who has been entrusted the project work by the central Government.

Articles 15: This article lays down that "Nothing in this Article shall prevent the state from making any special provision for women and children". It prohibits discrimination on grounds of religion, race, caste, sex or place of birth. Thus, the state is unfettered to make provisions for free children, or to take all necessary and reasonable measures for prevention of their exploitation. In doing so, the state shall not be deemed to be contravening the provisions of Articles 15. The study of constitutional provisions will be incomplete without reference to the welfare provisions for children provided in the Part IV of the constitution i.e. Directive principles of state policy.

Articles 39 of the constitution provide that "the state shall in particular, direct its policy towards securing". The health and strength of workers, men and women and the tender age of children are not abused and that citizens are not abused and that citizens are not forced by economic necessity to enter avocations unsuited to their age or strength. Children are given opportunity and facilities to develop in a healthy manner and in conditions of freedom and dignity and childhood and youths are protected against exploitation and against moral and material abandonment.

Article 45 provides that the state shall endeavour to provide within a period of the constitution, free and compulsory education for all children until they complete the age of fourteen years. Under this article, the state has undertaken to provide compulsory education; it is a right which must be available to all on equal terms and cannot be desired to any body. Children of socially disadvantaged groups such as the economically poor, scheduled castes and scheduled tribes should be given financial assistance for purchasing books, uniforms and stationary.

Legal Provisions for the Protection of Child Labour

The architects of independent India had dreamt of creating a free India to enable the children of tomorrow to avail the benefits of joys of living and laid down policy in the constitution providing facilities for the healthy development of children, for the protection of children and youth against exploitation, and for free and compulsory education within a period of ten years. The constitution has also made a provision to prohibit employment of children below the age of 14 years in all factories and mines and in all other hazardous occupations.

In the pre-independence years, much of what had been done by the state to protect the children, especially those engaged in hazardous occupation were said to be half-hearted, as the colonial power did not have their priority to protect the weaker sections of the society except when it substantially and materially affected their vested interests. Yet a number of legislations were enacted to protect the children against, neglect, cruelty, and exploitation. The fundamentals of laws pertaining to child labour have not undergone any drastic change since 1881, when the provisions regarding child labour had been added to the Factories Act for the first time in India. It was around the early 1880's that the youngest and most vulnerable members of the labour force were suffering from abuses in the textile mills of Bombay, Calcutta, Ahmadabad, Surat, Madras, Coimbatore, Wardha, and so on. The mushrooming growth of the textile industry was responsible for the imposition of excessively long hours and a cruel face of work on a large number of women and children.

The year 1920 marked a milestone in the history of child labour laws, as the Indian Factories Act was amended to incorporate the recommendations of the international labour convention for the minimum age of admission of children into employment, hours of work and night work of young persons and women. The definition of factory was expanded to cover any premises where 20 or more persons were employed and mechanized power was used. The working hour of children was limited by this Act to 6 hours a day with an interval of half an hour.

The Employment of Children (Pledging of Child) Act of 1933

This Act prohibits the making of agreement to pledge the labour of children for employment. A child in this Act is defined as a person who is under the age of fifteen years. An agreement to pledge the labour of a child is void under the Act. Further, a parent or a guardian making an agreement to pledge the labour of a child is subject to fine up to Rs.50/-. It also states that whoever makes with the parent or guardian of a child an agreement, whereby such person pledges child labour, shall be punished with fine up to Rs.200/-

The Employment of Children Act, 1938

This Act prohibits the employment of children in certain occupations, which are hazardous in nature, injurious to health and are outside the scope of factory legislation. Thus, child who has not completed 15 years of age can not be employed in the transport of passengers, goods or mail by railways, or a port authority within the limits of a port. The Act further lays down with the exception of children employed as apprentices or trainers, no child between ages of 15 and 17 can be employed or permitted to work or engage in the occupation unless he is allowed a rest at interval of 12 consecutive hours a day. By the amendment of 1939, the children below 14 years were prohibited to work where the work is carried on in the process of beedi making, carpet weaving, cement manufacture, cloth printing, dyeing and weaving, manufacture of matches, explosives, and fireworks, mica cutting and splitting, soap manufacture, canning, etc. For contravention of the provisions of the Act, the employer is punishable with simple imprisonment extending to one month or fine up to Rs.500/- or both.

However; it is noteworthy that before independence, the law pertaining to the employment of children in various sectors was failed due to the inadequacy of the inspecting staff to enforce the provisions of laws. No law with regard to child labour in agriculture, unregulated workshops, shops and commercial establishments was passed.

Post-Independence Legal Efforts

The focus on protecting the children from adverse effects of their employment on their physical and mental development was more progressive and sharpened, particularly after independence. The first step taken in this regard was amendment of the Factories Act, 1948.

The Factories Act, 1948

- Restricts employment of a child below 14 years in factory,
- Safeguards the health of young persons of above 14 years of age and below 18 years.

The main provisions of Act are enumerated below as:

Section 2 (c): Child means a person, who has not completed his fifteen years of age,

Section 22(2): No young persons shall be allowed to clean, lubricate or adjust any part of prime mover or any transmission machinery while the prime mover or transmission machinery in motion, if the cleaning, lubrication, or adjustment there of, would expose the young persons to risk of injury from any moving part of that machine.

Section 23(1): No young person shall work at any machine to which this section applies, unless has been fully instructed as to the dangers arising in connection with the machine and the prosecutions to be observed and (a) has received sufficient training in work at machine or (b) is under adequate supervision by a person who has a through knowledge and experience of the machine.

Section 23(2) (1): This sub-section shall apply to such machines as may be prescribed by the (state) Government, being machines, which in its opinion are of such a dangerous character that young persons ought not to work with them, unless the foregoing requirements are compelled with.

Section 27: No child shall be employed in any part of a factory for pressing cotton in which, a cotton opener is at work, provided that if the feed-end of a cotton opener is in a room separated from the delivery end by a partition extending to the root or to such height as the inspector may be employed on the side of the partition where the feed-ed is situated.

Section 34(2): The (state) government may make rules prescribing the maximum weights, which may be lifted, carried or moved by children employed in factories or in carrying or any specified process.

Section 67: No child who has not completed his fourteenth year shall not be required or allowed to work in any factory.

Section 71(a): No child shall be employed or permitted to work in any factory for more than 4 hours in a day.

Section 71(b): No child shall be employed or permitted to work in any factory during night.

The Minimum Wages Act, 1948

This Act provides for fixing of maximum rates of wages in certain establishments. This Act defines an 'adolescent' as a person who has completed his 15th year, and a 'child' as a person who has not completed his fifteenth year. This Act provides that different minimum rates of wages may be fixed for adults, adolescents, children etc.

Minimum Wages (Central) Rules, 1950

Section 24: Provides that the number of hours which shall constitute a normal working day shall be 4 ½ hours in case of a child. Any contraventions of the rules are publishable with fine which may extend to Rs.500.

Section 71(a): No child shall be employed or permitted to work in any factory for more than 4 hours in a day.

Section 71(b): No child shall be employed or permitted to work in any factory during night (Tripathy 1991).

The Plantation Labour Act, 1951

This Act covers all tea, coffee, rubber, cinchona and cardmory plantations, in which 30 or more are employed.

Section (2) (e) of the Act states that "child means a person who has not completed one's fifteenth year."

Section 24 states that no child who has not completed his twelfth year shall be required or allowed to work in any plantation.

Section 25 restricts a child above 12 years of age to be employed in any plantation between 6 a.m. to 7 p.m. except, with the permission of the state government.

Section 19 states that no child shall be required or allowed to work on any plantation for more than 27 hours in a week.

Section 26 states that every child above 15 years, but below 18 years may be in plantation provided, they obtain a certificate of fitness from a certifying surgeon. The Act casts an obligation on the state government to make rules requiring the employer to provide educational facilities for children.

The Mines Act, 1952

This Act includes all excavations where any operation for the purpose of searching for or obtaining mineral is carried out.

Section (2) (e) states that "child means a person who has not completed his fifteenth year".

Section 45(1) of this Act states that no child shall be employed in any mine or shall any child be allowed to be present in any part of mine which is below ground or any mining operation is being carried on.

Section 45(2) of this Act states that no child shall be allowed to be present in part of a mine above ground where any operation connected with or incidental to any operation is being carried on. An adolescent, 'a person who has completed his 15th years of age, but has not completed 18 years' is allowed to work in any part of a mine which is below ground, if he had a medical certificate from a surgeon, certifying that he is fit for work as adult and however shall not be employed in any mine except between the hours of 6 a.m. and 6 p.m. Any employer contravening the provisions of child labour is punishable with imprisonment up to three months or a fine up to Rs.1000, or both (Vishnupriya 1991).

The Merchant Shipping Act, 1958

Section 109 states the no person under fifteen years of age shall be engaged or carried to sea to work in any capacity in any ship except (a) in a school ship or training ship, in accordance with the prescribed conditions, or (b) in a ship in which persons employed are member of one family, or (c) in a home made ship of less than two hundred tones gross, or (d) where such person is to be in the charge of his father or other adult near male relative.

The Motor Transport Workers Act, 1961

This Act covers the motor transport undertakings which employ five or more transport workers. Under Section 21 of this Act, no child who has not completed fifteenth year shall be required to or allowed to work in any capacity. No adolescent shall be employed or required to work as a motor transport worker for more than 6 hours a day, including rest interval of half an hour between 10 p.m. and 6 a.m. (Tripathy 1991)

The Apprentices Act, 1961

The Act provides for the regulations and control of training of apprentices. Section 3 of the Act states that a person shall not qualified for being engaged as an apprentice, or to undergo apprenticeship training in any designated trade unless, he is not less than fourteen years of age and satisfies such standard of education and physical fitness as may be prescribed, provided that different standards may be prescribed in relation to apprentice training in different designated trades and for different categories of apprentices. This Act deals with matters like qualification for being engaged as apprentice, contract period of apprentices, obligations of employees and apprentices, payment and hours of work, health, safety and welfare of apprentice (Bare Act 2001).

The Atomic Energy Act, 1962

This Act prohibited the employment of persons less than 18 years of age as radiation workers, except with the permission of the competent authority.

The Beedi and Cigar Workers (Conditions of Employment) Act, 1966

The Act provides for the welfare of the workers in Beedi. Establishments and regulates the conditions of their work and for matters connected with them.

Section 2(b) states that, child is a person, who has not completed fourteen years of age. *Clause 2(g)* states that 'young person' means a person who has completed fourteen years of age, but has not completed eighteen years of age.

Section 24 strictly prohibits a child to work in any industrial premises.

Section 25 restricts women and young persons to work in any industrial premises except between 6 a.m. to 7 p.m.

State Shops and Commercial Establishments Acts

The minimum age prescribed for child labour under the Shops and Establishment Acts varies in different states and union territories. The age of a child for employment is 12 years in Goa, Daman and Diu, Rajasthan, Orissa, Delhi, Madhya Pradesh, Jammu & Kashmir, Tripura, Uttar Pradesh, Bihar and Karnataka. But this age is 14 years in Andhra Pradesh, Assam,

Tamil Nadu, Kerala, Punjab, Haryana and Himachal Pradesh. In Maharashtra, the minimum age for child in a shop or establishment is fifteen years. Night work foı children and young persons is prohibited under state laws relating to shops and commercial establishments. However the children have to work long hours extending up to 10 a.m. as mentioned in Table-5.

Table 5
Working Hours in the States

State	*A.M.*	*P.M.*
Andhra Pradesh, Gujarat, Maharashtra, Tamil Nadu	6	7
Bihar, Kerala	7	7
Jammu & Kashmir, Madhya Pradesh	7	9
Karnataka	6	8
Orissa, Rajasthan	6	10

The Employment of Children Act, 1978

In 1978, the Employment of Children Act was amended prohibiting the employment of a child below 15 years in occupations on railway premises such as cinder-picking or clearance of ash pits or building operations, in catering establishments and any other work which was carried on or in close proximity to or between the railway lines.

The Child Labour Act, 1986

This is an Act to prohibit the engagement of children in certain employments and to regulate the conditions of work of children in certain other employments. It was enacted by Parliament in the thirty-seventh year of the Republic of India. This Act consists of four parts. Part I contains definitions and Part II deals with the prohibition of employment of children in certain occupations and processes. Part III regulates the conditions of work of children while Part IV lists the penalties for violations of the Act. The Act restricts the work of children in certain process of following work:

- Beedi-making
- Carpet weaving,

- Cement manufacture, including bagging of cement,
- Cloth printing, dying and weaving;
- Manufacturing of matches, Explosives and fire-works.
- Mica-cutting and pilling.
- Shellac manufacture.
- Shop manufacture.
- Tanning.
- Wool-cleaning.
- Building construction industries.
- Manufacture of slate pencils (including packing).
- Manufacture of products from agate.
- Manufacturing process using toxic, metals, and substances such as Lead. Mercury, Manganese, Chromium, Cadamium, Benzene, Pesticides and Asbestos.

One of the limitations of the Act is that the word "hazardous" is not clearly defined in this act and it is left to the Technical Advisory Committee to define hazardous occupations of process. Also here is no provision in the act to seek the prohibition of child labour in an occupation or a process even if the request is backed by relevant data and no time fixed time to respond to such a request. The Act does not specify the minimum age of employment of children in occupations and process other than the prohibited ones. The central government takes up the task of revising the definition of "occupations" and "process" for the purpose of the making additions to the schedule in a time bound and planned manner. Besides, the adjective "hazardous" is held to have purely physical implications excluding the psychological, mental and emotional dangers that a job can mean to child workers in any given work. The very fact that childhood is snatched from a child and it is not prepared for, transforms every aspect of what should be an optimistic environment for a child into pessimistically hazardous one.

Walter Fernandez has rightly observed that the present Act legalizes the entry of children in hazardous occupation by regulating their employment in industries that are obviously non-hazardous for adults but are hazardous for children. Though the provision says that nothing in this section shall apply to any workshop where any process is carried on by the occupier with the aid of his family to any school established or receiving assistance or recognition from the government, when certain occupations and process are harmful to the health of children, it remains applicable even if children work as part of family entrepreneurial enterprises, or state managed/ established/aided/recognized schools. Once the occupations/ process have been identified as hazardous for the employment of children, any exemption made there of is the detriment of the children.

National Policy on Child Labour

Another milestone in the field of child labour legislation is National Policy on Child Labour approved in 1987. The constitution of India, both in the directive principles of the state policy and as a part of the fundamental rights, has laid down that state shall direct its policy towards securing the health and strength of workers, men, women, children and youths are to be protected against exploitation and no child below the age of 14 years shall be employed to work in any factory or mine or engaged in any other hazardous employment. The National Policy for Children Resolution, adopted in August 1974, further developed these ideas and set out a policy framework and measures aimed at providing adequate services for children. Free and compulsory education for all children up to the age of 14, provisions of health and nutritional programmes and services, providing alternative forms of education for children unable to take full advantage of formal school education for whatever reasons and measures for protecting children against neglect, cruelty and exploitation form part of the National Policy for children.

The anti-poverty policies, the national education policy, the national policy on health for all and on nutrition, as also the generally stepped provisions in social services in national plan outlays are all geared to tackle the problems of poverty, where too often, the origins and compulsions of child labour are rooted.

Child Labour Cell

A child labour cell, which was originally set up in 1979 to service the M.S. Gurupadaswamy Committee on child labour, is now a part of the regular ministry. It is associated with the formulation, coordination and implementation of policies and programmes for the welfare of child labour. The child labour cell is involved in the welfare of children at work through governmental and non-governmental action.

Grant in Aid

Child labour cell grants financial assistance to voluntary organization to take up action-oriented projects for child labour. These projects would aim at measures to maintain the health of the child while at work by providing supplementary nutrition, non-formal education and vocational training to help them better in their employment. During the year 1985-1986, 1986-1987 and 1987-1988, grants-in-aid have been released to the following surveys/ projects connected with the welfare of working children:

- Educational facility and improvement of health of child labour by Institute of Psychological and Educational Research, Calcutta.
- Setting up of pre-vocational training cum educational centre for children by Indian Institute of Rural Workers, Aurangabad.
- Setting up to Jaya Rajendra Rag Picker's Project by State Council for Child Welfare, Karnataka.
- Setting up of welfare/ development centres for working children in Bombay by International Council on Social Welfare, Bombay.
- Rehabilitation of child labour by Self-employed Women's Association, Ahmedabad.

- Sifting up a working children's community centre for package of services by Madhya Pradesh Shaskiya Karmachari Mahila Kalyan Samiti, Bhogal.

Committee on Child Labour, 1979

In order to look into the cause leading to the problems arising out of employment of children and to suggest suitable measures for their protection and welfare, the Ministry of Labour, Government of India, had set up a committee headed by Shri M. S. Gurupadaswamy in its resolution dated 6th February, 1979. The following were the terms of reference to the committee.

- Examine existing laws, their adequacy and implementation and suggest corrective actions to be taken to improve implementation and remedy for defects.
- Examine the dimensions of child labour, the occupations in which children are employed and suggest new areas where laws abolishing regulations of employment of children can be introduced.
- Suggest welfare measures, training and other facilities which would be introduced to benefit children in employment.

The committee had sketched a plan of action for making in depth and diagnostic studies on the nature and extent of the problem, adequacy of existing legal framework and the supportive measures for working children. The committee brought out a questionnaire to elicit information on child labour from the public, politicians, trade unions, social workers, welfare and other institutions, employers, parents of children and Government organizations. The information received from the questionnaire was tabulated and utilized in the report of the committee. The report of the committee was submitted to Government on 29.12.1979.

Studies Sponsored by the Committee

The committee has sponsored various studies to cater information on child labour which are as follows:

- A study on child labour in Varanasi Urban area by the Gandhian Institute of Studies, Varanasi.
- Studies on child labour at Ichalharanji in Kolhapur district by Maharastra Institute of Labour Studies.
- Stüdies of children in Beedi and Cottage institutions at Gondiain Bhandara district by the Tirupude College of Social Work, Nagpur.
- Studies of tribal children in agriculture in Akkalkwa by Tata Institute of Social Sciences, Bombay.

Central Advisory Board on Child Labour, 1981

In pursuance of one of the recommendations of the committee on child labour, the Central Advisory Board, which was set up in March 1981, has been reconstituted in July 1987 under the chairmanship of minister of labour to render advice on the problem of child labour. The following were the terms of reference:

- Review the implementation of the existing legislations administered by the Central Government.
- Suggest welfare measures and legislative measures for welfare of working children.
- Review the progress of welfare measures for working children; and
- Recommend the industries and areas where there must be a progressive elimination of child labour (Tripathy 1991).

Observations made by the committee are quite significant. In briefly, "the existing situation in respect of child labour in India can still be summarized as one of continuing drift". Though there is little evidence of children at work in the certain pockets in the country, as observed by the Whitleey Commission nearly 50 years ago. Bulk of children continued to be employed in the rural environment while most of them work without wage. An increasing number amongst them were of children employed for wages and also of many working on jobs which are hazardous.

The Task Force Report, 1989

The report of the task force on the implementation of the Child Labour (Prohibition of the Regulation) Act, 1986 and National Policy on child labour set up by the Child Labour Advisory Board, Ministry of Labour, under the chairmanship of Dr. I. M. Singhvi in December 1989, felt that 1986 Act and the NPCL have so far failed to yield any worthwhile results. The task force report provides a brief appraisal of one of the projects; i.e. Sivakasi, Tamil Nadu, on the basis of first hand information secured by the task force.

About Child Rights

Following are few rights in the immediate purview:

The Right to Education: 50% of Indian children aged 6-18 do not go to school. Dropout rates increase alarmingly from class III to V where it is 50% for boys and 58% for girls.

The Right to Expression: Every child has a right to express himself freely in his own way. Majority of children, however, are exploited by their elders and not allowed to express freely.

The Right to Information: Every child has a right to know his basic rights and his position in the society. High incidence of illiteracy and ignorance among the deprived and underprivileged children prevents them from having access to information about them and their society.

The Right to Nutrition: More than 50% of India's children are malnourished. According to estimation, one in every five adolescent boys is malnourished while one in every two girls in India is undernourished.

The Right to Health and Care: 58% of India's children below the age of 2 years are not fully vaccinated and 24% of them children do not receive any type of vaccination. Over 60% of children in India are anemic. 95 in every 1000 children born in India do not see their fifth birthday. 70 in every 1000 children born in India do not see their first birthday.

The Right to Protection from Abuse: There are approximately 2 million child commercial sex workers between the age of 5 and 15 years and about 3.3 million between 15 and 18 years.

They form about 40% of the total population of commercial sex workers in India. 500,000 children are forced into this trade every year.

The Right to Protection from Exploitation: As per official estimate, 17 million children are working in India. A study further reveals that children are sent to work by compulsion and not by choice, mostly by their parents, but with recruiter playing a crucial role in influencing decision. When working outside the family, children put in an average of 21 hours of labour per week. Poor and bounded families often "sell" their children to contractors who promise lucrative jobs in the cities and the children end up being employed in brothels, hotels and domestic work. Many run away and find a life on the streets.

The Right to Protection from Neglect: Every child has a right to lead a well protected and secure life away from neglect. However, children working under exploitative and inhuman conditions get neglected badly.

The Right to Development: Every child has the right to development which leads to explore her/his full potential. Unfavourable living conditions of underpriviledged children prevent them from growing in a free and uninhibited way.

The Right to Recreation: Every child has a right to spend some time on recreational pursuits like sports, entertainment and hobbies to explore and develop. Majority of poor children in India do not get time to spend on recreational activities.

The Right to Name and Nationality: Every child has a right to identify himself with a nation. A vast majority of underprivileged children in India are treated like commodities and exported to other countries as bonded labour or prostitutes.

The Right to Survival: Of the 12 million girls born in India, 3 million of them do not see their fifteenth birthday and one million of them are unable to survive even after their first birthday. Every sixth girl child's death is due to gender discrimination.

Prescriptions for Eradications of Child Labour

- Presently all the state and central governments under different schemes provide mid-day meal, uniform, books and other educational materials free of cost to the children but still the parents are unwilling to send their children to school. Hence, we suggest that the Government may provide an Educational Allowance to the families those who enroll their children in the school.

- The government bears enormous responsibility in ensuring the promotion and protection of the child right. Hence, there is need to establish a special "Child Rights Commission" on the lines of Women's Rights Commission.
- The Non-Government Organisations (NGOs) can play an important role in eradicating child labour. They can mould public opinion against the violation of child right. Hence there is need to encourage and support the NGOs that are working in this field.
- The problem of child labour is directly connected with the poverty and illiteracy of Indian masses. There should be every possible effort on the part of Government and NGOs.
- Most of rehabilitation programmes today aim at improving the working environment of the child and hence, are helping to perpetuate this evil. The ultimate aim has to be the abolition of child labour and all government programmes must work towards fulfilling this objective.
- Laws on child labour and education should be consistent in purpose and implemented in a mutually supportive way.
- Top priority should be given to universalisation and elementary education for children between 6 to 14 years within a time frame not exceeding more than 5 years. The other important programme would be non-formal education to help children who are unable or unwilling to attend full time school. These facilities should be provided by NGOs.
- Education policy needs a constructive change. Primary education should be made compulsory and free for all children below the age of 15. Curriculum should be reformed to suit local environment, school timings and

local community resources. "Earn-while you-learn" programmes should be introduced and expanded according to local requirements. Thus, education has become a part of the problem but it must be sorted out as a part of the solution on the above guidelines.

- Along with general education, vocational training should be imparted to the children to make them economically independent in their adulthood.
- There should be more budget allotment for increasing the prospects of child welfare. Children must be registered at the time of their birth. It will helpful in fixing their rights, accessing their education, health care and other services ın particular and provide information about their age evidence to their employers and government in general.

References

Agrawal, Suresh Chandra (2004), "Child Labour and Household Characteristics in Selected States", Estimate from NSS 55th Round, Paper in Economic and Political Weekly Jan 10, 2004, Vol. 39, No.2, pp. 173-185.

Ahmad, A.M. (1991), "Child Labour in Pakistan, A Study of the Lahore Area," Children Welfare, March-April, Vol. 70, No.2, pp. 269-283.

Anand Rajkumar, P. (2000), "Female Child Labour", A.P.H. Publishing Corporation, New Delhi.

Badami, A.R. (1990), Chronic Poverty and Its Consequential on Unemployment and Underemployment", Social Change, Vol. 27, No.3-4.

Baquele, A & Boyden, J. (1988), "Child Labour, Problems, Policies and Programmes, Combating Child Labour, Problems, Policies and Programmes, Combating Child Labour", ILO, Geneva.

Benjamas Prachankhadee, et.al.(1979), "Thailand" in Elias Mendelievich (ed), Children at Work, ILO, Geneva, p.140.

Children at Work (1993) ed. by Bhagwan Pd. Singh and Shukla Mohanty, B. R. Publishing Corporation, Delhi and ISLE, Patna.

Tapan Kumar Shandilya and Shakeel Ahmad Khan (2003), 'Child Labour: A Global Challenge' Deep & Deep Publications (P) Ltd., New Delhi.

Tapan Kumar Shandilya, Nayan Kumar and Navin Kumar (2006), 'Child Labour Eradication Problems, Awareness, Measures" Deep & Deep Publications (P) Ltd., New Delhi.

Alakh N. Sharma, Rajeev Sharma and Nikhil Raj (2004), Child Labour in Carpet Industry - Impact on Social Labeling in India, Institute for Human Development, New Delhi.

'Children, School and Work Glimpses from India (2005) by G.K. Listen, Anup K. Karan and Anoop K. Satpathy, Institute for Human Development, New Delhi and IREWOC Foundation, Amsterdan.

A. N. Sharma (1979), "Child Labour in Patna"

David Hayes (1980), "The Bane of Child Labour: Buying and Selling in Thailand", The Time of India, October 7.

Elias Mendelievich (ed) (1979), Children at Work, ILO, Geneva, p..94.

(a) Robin Porter, (1976), "Child Labour in Hong Kong", Social Welfare, November, pp.10-11.(b) Tara Ali Beg; Op.cit. p.66.

'The Working Children of Kathamandu, Nepal, Thailand, Bangkok: Child Workers in Asia' (1989) CWIN and CWA.

Tara Ali Beg (1979), "The Child in Asia", In Child in Third World, People's Publishing House, New Delhi, pp.64-65.

Theodora Papaflessa and Sophia Spiliotopoulos (1979), "Greece", in Elias Mendelievich (ed.) Children at Work, ILO, Geneva, p.74.

Government of India (2008), Yojana, November, Volume-52.

21

Child Labour—Experiences and Outcomes

Meera Verma and Vineeta Mishra

Introduction

Through an Act of Parliament, the Government of NCT Delhi has set up Delhi Commission for Protection of Child Rights (DCPCR). The Commission is meant to protect and fulfill the various rights for children enumerated under UN's Convention on Rights of Child (UNCRC) for their survival, protection, development and participation. The creation of Delhi Commission for Protection of Child Rights by the Delhi Govt. is a historic and pioneering initiative. The children who are reported to be extremely deprived, marginalized and poor suffer from multiple forms of abuse and exploitations. A large number of them are legally defined as "Children a Need of Care and Protection" under Juvenile Justice Act 2000. The Commission is committed to convert these children into "Supreme Assets", which they are actually meant to be the interventions and programmes recommended for the 11th Plan Period should include improving the reach and quality of existing programmes and formulating new schemes to address hitherto un-addressed areas and issues based on National Policy for Children, 1974, National Charter for Children, 2004 which makes special mention of the importance of protecting the rights and dignity of girl children, National Common Minimum Programme and the National Plan of Action for Children 2005.

Child Labour–International Experience

As the processes of globalisation have escalated, so too has the concern about child labour as the public has become more aware of the conditions under which children in the developing world are living. Heart-rendering pictures of working children have played on the sentiments of a westernized public. Cunningham (1999. p.14) notes how the results of studies on the problem of child labour by the Anti Slavery International (ASI) in the *1980s* revived images of child labourers as slaves in 'Dickensian' Britain around the year 1830 and 'tapped into a well of moral and emotional feeling'. This prompted the official organisations and NGOs to take action on the issue of child labour.

The growing awareness and concern about child labour has led activists and lobbying organisations in the West to force governments and the public to take action against countries where child labour is prevalent and condemn industries using child labour. Many trade unions and NGOs are also trying to gain support for boycott of products that are not made 'child labour free'.

Although well intentioned the following example reveals the problems that have been encountered when attempting to enforce the provisions that are based on the ILO standards under the wrong circumstances. In 1995, the textile workers in the United States angered by the alleged use of child labourers in these countries lobbied the US government to take action. The US government threatened to implement the US Child Labour Deterrence Act, proposed by Senator Harkin. This Act, better known as the Harkin Bill, would revoke trade privileges for textile exports to the US markets. In Bangladesh, this resulted in the dismissal of thou-sands of children from the textile factories. Humanitarian organisations curious about what had happened to these children, conducted a study a year following their dismissal. Their findings were disconcerting Children were not attending school and almost all had jobs in the informal sector, where working conditions were far worse than in the textile facto-ries. The children had to resort to working in the informal sectors of the economy, where they were breaking bricks, vending on streets, or engaged in prostitution (IWGCL. 1998a. p. 44).

A similar incident occurred in Marakesh, Morocco in 1997. A British television team, taking footage for what was to be a documentary on the subcontracting practices of Marc and Spencer's, stumbled across what they believed to be child labourers. Fearing the loss of business, the factory owner immediately dismissed the children concerned. An investigation into the well-being of these predominantly young women, who turned out to be around 14 or 15 years of age, revealed that many had been forced to return to their homes. To the young women, dismissal meant the loss of an opportunity to gain some independence by learning a skill and earning a wage; it meant a lost opportunity to escape the prospect of a lifetime of domestic work to which their culture and social structures had confined them (IWGCL, 1998b, p. 5).

Western and western-inspired activists who are concerned about child labour believe that it should be eliminated because 'it deprives children of their right to a childhood, prevents access to basic needs, undermines development and health and entails exploitative terms of employment' (Blancher, 1996, p. 74). Children whose experiences do not correspond with the modern ideal of childhood, which holds that children should be protected and provided for and that they should attend school and not work, are pitied for not having a childhood. This, however, sometimes leads to interventions such as those described above, which reveal a lack of knowledge about the dire realities of the developing countries.

The problem with these interventions is that they treat child labour as if it is a labour problem while it is, in essence, a welfare problem. In the West, the process of industrialization led to the development of social structures that could support the modern childhood ideal. Given the nature of the evolution of the international political economy and the socio-economic conditions within the developing nations, these processes will not simply repeat themselves in the same manner. The examples above reveal that legalistic approaches to the problem that compel the States and industries to enforce child labour laws that were developed in the West are insufficient in themselves and may not be in the best interests of the children and the families concerned. Such approaches also fail to reach those sectors in which much of child labour takes place and where conditions are most detrimental. These cases reflect a need for a better understanding of child labour and its underlying causes. The processes of globalization, rather than generating the socio-economic conditions that are necessary to reduce child labour, are in many ways perpetuating it. Child labour is a very complex problem, and any effort to address it must be contextually sensitive in that it takes into account the conditions that are driving children into work as well as the costs and benefits of work to children.

Child Labour – Indian Experience

The Eleventh Plan marks a big step forward in the area of Child Rights. It is entrenched in a Rights Framework that views children as agents and not as recipients. It recognizes and acknowledges multiple discriminations wherein the children are trapped in. This acceptance of the situation of the children can alone safeguard their rights and ensure better outcomes for children.

India's experience in promoting child rights points to three important lessons. First, the Indian experience illustrates that economic growth and all-round prosperity do not automatically translate into improvements in the lives of children. Even over the most recent seven-year period between 1998--99 and 2005-06 (coinciding with impressive economic expansion), we find, for instance, that:

- the proportion of under-weight children under three years under-weight fell from 47 to 46 percent;
- the proportion of fully immunized children 12-23 months went up from 42 to 44 percent; and

- the proportion of deliveries assisted by a health professional went up from 42 to 49 percent

In fact, the proportion of fully immunized children in urban India fell marginally from 61 percent in 1998-99 to 57 percent in 2005-06 suggesting that growing urban affluence is not always sufficient for advancing child rights.

Second, the Indian experience suggests that reductions in income poverty do not automatically translate into reductions in child poverty. In 1973-74, more than half (55 percent) of India's population lived below the poverty line. By 2000, the proportion had fallen to 26 percent. Despite this impressive reduction in income poverty, we find, for instance, that 46 percent of children under three are still underweight. Similarly, according to the Delhi Human Development Report 2006, Delhi is one of the richest Indian states in terms of per capita income and only 8 percent of Delhi's population lives below the poverty line. Yet, nearly 3-5 percent of children are underweight. Clearly, both income expansion and income poverty reduction do not automatically imply improved well-being of children.

Third, economic progress and improved literacy have not necessarily resulted in reducing discrimination against the girl child in India. The female-to-male ratio among children 0-6 years worsened from 947 girls per 1000 boys in 1991 to 927 in 2001. Particularly disturbing is the sharp decline in female-to-male ratios among children in the more affluent Indian states of Punjab, Haryana and Gujarat. Once again, the message is clear: there is no automatic linkage between increased opulence, improved standards of living and assurance of equal rights to children.

Child Labour–Recent Experience and Tangible Outcomes

India's recent experience with public action suggests five essentials that are needed to establish the linkages and ensure tangible outcomes for children.

First, issues of child rights need to be more politicized for them to receive appropriate policy attention. This has happened in some fields, as for example, with child labour, food security for children (brought centre stage by the Right to Food campaign), malnutrition, neonatal mortality, poor quality of education, child abuse and so on. But such efforts need to be encouraged for a whole range of neglected areas affecting children's lives. Second, the State must recognize the multi-dimensional nature of human poverty and initiate interventions that simultaneously address the many concerns of the poor including livelihoods, health, basic education, food security and children's nutrition. This, we find, is beginning to yield improved results for the poor especially as the benefits of interventions such as the National Rural Employment Guarantee Scheme, the National Rural Health Mission, the revamped Sarva Shiksha Abhiyan and the strengthened Integrated Child Development Services begin to reach the same families and communities at the same time. Third, the State needs to pay much greater attention to inclusive programming. This calls for special efforts to focus on promoting equity and accelerated progress for less privileged children. At the same time, more flexibility and innovation need to be built into programming initiatives to take note of contextual differences in the assurance of child rights. Fourth, society must pay more attention to improved accountability. Several steps are being taken in India to improve transparency in public decision making processes. The newly enacted Right to Information Act, for instance, is a major step forward in ensuring transparency and fairness in public decisions. There is great scope for better tapping the full potential of e-governance and use of information technology to establish new standards and norms of accountability. Lastly, the State must set up new institutions that specifically promote child rights at different levels. Government of India took a significant step when in 2007 it set up the National Commission for the Protection of Child Rights as a statutory body. State Governments must be encouraged to set up similar State Commissions for the protection of child rights. Such institutions can and should begin to play a pro-active role in order to ensure that all Indian children get a better deal in the coming years.

It is clear from the Indian experience that high rates of economic growth and reductions in income poverty do not automatically translate into improvements in the well-being of children. At the same time, public pressure is needed to ensure that the State intervenes not with one or two schemes, but with a range of programmes that address simultaneously the many dimensions of child and human poverty. And lastly, it is important for the State to establish and nurture new institutions that will focus specifically on promoting child rights. It is only then that sustained economic growth can get converted in good measure into accelerated improvements in the well-being of children.

Recently, people in the highly industrialized states considered child labour a thing of the past. The term conjured up images of children working in sweetshop conditions in the 19th century. Child labour in the industrialised countries was marginalised as result of changes in production processes that, in turn, led to changes in political and social structures. This led to a conception of childhood that has become predominant throughout the world. It holds that children's world is separate from those of adults and that children should attend school and not engages in waged labour. This conception is today considered to be universal. Yet, more than 50 per cent of the world's children are currently living at or under the poverty line and many of these children work to ensure their own and their family's survival (Bellamy, 2000, p. 15). This attests to the fact that most societies are far from achieving the goal of 'modernisation'.

Over the past three decades, the issue of child labour has re-emerged on the political agenda. Although globalisation is essentially an economic process that has been fuelled by the liberalisation and deregu-lation of market economies, it has profound political, social and cultural implications. Although the processes of globalization are leading to unprecedented levels of wealth throughout the world, they are also leading to higher levels of inequality within and between states. In a speech to mark the 10-year anniversary of the Rights of the Child Convention, Carol Bellamy, the Head of UNICEF, stated thus:

We have ended a century that has seen a staggering technological advance and the emergence of a global economy worth nearly $300 trillion. What is equally staggering-and wholly obscene is the gulf that now separates those who enjoy the fruits of this progress from those who do not-especially the hundreds of millions of women and children who are excluded and denied their fundamen-tal rights.

It shall be explored that what is being done to address the problem of child labour in the context of globalisation. Child labour is a social conse-quence of development and a symbol and symptom of poverty and in-equality. While some children are provided for and protected by their parents and the State, others must work to help provide for themselves and their families. Reducing child labour, therefore, means finding ways to ensure that, as phrased by Deacon *et.al* (1997, p.53), 'the productive potential of globalisation serve the goal of equity rather than subject society to competition and the deterioration of public social policy that is being brought about by neo-liberalism.'

Conclusion

Every child must enjoy her right to protection, development and childhood. Being out of schools, we are witness to how millions of children are in the labour force living lives of drudgery and exploitation working in agriculture, mining, construction, fishing, on garbage dumps, brick kilns, as domestic labour in our own homes and in countless other occupations, mainly in the informal sector. Large numbers of children are trafficked and abused subject to untold suffering and misery.

Overwhelmed by the magnitude of the problem at hand, child labour is tolerated and often even justified. If it is understood that child's rights have to be protected no matter what then solutions would emerge. An uncompromising stand on abolishing all forms of child labour with a rights based perspective would pave the way for children enjoying freedom and dignity in our country. However, the history will not excuse us if we are not awakened 'here and now' in the interest of the people at large by defending our human rights, on the one hand, and performing our human duties to others, on the other.

References

Bellamy, C. (2000), "The Roll of the Dice", Development, Vol. 43, No. 115-16.

Balancher, T. (1966), Lost Innocence, Stolen Childhood, University Press Limited Dhaka.

Cunningham, H. (1999), "The Rights of the Child and the Wrongs of Child Labour; An Historical Perspective", Paper presented at the IREWOC Workshop: Children, Work and Education, November 15-17 Amsterdam.

Deacon, B, Hulse, M. and Stubbs, P. (1977), Global Social Policy: International Organizations and the Future of Welfare, Sage, London.

IWGCL (1998a), Working Children, Reconsidering the Debates, International Working Group on Child Labour, DCI and ISPCAN, Amsterdam.

_____ (1998b), Forgotten on the Pyjama Trail, A Case Study of Young Garment Workers in Meknes (Morocco) dismissed from their jobs following Foreign Media Attention, DCI and ISPCAN, Amsterdam.

Index

D

E

SP/INV/S14783/54